Hi, my name is Jack

Hi, my name is Jack

One Man's Story of the
Tumultuous Road to Sobriety
and a Changed Life

JACK WATTS

HOWARD BOOKS
A DIVISION OF SIMON & SCHUSTER, INC.

NEW YORK   NASHVILLE   LONDON   TORONTO   SYDNEY   NEW DELHI

Howard Books
A Division of Simon & Schuster, Inc.
1230 Avenue of the Americas
New York, NY 10020

First Howard Books hardcover edition November 2011

HOWARD and colophon are trademarks of Simon & Schuster, Inc.

For information about special discounts for bulk purchases,
please contact Simon & Schuster Special Sales at
1-866-506-1949 or business@simonandschuster.com.

The Simon & Schuster Speakers Bureau can bring authors
to your live event. For more information or to book an event, contact
the Simon & Schuster Speakers Bureau at
1-866-248-3049 or visit our website at www.simonspeakers.com.

Designed by Akasha Archer

Manufactured in the United States of America

10   9   8   7   6   5   4   3   2   1

Library of Congress Cataloging-in-Publication Data

Watts, Jack (John T.)
    Hi, my name is Jack : one man's story of the tumultuous road to sobriety and a changed
life / Jack Watts.
        p.   cm.
    1. Watts, Jack (John T.)   2. Recovering alcoholics—United States—Biography.   I.
Title.
    HV5293.W37A3 2011
    362.292092—dc23   2011022059
    [B]

ISBN 978-1-4516-7189-6
ISBN 978-1-4391-9661-8 (ebook)

When I was a kid, there was a TV show called *The Naked City*, which I absolutely loved. Each week, it closed with the line *There are nine million stories in the naked city; this has been one of them.*

My path to recovery is like millions of others—unique, and yet surprisingly similar to everyone else's. It's to those who have walked this road—the road less traveled—that I dedicate my story.

If we are painstaking about this phase of our development, we will be amazed before we are halfway through. We are going to know a new freedom and a new happiness. We will not regret the past nor wish to shut the door on it. We will comprehend the word "serenity" and will know peace. No matter how far down the scale we have gone, we will see how our experience can benefit others. The feeling of uselessness and self-pity will disappear. We will lose interest in selfish things and gain interest in our fellows.

Are these extravagant promises? We think not. They are being fulfilled among us—sometimes quickly, sometimes slowly. They will always materialize if we work for them.

—"The Promises," from *The Big Book*

Good name in man and woman, dear my lord,
Is the immediate jewel of their souls:
Who steals my purse steals trash; 'tis something, nothing:
'Twas mine, 'tis his, and has been slave to thousands;
But, he that filches from me my good name
Robs me of that which not enriches him
And makes me poor indeed.

—William Shakespeare, *Othello*, Act 3, Scene 3

Contents

Acknowledgments

The primary tradition of Alcoholics Anonymous is this: anonymity is the spiritual foundation for all of our traditions, ever reminding us to place principles before personalities. *Hi, My Name Is Jack* adheres to this principle scrupulously. My story is true—not just parts of it, all of it. It's my family story, which doesn't include much about my career. I've written about that in *Pushing Jesus*, which also is true. *Recovering from Religious Abuse: 11 Steps to Spiritual Freedom*, which was my first published book, was inspired by my need for recovery.

I have written *Hi, My Name Is Jack* from my viewpoint, while steadfastly adhering to the spirit of anonymity to protect others who are part of my story. To ensure this, I have changed the names of many people as well as some places.

Others have helped me craft my story, and I'm indebted to each. To Gary, my best friend, and his wife, Paige, thanks for your persevering support throughout the process—the same to John and Patty Fitts, who have been steadfast friends since we were teens.

Thanks to Ditty Bell and Terry for all your help—the same to Pooh, Iggie, Kit, and the Mixons—even LuLu. Thanks also to Dwayne and Ernest, as well as Anne A. and Carolyn C. for valuable and essential editorial assistance. Thanks to David D. and Joel M. for encouraging me to move forward with the project. I want to give a special thanks to Jonathan and Wes, Philis and Jessica, Becky, Ashley, and especially to Nicci Jordan Hubert. To Allison and Chris, Kerin and Matthew, Jill, Monirah, Kevin and Angel, Art, Terrance and Merry, Ron, Heather, Joni, and others, thanks for your prayers, support, and a regular dose of reality.

To Robert A., Mack C., and Jud N., thanks for returning to my life after decades to give valuable counsel.

As you read my story, my advice is to take what you can use and feel free to leave the rest behind. It's a wild ride—that's for sure. Many things happened to me along the way, but I do not consider myself a victim—not even close. When I learned to take responsibility for all of it is when I stopped being a little boy and became a man.

Nothing but the Truth

"Hi, my name is Jack, and I am an alcoholic."

This is the way alcoholics introduce themselves at an AA meeting. I've done it thousands of times since my last drink, which was in the late spring of 1994—a long time ago and, in AA years, several lifetimes ago. It makes me an "old-timer" in the program. Stories from old-timers are often filled with tragedy, pain, and occasionally intrigue; but they also are filled with hope and encouragement because old-timers have seen it all.

One of the things you do in Alcoholics Anonymous is "tell your story" so that newcomers and others can get to know you better and, more important, so they can obtain confidence and motivation of their own "to turn their will and their lives over to the care of God." Therefore, nearly every successful story in AA is a God story.

My story, which spans many decades, is quite involved and often hard to believe. But it's the truth, and as Joe Friday from the fifties cop show *Dragnet* would say, it's "the whole truth and nothing but the truth." The story is like a mosaic—with each piece fitting together to make a complete and distinguishable whole. Ancient Greek philosophers used to argue about whether life was linear or circular, purposeful or random. My belief is that life is purposeful; and yet in the heat of the battle, it seems to be random most of the time.

By looking back, I can finally see how the pieces of the puzzle fit together. By doing this, I now realize that my life has indeed had a purpose and continues to have one. That's why the picture of a mosaic is so appropriate. If you look at a few pieces, a mosaic doesn't make sense;

but if you step back and look at it in its entirety, you can ascertain a divine design.

When you've finished reading my story, my hope is that you will be uplifted and encouraged, because it's a story of God's power and overarching purpose in the life of one guy who had no choice but to believe Him.

When America was attacked at Pearl Harbor, our enemies sought to destroy us. Although we staggered, we became stronger and more resolute than ever. We gained new purpose. The same has been true for me. I have become stronger because of my experiences—much stronger. That's what happens when you become sober in body, mind, and spirit: you gain strength you never thought possible. It has taken a long time—too long, perhaps—but there was no way to shorten the process. It is what it is.

Now let's begin. Perhaps the best place to start is the night I stopped drinking.

Chapter 1

"I've Only Had Three"

"Jack, I don't know how to say this gently; so here goes. If you want us to continue dating, you have to go to AA and stop drinking."

This ultimatum was delivered to me in the late spring of 1994 at a quaint Italian restaurant on Peachtree Street in downtown Atlanta, right above Underground Atlanta, by my long-standing girlfriend, Eleanor Benedict. We had been talking about Bill Clinton, who had taken office a little over a year before.

There had been no segue. She just blurted it out. When she did, I wasn't offended; I was surprised. I wasn't an alcoholic. "I've only had three beers," I said quickly and defensively.

"Tonight you've only had three beers, but your drinking has gotten out of hand. I can't go on like this. It has to stop, or we have to stop. The choice is yours. I'm serious about this," and I could tell that she was.

Now she had my attention. For me, three beers was nothing. I used to think of three beers as priming the pump before I started on Jack Daniel's. I would have anywhere from eight to ten of those and wind up the evening with one or two Grand Marniers. That was a normal evening routine for me.

Eleanor and I had been dating for three years—going on four—and Eleanor had been pressing me hard to marry her. Having been married twice, I was reluctant.

She was a medical doctor, finishing her residency at Emory and about to make substantial money as an internist. Eleanor was in her early thirties, redheaded, and had green, captivating eyes that were warm, alluring, and troubled. She was five three and always seemed to wear too much makeup. She wasn't beautiful—not in the traditional sense—but she was quite striking. She was also very exciting. There was never a dull moment with Eleanor.

At the time, I was doing quite well financially. I admit that I found the prospect of living a jet-setting, affluent life with a cute young doctor very attractive, but our relationship had its share of problems. One time, I was taking one of my daughters, Jordan, to the movies, and Eleanor came along to shop while we did. She and Jordan were fooling around in the car, and Eleanor bit Jordan. That's right. My girlfriend, the doctor, bit my daughter, who was only eight years old at the time. Jordan screamed because it was a hard bite, which both startled and hurt her. It was all I could do to keep the car on the road as Jordan reached over to cling to her daddy. Eleanor apologized, insisting that she was just being playful, but the scene was so bizarre that I began to rethink the possibility of a lifelong relationship with her.

This aberrant behavior was not an isolated incident. Another time, Eleanor and I planned to go to a bed-and-breakfast inn for a long weekend in Savannah. One of my older daughters, Brenn, who was twenty-two at the time, asked me if we could drive her there and back. Brenn planned to stay with a girlfriend of hers who just happened to be the hostess at the same B&B where Eleanor and I were registered. Naturally, I said yes. Frankly, I thought nothing of it and looked forward to the long drive down and back, with Brenn along for the ride. She was a lot of fun. For this trip, we drove in Eleanor's car instead of mine, which was in the shop.

Although Eleanor readily agreed that it would be wonderful having Brenn, she was secretly seething. When we arrived at the B&B, Brenn's friend Jennifer, who was a very attractive young lady, gave me a hug, which was apparently a little too close and a little too long for Eleanor's comfort. Having known Jennifer since she was fourteen, I didn't think a thing about it—nor would anybody else in their right mind. Yet Eleanor, who had more and more frequently acted as if she had some kind of personality disorder, was not behaving like she was in her right mind—she was acting insecure and jealous. Although she didn't say anything then and there, her discomfort quickly turned to anger. When Brenn left to spend the weekend with Jennifer, Eleanor unleashed a tirade of obscenities that would have made a sailor blush. I was stunned, but there was no appeasing the doctor.

I retreated to the bathroom to take a shower and to avoid further battle. My fear was that every other guest would overhear her shouting, making it impossible to look others in the face at breakfast the following morning. While I was in the shower, Eleanor hurriedly gathered her things, threw them in her car, and left.

I will never forget how I felt when I realized what had happened—like an absolute fool. There I was, a forty-nine-year-old man with his twenty-two-year-old daughter, stranded in Savannah—250 miles from home. I not only felt like a fool, I also looked like one for being in a significant relationship with someone who was that volatile.

Within an hour, I rented a car for Brenn and me to drive back to Atlanta, cutting the trip short by two days. While on the road, I left a message for Eleanor, telling her it was over, which was the healthy, appropriate thing to do.

But I wasn't healthy. Although I did not realize it at the time, I was an alcoholic. Therefore I reconciled with her two weeks later when she came to see me—remorseful and in tears. That is what alcoholics do; it's who we are. Even when there is no alcohol in our system, we still think like alcoholics, and it costs us. I was a rescuer, and my alcoholism clouded my judgment regularly and repeatedly.

It's funny because Eleanor thought all of our "issues" were based on my drinking and not hers, but that wasn't true. I think she had problems with alcohol as well, and like nearly every problem drinker, she was in complete denial. During our last Thanksgiving together, my family came to eat at my house in the Buckhead section of Atlanta. Being the host for all four of my daughters and their families, I didn't have anything to drink. I was much too busy. By the way, this is also one reason I denied having a drinking problem for so long. I didn't have to drink on every social occasion. There were many times when I never touched it, but in truth, these times of abstinence were becoming less frequent.

Before the meal, everyone was talking and mixing very well when Eleanor, who was feeling no pain, spilled her red wine on my beautiful new white Burberry rug in front of everybody. I asked her to clean it up right away.

"Let the maid do it when she comes next week," she said with a dismissive, haughty laugh.

Immediately I got a sponge and started cleaning it myself. Victoria, my second daughter, who was twenty-four, marched up and said, "Dad, why are you cleaning that and not her?"

Eleanor heard this, and the battle was on. They went into another room and let it rip. It was awful, and it seemed to go on for hours. Every once in a while, Eleanor would come out and refill her glass to keep her throat moist for the next round. By the time the doctor left to go on duty, there was nothing left to be thankful for. The holiday was ruined.

She called in the early evening after everyone had left and said, "It wasn't that bad." She added, "The first two cases I saw today were Thanksgiving gunshot wounds."

"So I should be grateful that we didn't have gunplay?" I said, still infuriated that the holiday had been destroyed.

There were dozens of other examples I could describe, but everybody could see this relationship was unhealthy—that is, everyone but me. I met Eleanor at a Bible study, and we were attracted to each other at first sight. She was a petite beauty and obviously quite intelligent. I kept hoping things would turn around with her, but they never did.

So when she gave me the ultimatum to go to AA, I went. I found a noon meeting at the Triangle Club, which was right behind a huge liquor store that I frequented often. When I went to the first meeting, I was surprised to see so many sharp people and virtually no street people. At the end of the meeting, I went forward and picked up a white chip, which signaled my acknowledgment of being an alcoholic and my willingness to surrender my problem with alcohol to God.

My relief was instantaneous. I felt a burden lift from my back, and I was certain I was in the right place. Ever since I was in high school, when I first started drinking excessively, I knew I was different. I didn't fit in— not really. At AA I was finally with people who were like me—people who thought like me. It's definitely where I belonged.

On the outside—the side I allowed people to see—I looked fine. In fact, I looked better than fine. I looked good. On the inside, however, I was a mess, and I knew it. In the second step of AA's 12-Step program, it says that God can restore an alcoholic to sanity. At first this seemed a little extreme, but I soon realized how crazy I had become. Take my anger, for example. I would sit in a meeting and, if a guy looked at me in a way I didn't like, I would say to myself, *I can take him. If he even looks at me again, I'll beat the crap out of him.*

I always thought like this and was surprised to find that most people don't. Even people who have a problem with anger aren't *that* angry. My anger seemed normal to me, which is a pretty good definition of insanity. By the way, if a girl looked at me, I thought, *She wants me.* Sadly, I still think that way, which is pretty typical for a guy—even an older one.

In those first few months, AA was my life. People seemed genuine and more willing to be transparent than any people I had ever seen before. At Triangle, there was a guy who led quite a few meetings. He was kind, accepting, insightful, and had an obvious desire to help others. He seemed genuinely humble, which came from deep within him. He was also gay and had AIDS. It was clear to me that he had a better relationship with God than I had. Before I went to AA, I'm sad to admit that I thought AIDS was God's punishment for being gay, but not after I saw God's love come from this man—unconditional love. He spent his final days of life in service to others, constantly giving and never bemoaning his fate.

He died soon after I met him. I can't even remember his name, but I'll never forget the character qualities he possessed—qualities I coveted. As a result of being in meetings he led, I started to realize that God's love was greater than the box to which I had confined Him. I knew I didn't love people the way the gay guy did—not even close. I needed help with more than my drinking. I needed character transformation as well. I wanted this kind of love to come from me, not the anger I had always harbored.

I also started to realize just how destructive my life with Eleanor had become. As I became more involved with AA, I began to see that I wasn't responsible for fixing her. I had enough problems of my own. One evening, six weeks into the program, I broke up with her and never looked back. I had been sober for only a short time, but I knew I wouldn't maintain my resolve while still dating her. I'll always be grateful that she initiated my visit to AA, but marrying her was certainly not the way to express that gratitude. I needed a fresh start.

As part of my AA program, I began to take a complete—painstakingly honest—inventory of my life. In so doing, I asked myself exactly when I became an alcoholic. I decided that it was in 1933—eleven years before I was born.

Chapter 2

I Was Wanted

Los Angeles may be the city of charm and opportunity today, but in the 1930s the place to be was Chicago. My mother, Mary Catherine Reagan, knew this, and being the youngest of six children from a dairy farm in Maxwell, Illinois, Mary anxiously headed to the city as soon as she graduated from high school. Her shorthand was good and her typing skills a little better, but Mary's greatest asset was her charm—pure Irish.

Prohibition had just ended; the Depression was in full swing; Hitler was coming to power in Germany; but regardless of what was happening in the world, you could always find a party in the Windy City. And that's exactly what Mary did every Friday and Saturday night. One evening, when Mary had had a little too much to drink, she carelessly locked herself in a bathroom and couldn't get out.

A handsome young man from St. Louis, Missouri, was there and quickly came to her rescue. He climbed outside a living-room window, walked carefully along a ledge six stories up, and entered the bathroom through the small window above the commode. In his hand was a key to open the door, and thus he saved the damsel in distress. His name was William Houston Watts, my father.

Some say it was the last truly athletic thing Bill Watts ever did. Nevertheless, he and Mary started dating and quickly became a couple. The story they told us was that they married in 1934 and my older brother, Danny, was born in 1935. This story was unquestioned for nearly seventy years until my dad's younger sister, whom we called Sweetie Pie, inadvertently revealed that they were actually married in the spring of 1935—just a few months before Danny was born.

At first you might think this little revelation to be insignificant, but in the dynamics of our family, it has proven to be of monumental importance. Like a clue to a Sherlock Holmes mystery, it helped unlock my understanding to nearly everything that has transpired since.

You see, my dad was a very bright and talented man, a man of great promise. He was a freshman in college, a young man who had just taken a trip to Chicago to have a little fun. He had no plans to marry anybody, but when Mary turned up pregnant, he did what was right. He married her—just like nearly any other guy from his generation would have done. His sister finished college and eventually received her PhD. Six years younger than Dad, Sweetie Pie became a renowned artist and college professor, accomplishments her older brother envied but never equaled.

The pregnancy meant he had to quit college, go to work, and raise a family. He did what was expected of him, but his heart bore deep resentment toward Mary for getting pregnant. But his resentment didn't stop there. He reserved a special place of hatred in his heart for his newborn son, Danny. He blamed Danny for the lot in life he was forced to endure. Danny could do no right in his father's eyes, no matter how hard he tried. My dad would use the least provocation to scream obscenities at him, undermine his self-worth, and make him the brunt of his cruel and sarcastic humor. This abuse not only undermined Danny's character and confidence, but it also twisted him at the core of his being in dark ways that would come to light decades later. You might say that even in his youth, Danny had a black spot on his soul.

Danny grew up despising our father, and the two of them became enemies for life. To this day, more than three decades after Dad's death, any conversation with my brother Danny invariably turns into a diatribe about our father's real or perceived faults. Now, in his late seventies, Danny is still rebelling against paternal authority. It's probably at the root of Danny's lifelong problem with alcohol and cocaine. As you can imagine, this bitter enmity and rivalry caused significant problems, some of which will never be resolved.

Mom, like all good Irish Catholic girls—and in spite of the constant warfare between Dad and Danny—wanted more children. A second pregnancy, however, eluded her until a year after her mother, Bridget, died in 1943.

Mom's nickname was Murph—a tribute to her Irish charm. This sobriquet was not derisive but endearing—so endearing, in fact, that her children called her Murph. We even pinched her fanny when she walked by, just like her husband often did. Even in the midst of this highly conflicted family, Murph was a lot of fun. Just a little over five feet, Murph was formidable, with a fierce Irish temper.

She was fond of telling me, "When my mother died, she went to heaven and asked Mary to ask Jesus if I could have another child. And, Jacky, God sent us you. We wanted you so much." My mom had that kind of simplicity, purity, and superstition that is uniquely Irish. As you can imagine, we teased her unmercifully about such statements.

As cute as this was, it also was important. When I came into the world, I was wanted, which didn't go unnoticed by Danny, who was nine at the time. He was keenly aware of the difference between the two of us. I was wanted; he was not. Shortly thereafter, my mom became pregnant again, and my brother Dick arrived on VJ Day (victory over Japan in World War II). I was fourteen months old. Dick was very sickly, receiving extreme unction (now known as anointing of the sick) and a hurried Catholic baptism because he wasn't expected to live. My mother poured herself into his care. Dick not only survived, he also thrived.

Because she nearly lost him, the bond between my mom and Dick was so strong that they became extremely close for the rest of her life. Once she gave Dick a T-shirt that said, "Mom Loves Me Best." No kidding, she really did this—and she was surprised that the rest of her children were openly incredulous and inwardly resentful! That was Murph—you had to love her.

My parents used to say that my dad liked me the best, but I never believed that was true. When I was only three, however, he did take me to a bar with him on Saturday afternoons to drink with his friends, and I felt special then. He would sit me right up on the bar, like I was one of the boys—along with the beer, whiskey, smoke, hacking coughs, uproarious laughter, and lewd stories. They would give me the last sip of beer and think it was hysterical to see such a cute little boy drain the last drops from a bottle. It was my introduction to alcohol—at three. Looking back, it's hard to imagine such irresponsibility, but at the time they didn't think a thing about it.

Because Dad's company transferred him often, Danny and I were born in Iowa, then Dick in St. Louis. In 1949 we moved to Newton, Massachusetts, a suburb of Boston, where we bought a small three-bedroom, one-and-a-half-bathroom house. The conflicts between Danny and Dad intensified. Because Danny was now a teenager, he was able to hold his own in verbal combat. He started lifting weights in the basement and went from a scrawny kid to a full-fledged bully in just a few months.

His bullying was no novelty to either Dick or me because Danny used every opportunity he could find to inflict minor physical pain or major emotional cruelty. In spite of this, we loved him dearly. He was our big brother, our hero, our champion in standing up to Dad. He couldn't see the intensity of our loyalty because he was a bully, and since bullies are obtuse by nature, they often can't see or understand what's going on around them. They're too busy with the corporal dimension of pain to comprehend the emotional side of life.

Dick and I, on the other hand, were happy, carefree, and as mischievous as Tom Sawyer and Huckleberry Finn. We were into everything. Dad was hard on us—make no mistake about it—but we had each other. When he would send us to our room, which we shared, we didn't sulk and brood like Danny did, because we had each other to play with. So our punishments were just opportunities for some new adventure.

By 1953, we were well settled in Massachusetts. Danny was nearing the end of his high school education—not because of graduation but because he was nearing his eighteenth birthday. He received one D in his junior year, his only passing grade, and that was in PE. He got into fights constantly and was finally arrested for one particularly nasty incident where several kids were hospitalized with broken bones. The judge said he could either go to jail or go into the service. So the day Danny turned eighteen, he joined the Marine Corps and was quickly shipped off to Parris Island, South Carolina, for basic training.

At about the same time, Mom became pregnant with her fourth child—my sister, Terry Jean. I came up with the name because I loved the comic strip *Terry and the Pirates*, but she was always called Jean. Because there were eighteen years between her oldest and youngest, Mom was fond of saying, "I've been stuck at home with you kids all my life." This reproachful statement might have destroyed the psyche of most, but Dick and I laughed and wore it proudly as a badge of honor.

To most families, education or athletics is the most important role for children. For us, it was earning money. From the time I was old enough to carry a bag, I caddied for Dad when he played golf every Saturday and

Sunday. On Sunday mornings, we would be at Mass, and just as soon as the priest washed his hands, Dad rushed me out of church so we wouldn't miss our tee time. This cut church short by about twenty minutes, but he got no argument from me.

I liked caddying for my dad because he was with his friends, and he would never embarrass himself by yelling at me in front of them. I also loved talking to these men—all of whom were World War II veterans with incredible tales from Europe and the South Pacific. One of my favorites was Bill Sullivan, the original owner of the New England Patriots. I caddied for him a hundred times.

I remember asking my dad what he did in the war, and he said, "I did your mother." He was the only nonveteran in the crowd.

Once, when I was fourteen, we were on the eleventh tee when the entire foursome started talking about my future—where I would go to college, what I would be, and what kind of girl I would marry. One of the golfers— a man with a distinct southern accent—commented, "Jack should go to the University of Georgia. I like that. It has a nice sound to it." No one paid any attention to it but me. It did have a nice sound to it, so I made up my mind right then and there to go to UGA. It was a decision that would have life-long implications, and I made it capriciously—with no more thought than it had a nice sound to it.

I also worked at a gas station for a short time on Sundays when I was sixteen. Once, when locking up, I left the windshield display out all night, and it was stolen. The owner noticed it was missing right away and came by our house early on Monday morning. He wanted to make me pay for the display, wipers, and several other things. Dad did a little investigating and discovered that the display unit was provided by the wiper company and would be replaced without cost. So the guy was trying to use this opportunity to make a cash bonus for himself because of my mistake.

Upon learning this, I wanted to confront him immediately; but my dad wanted us to pay for it and then threaten to go to the senior management of the gas company. Reasoning that we could make the guy pay us to keep our mouths shut, we would turn the table on him. "It's not blackmail, Jacky," Dad explained. "It's just a little free gas, a tune-up, or something like that." I was appalled, but that was my old man—always looking for an angle and proud of it. He thought this was a laudable quality rather than a character flaw, and he was contemptuous of me for not seeing it his way.

In fact, he was so proud of his penchant for looking for an angle that I always found it ironic that he put up this plaque right over the dirty-clothes hamper for all of us to see every day:

The Darkest Hour in Any Man's Life
Is When He Sits Down
To Plan How to Get Money
Without Earning It.
                    —Horace Greeley

My dad was always trying to get money without earning it, so the plaque was like spouting the virtues of abstinence while being a closet drinker. By the way, I never paid for the windshield wipers or anything else in the matter, because we never could get any straight answers out of the gas station manager.

It's funny, but if you look back, you can nearly always discern patterns of thought and behavior that have had a profoundly negative impact on your life. You think, *I should have said no right then and there*, or *How could I have let him do that to me?* That's how I have always felt about my dad's sneaky little deals and attempts to get something for nothing.

Inside, I knew his plan was wrong. Something was desperately wrong in our family. The leader, my dad, was not honorable. We were being trained to connive, to look for angles, to exploit and manipulate rather than to do what was right. More than anything, I wanted to do what was right. I felt like Oliver Twist being led about by the artful but malevolent Fagin and his henchman, the Dodger. I tried to watch out for Dick—to protect him from all the dysfunction surrounding us; that's all I could do.

Chapter 3

The Same Penny

One Saturday afternoon in the late fifties when I was fourteen, I was caddying for Dad, and I did something he didn't like—a rarity on the golf course because I was a very good caddy. I can't remember what it was, but I do remember what he said on the thirteenth tee in front of the entire foursome. "Jack, you know what you are?"

Puzzled, I just looked at him and shrugged my shoulders. "You're a sexual intellectual," he announced, knowing I would be intrigued.

"What's that?" I said—genuinely captivated because, like every fourteen-year-old, sex was an all-consuming topic. Until that moment, there had never been a hint that I was an intellectual about anything—let alone my favorite subject.

Without missing a beat, he said, "You're an f-in' know-it-all!" But he didn't say "f-in'"; he used the whole word.

Everyone erupted with laughter, including me, but as I continued carrying his bag around the course, the indignation of my public ridicule began to build. When I finished the loop, I was walking home, reliving my humiliation and thinking of comebacks that would have turned the table, when a friend came up to me and said, "Jacky, I need to talk to you. It's very important."

It was Bobby Marconi, a classmate and someone I hung out with from time to time. He insisted we walk into the woods near my house where we could be assured of complete privacy. Although his request seemed ridiculous, I was curious and went with him.

When we got to a certain spot, he said, "Promise me that you won't get mad at me?" I did. Then he asked, "You know Timmy Brinson, don't you?"

I nodded yes. Of course, I knew him; we went to the same school, Warren Junior High, and to the same church, St. John's.

"Well, Timmy brought your sister right here and gave her a penny to take her underpants down."

He had my complete attention. "What happened, Bobby?" I said menacingly, "and what did you do to stop it?"

He could see that I was ready to beat the crap out of him.

"You promised you wouldn't be mad at me, Jacky, and I didn't have to tell you anything." He was right and I acknowledged it, so I decided to forget about Bobby and focus on Brinson. He told me the rest of the story but had little else of value to add. I told him I would call him later when I had decided what to do.

I went home and walked up the stairs to my five-year-old sister's room. She wasn't there, so I called, "Jean, come here."

When she came into the room, I pulled a penny out of my pocket and asked her, "Jean, where did you get this?" It wasn't the same penny, but she was only five and I reasoned, *How hard can it be to bluff a five-year-old?*

As it turned out, it wasn't hard at all. "How did you find out about that, Jacky? Timmy gave it to me to see my 'cookie,'" she said.

It was true. Jean called her vagina her cookie—something Murph dreamed up. My throat was dry and my heart raced, but I didn't say a word. I just waited to see what else she would say. After a minute, sheepishly she asked, "Jacky, what's that white stuff?" So it had been more than having her pull down her underpants. He had masturbated in front of her. I didn't answer but hugged her and left the room.

I found Dick, told him, and proverbially threatened him with his life if he informed Mom or Dad. My brother, recognizing that this situation would be best resolved by us, didn't say a word.

Being Saturday, our parents had planned to go out that evening, and Dick and I had to babysit for Jean. We were forbidden to have anybody over, but just as soon as the car left the street, I called several friends and told them to come over so that "we could play football in the backyard under the floodlights." I called Timmy Brinson and invited him to come over.

Mom and Dad left at 6:30 P.M., and by 7:00 P.M., all the kids had arrived. We picked up teams, and Timmy—as predetermined—was not on my team. We kicked off to him, and as Timmy started up the field, I hit him like a linebacker. The next play, he caught a pass, and I creamed him again.

Indignantly, he got up and said he didn't want to play anymore and was going home. That's when I confronted him. "Brinson, what were you doing in the woods with Jean?" He froze, and I could see cold terror in his eyes.

"What were you doing, Brinson," I pressed. It was no longer a question but an indictment.

"Nothing!"

"Marconi saw you."

"I . . . I . . . I . . ." He never finished his stammering sentence. I hit him square in the mouth and knocked him flat on his back. He tried to get up, but I hit him again and again and again. I told Dick to hit him, but he said I was doing just fine by myself.

Brinson cried. He pleaded. And then he confessed. I had made him afraid. I made him hurt. But I didn't do anything irreparable. It was just a "good, ol'-fashion lickin'," and he deserved it. When it was over, I let him go home.

The next morning, the phone rang at 7:00 A.M. My dad—already up, drinking coffee, and reading the paper—answered it. Ten seconds later, he yelled upstairs, "Jack, get your ass down here right now!" I jumped out of bed—instantly awake—and went downstairs, as did everybody else.

"Timmy Brinson's mother just called and said you beat up her son last night. They may have to take him to the hospital. She says she's going to call the Newton Police."

"I don't care," I said. "I'm glad I did it!"

I stood there in complete defiance of my father's impending fury and rage. He started to come after me and I braced myself for a beating, but that didn't happen. Of all things, Jean, my five-year-old sister, intervened and came to my defense.

Full of righteous indignation, this little girl blurted, "Daddy, don't spank Jacky. He hit Timmy because of what he did to me." Stunned, my father stopped in his tracks as the whole story unfolded from the lips of this little girl. To his credit and for once in his life, Dad listened to the entire story before going off half-cocked.

Ten minutes later, Dad called Timmy's mother and graphically told her what had happened. "Maybe *we* should call the police," he said. In terrified horror, the Brinsons—mother, father, and son—came right over and begged Dad not to go to the authorities. He didn't, and it ended right there with the promise that Timmy would get counseling immediately.

It ended there for the grown-ups anyway, but it didn't end for Timmy.

At school he was endlessly teased, taunted, and called a pervert by everybody for as long as I can remember. Whenever he saw me, he turned and went in another direction. To my knowledge, Jean never saw him again.

Years later, Jean had no memory of this incident and, to this day, she still doesn't. I asked a counselor how she could forget about something that important, that vivid in our childhood. The counselor said, "Jean was five. The trauma was handled promptly and appropriately. She didn't have any reason to remember it."

Looking back as an adult, I have often thought about Timmy Brinson. I didn't tell my dad because I was mad at him for cutting me down on the golf course. I wanted to make sure that something was done about it, and I couldn't depend on him to do it. I also have thought about how Dick and I took control of the situation and put a stop to Timmy's deviant behavior. I wonder how many other young girls were spared molestation because we publicly exposed Timmy Brinson.

As I now see it, Dad didn't do the right thing. He let Brinson go with only a promise to get counseling. Jean was the joy of his life, but my dad didn't go to the police. He didn't have Timmy put in jail; he didn't do anything. He toyed with the idea of a civil suit, but they didn't have any money. Once again, Dad was looking for an angle—a way to get money without earning it. I was fourteen and knew nothing about the legal process, but I knew it was my responsibility to take care of my sister. In my heart I knew I couldn't let Brinson get away with it, and I didn't. If I had it to do over again, I would do the same thing.

I remember thinking I had to be more vigilant. I said to myself, *I would never let this happen to a daughter of mine.*

Of course, it's easy to pontificate about what's noble. Real life, however, is never that straightforward and clear—as I was to find out repeatedly over the years.

Conspicuously absent from this incident was Murph. She was there in body, but she had absolutely no impact on the events or the outcome. The reason is one word: alcohol. My mom was an alcoholic and had been for years. We all loved her, defended her, and protected her. We enabled her repeatedly. It was what we were expected to do. In many ways, as a teenager, I had parental responsibility for my mom, which seemed normal at the time. I suppose it's where I got the idea that rescuing women was my responsibility.

Years earlier, Mom started having a glass of port wine while doing her daily housework. Within a short period, that turned into a quart of beer. Because that made her gain weight, she turned to Fleishmann's Preferred Whiskey and then to the love of her life, Fleishmann's Vodka. Dad worked for Standard Brands, which owned Fleishmann's, so Murph was showing her loyalty to the company by consuming large quantities of its products. If nothing else, Murph was loyal.

Mom didn't just drink a lot. She got drunk and passed out twice a day— not once, twice. Depending on where she was in her drinking cycle, she would be the sweetest person you would ever know or the meanest, cruelest witch with an acerbic tongue. Every day was like this—not just some days. We learned we couldn't depend on Mom for anything. If I asked her to give me a ride somewhere, she would say, "You've got a thumb. Use it!" I hitchhiked for transportation starting at age twelve. It was my only form of transportation, and I did it every day for years.

In spite of all this, we loved and protected Murph like you would never believe. If she got mad at someone, which was daily, she would "shoot them a bird" with her little, crooked arthritic finger. If they took umbrage, the verbal battle was on with Murph—all five feet of her—right in their face. We always had her back—even when she was wrong, which was nearly all the time.

She used to tell me, "Jacky, I want you to have this put on my tombstone: 'Anybody can sh*! on me once, but I'll be damned if they'll sh*! on me twice.'" Good old Murph. No slight was ever too small to disregard.

It's no wonder that none of her sons has had much luck with women. The problem wasn't getting into a relationship but *staying* in a relationship. She was our model, which made women who were a little crazy seem normal, even desirable. What was attractive to us were women with an edge to them—not women like the mother on *Father Knows Best*. From the get-go, my ability to choose was flawed.

Chapter 4

No Match for Kids

Our teenage years were fairly typical—that is, for wild, undisciplined Irish Catholic kids from Boston. We started smoking by thirteen. I smoked Old Gold Straights; Dick smoked Lucky Strikes. I went from one brand to another until Marlboro introduced the Marlboro Man and the theme music from *The Magnificent Seven*. After that, I stuck with Marlboros.

We drank whenever we could obtain it, and we talked incessantly about "getting some off" this girl or that girl. They were all lies, of course, but there was an unspoken rule that went something like this: *you believe my stories, and I'll believe yours.* It was a matter of honor for us to validate one another and impart "studhood" by saying, "He's gettin' some." It rarely was true and it never happened with me, but heaven help anyone who challenged these wild, lurid tales. It never occurred to us, of course, that we were degrading hundreds of innocent girls just to inflate our status with one another. But none of us were ever accused of being deep thinkers when we were in our midteens.

The nice thing about Massachusetts is that it has four seasons—winter, June, July, and August. You might think we would forgo drinking cold beer when it was below freezing, but you would be wrong. We would park behind a snowdrift on the golf course and be assured that no one would find out. Shivering, we drank and talked and drank some more. Those were some grand times.

A couple of years earlier, when I was twelve, Danny came home from the Marine Corps and decided he wanted to be educated rather than spend the rest of his life as a thug. So he finished high school, went to junior college, and then on to college at Boston University, where he eventually received a master's degree in business administration—years before it became fashionable. This meant he could make a fortune, which was exactly what he wanted to do; but he never abandoned his first calling: being a bully.

He also got a girlfriend, Erica Rose, nicknamed "Nicotine Nose Rose" because of the way she would French-inhale cigarettes. I know it sounds gross now, but back then it was sexy. One day Danny came home and said he and Erica were getting married in two weeks.

This seemed quick, but they were determined. They had a nice little wedding, with the reception at our house. I was the bartender who found it necessary to sample each drink poured.

They rented a small apartment, but that ended up being a disastrous arrangement, so they moved back into our house and took Dick's and my room. We didn't mind; it was an adventure. After dinner nearly every night, they would get tired at about 7:15 P.M. and go to bed for the night. This meant Dick and I had to do the dishes, but we didn't complain. We volunteered. Mom used to say, "Jacky and Dicky are so sweet to do all the cleaning up so that Danny and Erica can have some private time together."

Right! They were having their "private time" in our room, and we knew that the door was out of alignment and would not close all the way. So Dick and I would slowly, carefully, methodically, and silently creep up the stairs and watch them through the crack in the door. One time Danny was really going at it fast, and Erica put both hands on his rear end. Dick whispered in my ear, "She's trying to slow him down."

As you can imagine, we got caught, but to our genuine surprise and relief, Dad thought it was funny and didn't punish us. Danny was mad, but it was Erica who was really mad. They moved out shortly thereafter, and Erica announced she was pregnant. Six months after the wedding, they had a "premature" baby, weighing eight pounds.

Mom had a fit. "Why didn't you tell me she was pregnant and you had to get married?" There was no defense, and Murph railed in righteous indignation. Of course, there was only one difference between Mom and Erica: Erica got caught, and Mom didn't—at least not during her lifetime. Murph missed a great opportunity for compassion, healing, and bonding, but pointing out the flaws of another, especially a daughter-in-law, was much more her style.

By the time I got to high school, I didn't get into trouble anymore—not because I had matured but because Newton High had a trade school that was five hundred strong. The trade school was a feeder for the Mafia and Walpole State Prison. It was a small part of the student body, however, because there were three thousand kids—nearly all of whom went on to prestigious schools in the Northeast. I was in Curriculum I with all the brightest kids, because—in spite of my dad's continuous prophetic utterances that I would amount to nothing—I wasn't stupid.

Don't get me wrong. I didn't study, but I did pay attention in class. These days, educators would call me an audio learner. Back then they had lots of other names for me, none of them good. I was very social and, in my senior year, became vice president of the student body. I beat out two girls because I had the seniors, Dick had his crew who were all juniors, and the trade school kids would never vote for a girl.

I had played football in junior high but not in high school. Instead, I joined the gymnastics team, specializing on the still rings, which allowed me to build significant upper-body strength. One Friday after practice, when I was sixteen, I hitchhiked home and didn't arrive until about 8:00 P.M. My dad had not yet come home. As the night wore on, my mother started to get mad, and her anger increased as the hours passed. At about 11:00 P.M., Dad walked in the back door—drunk but in a lighthearted, playful mood. That ended as soon as the door shut behind him. Murph was on him with a tirade of wrath and obscenities that was even difficult for him to handle. She accused him of being with Maxine—whoever that was. Having had enough, he finally snapped and gave her a backhand right across the face.

I was sitting in the living room, watching the whole episode unfold. When he hit her, I slowly got up and started walking toward him. Recognizing he was being stalked, Dad turned around and said, "Think you're big enough to take on the old man, huh?"

Upon reaching him, our hands interlocked over his head, and I forced him back across the kitchen table with little effort. Then, from the corner, my mom said, "Don't hit him, Jacky. You'll kill him; then what will we do?"

I didn't hit him. I just let him go, but two things changed from that time forward. One, he never threatened me physically again. Two, he never raised his hand to Mom again. Dad stopped being a bully from that point forward, but his verbal cruelty continued unabated—cleverly disguised as humor. Dad often told "funny" stories or engaged in offensive antics to ingratiate himself with friends and acquaintances, and it was always at the expense of his family. We laughed along with him, but looking back, I can see how each of these incidents—and there were thousands of them—took a little piece of our souls.

One day during gymnastics practice, the drama teacher came in to find a boy to help out with the senior play. I was chosen. All I had to do was be a G-man and carry the heroine down a short flight of stairs over my shoulder and carefully set her down without letting her skirt ride up to show her underwear and rear end.

That was an easy enough assignment, and I did it in rehearsal for weeks. During the final days before the play, however, guys started coming up to me by the dozens, saying I shouldn't miss this opportunity to get a good laugh. I should let her down but hold on to her skirt. "Let the whole world see her ass! What do you care? We're graduating in a few weeks anyway," they implored.

The night of the play, I made my decision and held on to her skirt as I put her down. Her skirt rode all the way up to her waist as she squirmed valiantly to push it back down. Unfortunately for her, I had leverage and my right arm held her tight. The audience roared with laughter and approval. I was a hero to everyone—except for the girl, her parents, and the drama teacher. Even though I didn't have one speaking line, I received a standing ovation when the cast took their bows. In the cafeteria the next week, kids came up to me in droves to tell me how much they liked what I did.

The girl's name was Jane, and she never spoke to me again. I can still see the look of pain and humiliation on her face. I wince every time I think of her because she did not deserve what I did. She was innocent, trusting, and vulnerable, and I used her to get a good laugh. I was becoming like my father, getting a good laugh at the expense of another, but it was years before I would come to realize it. If I knew how to find Jane now, I would apologize and make amends, even though it has been more than two generations since it happened.

Predictably, Danny thought I was a hero, too. By this time he was just starting his MBA program at Boston University, where he was being mentored by Dean Ebersole, who referred to Danny as "the apple of my eye." Wanting me to get the best advice about education possible, Danny arranged for me to go to Boston University to meet with the dean. He was old, fat, and bald, with Coke bottles for glasses; and he played with himself the entire time I was there, which made me cringe.

It had been prearranged for the dean to drive me home after the interview, and he kept trying to put his hand on my leg the whole time. There were no seat belts back then, so I kept as close to the door as I possibly could. I escaped and told Danny and Erica what had happened. They called me a liar and a monumental ingrate for not availing myself of the dean's mentoring. Yeah, right.

The following year, Danny sent Dick, who was one year behind me in school, to see the dean for educational counseling. I warned Dick in specific detail about what the dean would do; and sure enough, Dick confirmed that the dean's counseling included blatant sexual advances.

Even with this, Danny insisted we were both lying. We trusted Danny to take care of us and to have our best interests at heart. He didn't. At the time, it didn't occur to either of us that Danny could possibly have compromised our safety on purpose, or that his relationship with the dean had more to it than we assumed.

My final two weeks at Newton High were momentous, to say the least. For whatever reason, some school janitor got fired, and the union was up in arms about it. They said it was this man's job to monitor the boiler room and, without him, the school could explode. It was late May; so there was no chance that the boilers, which produced steam heat, could explode. All that was burning was the pilot light. Nevertheless, this problem was serious, according to the union, and a perfect reason for the students to have a demonstration. We loved the idea, fighting injustice and all that.

Being the student body vice president, I was at the epicenter of the impending storm. The principal wanted the student leadership—the president and me—to squelch the movement. We wanted a little excitement and to be remembered, so we gave lip service to the principal and plotted a massive student uprising the last day before final exams.

The morning before tests began, we had football players stationed at every entrance to the school so that wimps and girls couldn't go in. The entire student body—three thousand kids—was outside when the bell rang. By 8:30 A.M., all were chanting, "Blow . . . Blow . . . Blow." Nothing happened, of course, but when a single police car arrived, everything changed. The kids from the trade school started rocking the police car back and forth. The cops called for reinforcements, and the school president and I lost control.

We wanted a little harmless fun, but what we got was a full-blown riot—several years before riots about Vietnam became fashionable. The trade school kids marched on City Hall, three blocks away, to lynch the mayor. They were greeted with fire hoses, and the riot quickly disintegrated. By this time I was in class along with nearly every other sane student.

But it didn't end there. Detectives from the Newton Police Department arrived and determined I was a leading instigator. I had several interviews with them, and they learned I had a "provisional acceptance" to the University of Massachusetts. One call from them and that changed. I was out at UMass, the school my father wanted me to attend.

They asked if I had been accepted anywhere else, and I said I had not. I lied. Georgia, which was my security school and where I wanted to go— thanks to the comment from my dad's golfing buddy years earlier—had accepted me. I was called in for questioning one more time, but there were no arrests and nothing else came of it. The detective called me a negative leader, coming to that conclusion because he remembered what a thug Danny had been a decade earlier. He just assumed I was like my brother.

Gratefully, graduation came and went, and I laid low for the remainder of the summer. In August, I boarded a Greyhound Bus—headed for Athens, the University of Georgia, and a new life.

Chapter 5

Let's Have a Party

I arrived in Athens, for the first time in my life, forty-two hours after boarding a Greyhound bus. On the journey, I received a tour of many farming communities in the rural South and learned that the earth could be a rusty color of red. It was late August 1962, and I had never experienced such heat in my life. When I arrived at the university, I learned I would be rooming with a blind student.

In my room, which was not air-conditioned, there sat Bubba Racine—naked, sitting on a chair, picking at his toes, and listening to a book on record. This was not a onetime occurrence. He always sat in our room naked, picking at his toes, with the record player on. There were two chairs in the room, and he sat on both of them—naked, always naked—without putting a towel down or anything else to cover the seat. I never sat in my own dorm room—not once, ever. Just the thought of it still makes me shudder.

It was quite an experience, but I was so relieved to be away from Newton that nothing could dash my enthusiasm. I stayed away from my dorm room as much as possible, and I took the top bunk, which was the only spot that seemed to be off-limits to toe-picking Bubba.

Rush started, and I signed up for it immediately. Pledging Kappa Sigma, I felt a sense of belonging for the first time in my life. Because I was the only Yankee in the fraternity, my required metamorphosis to southerner encompassed every aspect of my being. The first things to go were my white socks, which I wore with everything, including suits. It was all I had, so I was required to buy Gold Cup socks. To me, they seemed better suited for old men, but after being paddled a few times, I saw the error of my ways. Next, I had to buy cardigan sweaters—you know, like Mr. Rogers always wore.

A graduate student in English, Juddy Blount, gave me speech lessons so I wouldn't say At-lant-A but a much more subdued At-lan-a, where the second *t* was silent. Eager to please, I did as he directed.

My dorm room was in Reed Hall. Staying down the adjacent corridor from me was Harold Black, one of the first African American male students ever admitted to the University of Georgia. He was a nice guy—shy and scared to death, so I befriended him. We started eating together at the cafeteria in the mornings. Several members of my pledge class from South Georgia gave me a very hard time about it, so I reluctantly started avoiding Harold. To this day, I'm ashamed of what I did.

At Kappa Sigma, we drank practically every night. There was always something to do, and the classes seemed easier than high school. That didn't mean I made good grades; it just meant I really didn't need to work very hard to pass.

Once, in the fall, we had a party on a Thursday night. It was called the Golden Grain Party, which I thought had to do with harvest time. Boy, was I wrong. It was called Golden Grain because that's what was served in the enormous punch bowl. At that time, Athens was a dry county. Consequently, some of the brothers drove to South Carolina, where they bought Golden Grain alcohol. You couldn't even buy it in Georgia. It was 190 proof—almost pure alcohol. When they brought it back to the fraternity, they gave it to Johnny, our "houseboy," to mix for the party. Johnny was illiterate and thought it was vodka, so he mixed it in the bowl three parts grapefruit juice to one part Golden Grain. It should have been mixed twelve to one, but because pure alcohol is almost tasteless, nobody could tell how potent it was.

The party lasted about forty-five minutes. After that, nearly everybody had passed out. Fortunately, nobody died. I don't remember going back to my dorm, but I do remember waking up at about 2:30 A.M., needing desperately to go to the bathroom. Still completely drunk, I hopped down from the top bunk. I went to the door to go down the hall to the bathroom, but I couldn't figure out how to get our door unlocked. Try as I might, I couldn't get it opened, so in my inebriated state, I just started going right there. Bubba got out of bed to open the door for me, but being blind, he walked straight into the line of fire. Enraged, he started slapping at me like a girl. I just went back to bed.

Early the next morning, however, Bubba, screaming like a banshee, startled me awake. He had stepped right into the puddle, which, understandably, infuriated him.

I had to take a final exam at nine, which I don't even remember taking, but I did receive a C+ for my effort. After the exam, I was called to Dean Tate's office, where I narrowly avoided being kicked out of school for using my roommate as a urinal. But I was required to get a new roommate and make a $100 charitable contribution to the school.

Finding a new roommate was easy, but I had to borrow some money from friends to make the $100 charitable contribution. Back then, $100 was a lot of money. Now I'm certain this system violated my constitutional rights or something like that, but it kept thousands of crazy kids like me in line. It hurt, but it seemed fair.

Once, about thirty rednecks from Payne Hall said they were going to lynch Harold Black. They were all congregating in the parking lot between buildings, drinking beer and talking about what they were going to do to that "damned n*****." Dean Tate pulled up in his car, got out, and in a booming, authoritative voice said, "All right, boys. Let me see your IDs." Knowing what that meant, they scattered in every direction, and no threat like this was ever made again.

As a Kappa Sigma pledge, my main purpose in life was to do whatever any brother asked of me. I shined more shoes than the guy at the airport. I also was supposed to have a deferential demeanor, which was a challenge on my best day. "Watts," a brother would bellow, "you didn't make my bed the way I like. Give me twenty push-ups."

"Yes, sir. One hand or two?"

"You cocky Yankee, give 'em to me one-handed."

"Yes, sir. Right or left?" What really pissed them off is I could do it. My cockiness cost me dearly, however, because I would catch a lick with the paddle half a dozen times a day—maybe more. From September to March, I always had a bruise or two on my "skinny Yankee ass."

When Hell Week came along, I was elated but apprehensive—elated because I would be an initiate at the end of it, apprehensive because no fewer than ten brothers said they were going to make it their personal responsibility to break me. I believed them.

Hazing was steadfastly forbidden by university rules; so was drinking at football games, but nobody paid attention to that one either. They paddled us, made us drink mineral oil, and a number of other degrading things; but the scavenger hunt was actually fun. My group of three was sent to Atlanta, where glamour queen Jayne Mansfield was playing at the Copacabana on Ponce De Leon Avenue. We were "required" to bring back her panties.

As soon as we got into the car, I told the guys I knew how we could accomplish our mission. When we arrived at the nightclub, I asked to speak to her husband, Mickey Hargitay, who had been Mr. Universe in 1956. I told him my brother Danny had worked out with him often in California and was still training in Boston. "Yeah, I think I remember him," said Mickey, who obviously didn't have a clue who Danny was.

"We sure would like to meet your wife, Mr. Hargitay. Can we?"

"She's onstage right now, but I'll ask her," he said, using his only compound sentence of the night. "Wait right here."

Twenty minutes later, he brought us in to see his wife, Jayne Mansfield, who was a certified glamorous queen in the spring of 1963. "I just love fraternity boys," she said, jiggling her breasts as she said it. I looked at her and was mystified. She looked old, harried, and flaccid rather than alluring and voluptuous, with thinning hair. But I digress; we were on an important assignment.

I said, "Miss Mansfield, we need a pair of your panties for our fraternity scavenger hunt. May we have a pair? We'll pay for them—if you like."

"I'd love to boys, but I don't wear panties," she said without the least bit of embarrassment. At this point, one of my pledge companions dropped a pen and tried to sneak a peek. I quickly stepped in front of him because, although Mickey's Alka-Seltzer might have lost a lot of its fizz, he was sure to figure that one out.

I thought for a moment, then countered, "How about a bra? We could bring that back instead."

"Okay, I can do that." Turning, she went to a large trunk and pulled out a performance bra—complete with sequins that she used onstage. On one cup she wrote "Lovingly . . . Jayne Mansfield" and on the other "Affectionately . . . Jayne Mansfield." When we returned to Athens, we were heroes.

Because of our victory in the scavenger hunt, we were given our choice of which sorority we would visit for dinner that Sunday evening. Our Sweetheart was a Chi Omega, so I chose that one. Lots of cute girls were there, but one heavyset girl named Nancy talked to me the whole evening. We talked for hours. My primary motivation wasn't romance but survival.

I knew that as long as I was there and it didn't look like I was stalling, I would not have to go back to the fraternity house and get my butt beat.

One requirement during Hell Week had me concerned. We had to have a date for the Hawaiian Luau Party the following Friday, but we weren't allowed to talk to any girls to ask them out. Most of the pledges had girlfriends so they didn't have to worry, but I didn't have a clue about how to take care of this. The only girl we could talk to was the Sweetheart, Libby Freeman—as lovely a young woman as you would ever want to meet.

I walked into the fraternity Monday afternoon, braced for more ignominious hazing; but to my utter shock and surprise, Libby was in the living room and came running up to me—a pledge, a freshman, and a Yankee. She ran up to *me*! My stock went right through the roof with all the guys because this beautiful senior ran right up to me. She said, "Jack, do you have a date for the luau yet?" Without waiting for a reply, she continued, "Because if you don't, one of my sorority sisters wants to go out with you. She thought you were real cute. You'll take her, won't you?"

"Sure" was all I could get out, but it was all I needed. I had a date, and my last worry was gone. I thought my date would be the heavyset girl I talked to for so long, but it wasn't.

Chapter 6

The Girl for Me

Having just finished Hell Week and been initiated into the Kappa Sigma fraternity as a brother, I was feeling pretty confident and self-assured as I drove up to Chi Omega to pick up my date for the luau. Upon arrival, I called for her in the formal way required by sororities in the South. Then I went into the tastefully appointed reception room and waited for her to come downstairs. I waited twenty minutes . . . forty . . . sixty . . . ninety minutes. I was worried that all the free liquor would have been consumed and that the party would be half over. Then someone said, "Mona's coming down the stairs to meet you."

Calming myself, I walked to the stairs and looked up. She wasn't the heavyset girl I expected. Instead it was the most beautiful girl I had ever seen in my life—Mona Everett. The first thing I noticed was her magnificent blue eyes—followed very closely by her perfectly proportioned figure, medium-length frosted blond hair, and chin that jutted out just a little too far. She was gorgeous with a very confident, sensuous demeanor. As she came down the stairs, she was smiling, and I said to myself, *I'm going to marry this girl.* I'll never forget it. I wasn't yet nineteen and had virtually no real experience with women, but I knew instantly this was the girl for me.

When we went to the party, every eye turned when I brought Mona into the room. They couldn't believe I was with such a beauty, and neither could I. She was from Colquitt, Georgia, a small agricultural community in the southwestern corner of the state. You couldn't get more South Georgia than Colquitt.

Mona was a sophomore who had been dating a tailback from the Clemson football team for years. His name was Ted Winston. Neither was ready to settle down and get married, so they decided to date other people when they weren't with each other. To Mona, I was a cute boy to have some fun with. To me, it was much more right from the start. We started seeing a lot of each other—movies, tennis, studying, or my personal favorite, making out. We did a lot of that.

When the school year ended, it nearly killed me to go back to Boston. Mom sent me $36 for the bus fare, which I cashed and hitchhiked home. It took me twenty-two hours instead of forty-two hours on the bus—with the added bonus that I pocketed the money. Hitchhiking was easy for me. I would do it with another student. We would wear a sports coat and tie and carry a sign that said: "BOSTON . . . *Help Save Our Soles!*" People loved it. They would stop, and some went many miles out of their way to accommodate us. I would just show up at the front door in Newton and announce I was home.

I was particularly interested to see Dick. I was a little worried about him. In the middle of winter, Mom had called, saying Dick was in the hospital. He was going to see his friend Jimmy Callahan in Auburndale one night, and he rode a Raleigh bike he had found to get there. Realizing it was well below freezing, Dick went down a hill very fast to lessen his exposed time to the cold. A taxi pulled out of a side street, hitting him straight on. Dick went through the windshield.

The cabdriver wasn't hurt, but he was badly shaken by the incident. He took Dick to the hospital, where he was admitted. The cabdriver had alcohol on his breath, according to several hospital employees, so he quietly slipped out before the police arrived.

As it turned out, Dick was fine—just a little sore from the force of the impact, which was blunted by his heavy winter coat. When he was released, Dick asked Dad if the cab company would replace his bike. "We'll see, son" was the answer Dad gave him. Periodically, Dick would ask again if he was going to get another bike, but Dad was always evasive. Finally, Dad told Dick his bike wouldn't be replaced. According to Dad, the window of opportunity had passed.

At any rate, I arrived in Newton in late May, and my dad had secured a job for me working at the Stop & Shop Bakery next to the famed Boston Garden, home of the World Champion Celtics. The area sounds glamorous, but it was a dump—at least in the summer of 1963. I worked from 3:00 P.M. to 11:00 P.M. in the oven section, which was never below 130 degrees, and I had to ride the Metropolitan Transit Authority (MTA) to and from work.

Because of the hours, I had no social life and never saw any of my friends from high school. In my off time in the morning, I would read classic novels and found—to my surprise—that I had more comprehension than I had gotten credit for.

With no social life and living at home, I saved nearly $1,200, which was 60 percent of what it cost for a year at UGA. I didn't know it at the time, but my dad would never send me another dime for college. I had just turned nineteen, and I was on my own.

In late August, I received $36 from my mom for the bus, had her drop me off at Greyhound, waited until she left, cashed in the ticket, and then hitchhiked to Athens. It took twenty-six hours going back. As soon as I arrived, I called Mona, who was not nearly as excited to hear from me as I was to talk to her—probably because she had spent a lot of time over the summer with the Clemson tailback.

Regardless, rush started—followed by football, classes, parties, and the full swing of college life at UGA. In November I was playing bridge, which I did for hours every day, when one of the brothers hurriedly came out of the TV room. "The president's been shot!" was all he said. Instantly, the TV room was full, as we all watched the events at Dealey Plaza unfold before our eyes—narrated by Walter Cronkite. Finally, they announced that President Kennedy was dead. My bridge partner, said, "He's dead. We can't help him now. I've bid six spades—a baby slam, and I want to play the hand." We all went back and played the hand, which I've been embarrassed to admit ever since.

Kids at UGA, like Americans everywhere, were devastated by the assassination; and for a short period of time, sobriety reigned at Kappa Sigma. With classes canceled for three days, Mona and I spent substantial time together and continued to do so until the end of the quarter. Making the best grades so far, I went home for Christmas, not realizing I was spending the last carefree days of my youth.

Chapter 7

"It's Been Thirty-Three Days"

My mother discovered I wasn't going back and forth to school on Greyhound. To this day, I don't know how she figured it out, but that was the end of my $36 bonus. Refusing to ante up for a $76 airplane ticket, which I would have used, and with my steadfast refusal to get on the forty-two-hour bus ride, Murph dropped me off at the Mass Pike at 2:00 A.M. on New Year's Eve to hitchhike. It was well below freezing. I got a ride in about three minutes, which carried me all the way to Virginia. I arrived at school in the middle of a terrible snowstorm, a rarity for Georgia.

I slept for a few hours and then called Mona. We picked up right where we left off, seeing each other every day. One Saturday night in early January, we went to a drive-in to see some really boring movie. Because it was so cold in the car and the movie was not interesting, we snuggled and started making out more than usual, which was fine with me. We were in the front seat of her Nash—the ugliest car at UGA. Because it was so uncomfortable, she actually got on top of me, straddling my legs. I couldn't figure out what she was doing, but then it dawned on me: she wanted to have sex!

I remember thinking, *There's no downside to this.* It was the most wonderful, thrilling, fulfilling fourteen seconds of my life.

And that's not all. At that exact quarter minute, a fraternity brother, recognizing the ugly, split-pea-soup-green Nash, came to the window to say hello. Realizing he shouldn't disturb us, he quietly went away. Upon returning to the fraternity that night, however, it was a different story. He greeted me with an enormous smirk on his face and, in front of several others, said, "Jack's getting some from Mona. Way to go."

Without hesitation, I responded, "No, I'm not."

"I *saw* you" was all he said. As he and the others walked off, each sported a smile of profound approbation. As long as I could remember, I wanted guys to think I was "getting some"; but when it finally happened— for the first time, I might add—all I could do was deny it. I didn't want anybody to think badly of Mona.

As it turned out, and much to my disappointment, it was a onetime thing. We still saw each other daily, but she was careful to avoid getting into a compromising situation. For me, that was okay, because I was deeply in love with her and nothing could reverse my feelings.

Toward the end of January, she started breaking up with me, and I was very upset. During one telephone call she said, "Jack, it's been thirty-three days." That's all she said and ended the conversation shortly thereafter. I had no idea what she was talking about and went to bed.

At 3:30 A.M., I opened my eyes—wide awake. "Oh, my God" was all I could say. She might be pregnant. This realization froze me with a sharp pang of trepidation.

Several days later, I took her to a local gynecologist who did a frog test, where the doctor injected some of Mona's urine into a frog. If the frog produced eggs within twenty-four hours, it would confirm Mona was pregnant. The frog quickly produced eggs. I told Mona that I loved her and wanted to marry her. She responded coldly, "I want an abortion."

Stunned and Catholic, I said, "That's wrong, and they'll put us in jail if we're caught." Very few decent people received abortions in 1964; they got married like my dad and older brother. Like them, I was eager to do what was right.

Each day Mona grew more distant. By early February, I was very unhappy and couldn't concentrate on schoolwork. My grades suffered badly. I didn't care. One night, a group from Campus Crusade for Christ was scheduled to visit Chi Omega. Attendance was mandatory, so Mona went to hear what they had to say.

The next day she called, and we had lunch. "I don't want an abortion; I want to have the baby and give it up for adoption," she said. I was speechless. She had been adamant about getting an abortion the day before, and now she was just as adamant about adoption.

Turning to me, she meekly asked, "Would you like to talk to the man from Campus Crusade?"

"Yeah, I would."

Chapter 8

The First Time in My Life

The very next night, after a meeting at the Sigma Chi house, Carl McMurray, the regional director of Campus Crusade, came to see me at 11:30 P.M. We sat in the Chapter Room of Kappa Sigma and talked for hours. Not knowing what to expect, I began the meeting by saying, "If you're going to try and talk me out of being a Catholic, I'm not interested." I knew practically nothing about any other form of Christianity, but I was fiercely loyal to the One, True, Holy, Catholic, and Apostolic Church. It had been drummed into me my entire life.

"I'm not going to try and talk you out of being a Catholic, Jack. Mona told me she was in trouble. Would you like to know what God wants you to do about that?" Carl asked very candidly and matter-of-factly.

"Yes, I would," and that's exactly what he did.

We talked for hours. I knew little about God, but I was very open and eager to hear all that Carl had to say. Upon completion, he asked me if I would like to pray with him—right then and there—to invite Christ to come into my life.

"No, absolutely not," I said. I had never prayed openly in my life. The very thought of it was appalling—as it would have been for any pre-Vatican II Catholic. So at 2:45 A.M. he left to drive back to Atlanta, discouraged because he had not closed the deal. For me, however, the night had just begun.

Carl had written down one Scripture verse for me to look up. I didn't have a Bible. I didn't know the difference between the Old and New Testaments, but I did know where I could find a Bible. I went into a drinking buddy's room and asked if he had one. Cursing at me for waking him up, Ron opened his trunk, rummaged around, and handed me an old leather

Bible. Thanking him, I went back to the Chapter Room, closed the door, put the jukebox on full blast, lit a cigarette, and started reading the Scriptures for the first time in my life.

I had no idea where to begin, so I just opened the Bible and started reading. I went from one passage to the next—each more poignant and on target than the previous one. I felt like my hands were being gently guided every time I would flip through the pages. I read until 7:00 A.M., smoked a pack of Marlboros, and made my decision to invite Christ to come into my life. I did so, kneeling and saying Hail Marys in the Chapter Room of Kappa Sigma fraternity with a song blaring from the jukebox, "Hey, Won't You Stay Just a Little Bit Longer?" I had not slept at all, but I was invigorated. Something had changed in me, and I knew it. I felt empowered, clean, purposeful, and resilient.

Christians, or so it seems to me, like to think that once a person invites Christ into his or her life, everything changes dramatically, flawlessly, and nearly overnight. But it's simply not true. That night, however, what changed for me was my belief system. I was now a Bible-believing Christian, and what the Scriptures said was important—actually, more than important; it was foundational. It reshaped the core of who Jack Watts was, how I thought, and what I would do with my life.

The subsequent decades have been about change and healing—with numerous failures mixed in. I think of it like eating the petals of an artichoke, which need to be pulled off one by one before you get to the juicy heart. Each problematic issue in my life, like a petal, had to be recognized, acknowledged, and solved before core attitudinal issues could be addressed. I couldn't get to the heart of my problems quickly. I had to take things one at a time—like the petals of the artichoke. I wanted to "be fixed immediately." I even insisted on it in my prayers, but that's not the way life works. At times I thought I would never heal or mature; at other times I was certain of it. Many years later, however, the transformation has indeed been substantial—closer by far to the "tasty heart" of the artichoke.

If the ghost of Jacob Marley, in Dickens's *A Christmas Carol*, was forced to carry the weight of the chains he had forged by a lifetime of greed, then like the rest of my family, I have been forced to carry the chains of my "Wattsness." Some of the character qualities have been positive, but there has been enough negative dysfunction, stemming from low self-esteem and deep-seated anger, to make every following year interesting.

Chapter 9

"Keep Your Coattails Down"

I called Mona later that day and told her what had happened. She was surprised and called Carl McMurray. The next day, Carl came to visit and asked me—over and over again—if I would like to pray with him to make certain Christ had come into my life.

"Do you have to invite Christ in more than once?" I inquired innocently.

"No, once is all you need," he conceded, reluctantly dropping the subject.

Carl started coming to see me three or four times a week. He also started counseling each of us separately and then together about living honorably and about general Christian principles. By the end of February he became very specific when he said, "Mona, if you want to do God's will, marry Jack." Quoting Deuteronomy 22:28–29 (NASB), Carl said, "If a man finds a girl who is a virgin, who is not engaged, and seizes her and lies with her and they are discovered, then the man who lay with her shall give to the girl's father fifty shekels of silver, and she shall become his wife because he has violated her; he cannot divorce her all his days."

When she heard this, Mona's response was immediate and crushing, "But I wasn't a virgin." This is how I discovered that the love of my life had been having sex with Ted—the Clemson tailback—for years. Because he never wore protection, I learned, Mona assumed getting pregnant was difficult. To add insult to injury, she added, "I don't love Jack, and I don't want to marry him. He's a little boy."

Carl said, "The point here is that this pregnancy has humbled you. You've asked what God wants? He wants you to marry Jack. It's as simple as that."

"I don't believe that's what He wants, and I'm not going to do it," Mona replied. A Taurus, and as immovable as a bull, she could not be budged, countering, "We can go away together without anybody knowing, have the baby, give it up, and come back to school next year with nobody the wiser."

Carl finally stopped trying to convince her but said we needed to tell her parents what was happening. We would never be able to keep it a secret from them, he reasoned. So it was determined that Mona and I would get in her car at noon on Friday and drive to Colquitt, where I would tell her family I had knocked up their precious baby daughter.

We left right on schedule. As we drove through rural South Georgia, I was struck by how poor this part of the country really was. When we pulled up to her house, the first thing I noticed was that it was on stilts, which meant the floors slanted in nearly every direction.

Her mother, Rose, came out to greet us. She was about four eleven and weighed 250 pounds. I'm not exaggerating—250 pounds. I was not prepared for this. Her dad, Lucian Everett—a rural route postman—was a little heavyset but was actually quite distinguished-looking.

After dinner, as we sat in the living room, all eyes fell on me. Recognizing my cue, I began telling them how we had both come to Christ and how much this impact was having on our lives. Waxing eloquent for quite a spell, I ended by saying, "All these positive things came about when we realized that Mona was pregnant."

"Ah, what was that last part again?" her father, Mr. Lucian, quizzed.

I repeated it, and her mother burst into tears. Sobbing, she said, "Oh, Mona, why couldn't you learn to keep your coattails down?"

As you can imagine, we talked for a long time after that, and Mona told them she had no intention of marrying me. In front of me, as if I weren't there, Rose said, "Why don't you tell Ted it's his and marry him?"

"Because it can't be his," Mona protested defensively.

"A girl who will do one will do the other. Tell Ted it's his," Rose insisted.

"Ted and I have never had a relationship like that, Mama, and I'm insulted that you would accuse me of such a thing," Mona said as her nostrils flared. I kept my mouth shut, but I could see that this simple country-woman was no fool—unlike the Yankee in her living room.

The next morning, Mona awakened me early by saying, "Jack, you've got to get up. Daddy's gone to work, and he wants you out of the house and gone before he gets home for lunch."

I was surprised, but by the time I got up and dressed, Mona had the car running to carry me out to the highway. The highway wasn't much more than a dirt road. When she dropped me off, I never felt more alone in my life. It was sweltering, I hadn't eaten, and there was virtually no traffic. I walked a couple of miles and was finally picked up.

I hitchhiked to Carl McMurray's house in Atlanta. My plan was to stay there a couple of days before hitchhiking back to Boston to get a job and pay for Mona's upkeep until the baby was born and put up for adoption. When I arrived at Carl's, they were thrilled to see me. Carl's wife, Mary Jo, one of my all-time favorite people, excitedly said, "Mona just called ten minutes ago. She's changed her mind. She wants to marry you, and she wants you to go back to Colquitt right away."

To say I was surprised was an obvious understatement. Carl said, "Mary Jo and I wondered how long it would take her to come to her senses. It didn't take long. You couldn't have been gone more than a couple of hours before she realized how alone she really was."

So, first thing the next morning, I hitchhiked back to Colquitt, arriving in the late afternoon. The atmosphere was tense at Mona's house—with Rose ranting about her daughter marrying a Catholic from Boston one minute and beaming at the prospect about being a granny the next.

Mr. Lucian arrived at suppertime. We all sat down, but he would neither look at me nor speak to me. Quietly, we ate. Near the end of the meal, Mr. Lucian turned to me and said, "Would you care for some of Rose's homemade tomato and okra relish?"

The ice was broken and the tension subsided. I answered, "Yes, I'd love some relish." I took a huge helping of that wretched, foul-smelling, slimy stuff, and suppressed my gag reflex as I ate it with a smile.

The next day, Mona and I drove to Albany, Georgia, and bought two wedding bands for $19.95 each. It was all we could afford. Going back, we went to see the Methodist minister and arranged to be married in the little church that had stood in Colquitt since the Civil War. We planned a simple, quiet, and quick wedding.

Her two sisters, Biddy and Beebe, arrived with their husbands—as well as her brother, Charles. Mona was much younger than any of her siblings, each of whom tried to talk her out of marrying a Yankee from Boston. None was successful.

Finally, the morning of the wedding arrived. As I walked into the kitchen to get a cup of coffee, one of her sisters screamed, "Daddy's having a heart attack! Call the ambulance quick!"

The ambulance arrived, and Mr. Lucian was rushed to Tallahassee

Memorial Hospital. We all went down there with him and stayed in the waiting room for hours. In the late afternoon, Mona's sister Biddy and her husband, who were from Jacksonville, Florida, had to return home. I was asked to go to the cafeteria and get them Cokes for the trip.

When I returned with the soft drinks, Biddy and her husband had gone and taken Mona with them. I was told caustically by her sister Beebe, "Mona isn't going to marry you. It would kill Daddy." That was it. No debate, no compromise, and no good-byes. As it turned out, there wasn't anything wrong with Mr. Lucian's heart—other than it was too hard.

Her brother, Charles, drove me back to Colquitt to spend the night at the family house. I had expected this to be my wedding night, but when I went to bed, Charles tried to get in bed with me—dressed only in his underpants. Clearly excited, he smiled lasciviously, which shocked and repulsed me. I jumped out of bed and went to another room, but he followed me there as well. I pushed him away and told him I was not interested in his sexual advances. Undeterred, he went into the living room, retrieving a sword from over the mantel to threaten me. I told him if he didn't put it down immediately, he would never have to worry about getting an erection again. Realizing how serious I was, he finally left me alone. Years later, I discovered he had just been released from a federal prison where he had been incarcerated for several years for embezzling from the IRS.

I didn't sleep well and left quietly—very early the next morning while it was still dark. Once again, I was back on the road, hitchhiking to Atlanta for a quick stop before going to Boston. I was crushed and worried sick about what was going to happen to Mona. I wondered what giving up her baby would do to her in the long run. I also wondered if there was anything I could have done differently.

A new concern started to surface as well: What was going to happen to my unborn child? This concern grew and became an overwhelming pain deep in my heart, but there was absolutely nothing I could do to prevent what was happening. I had no recourse. As I realized I had no choice but to give the baby up, I prayed, *Father, I give You my child. Please take care of it.* As I did, a peace that I did not understand and had never experienced before overwhelmed me. I knew I would find my child one day.

Chapter 10

Questions about Your Position

My stay in Boston lasted only three months. That's all I could stand. Once again, Dad found me a job—this time driving a Wonder Bread truck as a route salesman. My boss was very excited to have me and told me I would qualify to be a supervisor if I was successful on the route for five years. I had to be at work at 3:30 A.M. five days a week. Half my paycheck went to support Mona, who was expressly forbidden by her family to communicate with me in any way. All I was allowed to do was pay for everything. I was on academic probation at UGA, so further schooling seemed improbable. I was just nineteen, but my life was already miserable.

Add to that scenario Murph's alcoholism, which was totally out of control, with Dad quickly catching up, and it was easy to see why I felt lonely and hopeless. In addition, Dick was in the navy somewhere in the Mediterranean, so I didn't even have my brother for support. I started to carouse with my old friends from high school, drinking nearly every night.

Living in this situation was not good for me, and I knew it. So I packed everything I owned, put it in my 1958 Olds 88 convertible—white and powder blue—and took off for Jacksonville to find Mona. It was June, so school was out for the summer. Upon arriving, I stayed with a fraternity brother, found out where Mona was living, and showed up at her sister's house one weekday midmorning unannounced.

Mona was the only person at home, and she was thrilled to see me. For days, I came and went secretly, which seemed to be particularly pleasing to her but very uncomfortable for me. I had a fleeting thought that being her *secret* boyfriend was the most attractive quality about me. She acted as if we were a nice, young married couple, expecting our first child, which seemed a little bizarre, given the situation. By now she was showing and, like most young pregnant women, radiated. I did not want to give the baby away and did everything I could to get her to change her mind, but she wouldn't budge. Finally, Biddy and her husband discovered I was there and put a stop to me seeing her.

Reluctantly, I got into the convertible and headed for Carl McMurray's house in Atlanta again. By that time, however, I was out of money and didn't have enough gas to make the 375-mile trip. I picked up a hitchhiker who filled the tank at $0.29 a gallon, and we headed off for Atlanta. After dropping the guy off at his doorstep, I went to the McMurrays, who welcomed me without reservation.

I had no money, no job, no place to stay, and substantial regular expenses for Mona's upkeep. But I wasn't concerned or worried. My life was just beginning for a second time, and I was determined to do a better job with it. I secured employment the following day selling women's fashion shoes at Davison's, a Macy's company, and I moved in with several staff members from Campus Crusade.

I did extremely well selling shoes because I was young, energetic, and loved talking to women. I developed numerous "call customers," including Alberta Williams King, the mother of Dr. Martin Luther King Jr. She was a delightfully kind woman who loved beautiful shoes but had difficult feet to fit. Actually, they were more than difficult—they were nearly impossible. I worked with her for what seemed like hours, and she was genuinely appreciative. I would see her son around town often, and he would always shake my hand or nod while he was passing. Although already prominent in 1964, I had no idea how important Dr. King would eventually be to America and the world, but I knew I liked his mom. Perhaps his mom told him about me; I like to think that, anyway.

During this period, I didn't drink at all. I worked hard all the time, and I continued sending Mona money for a while longer but finally stopped. I sent her relatives a letter, telling them I wouldn't send any more money if I wouldn't be allowed to communicate with Mona regularly. They refused, so I stopped.

I spent a great deal of time at church. I went to a very conservative church, where they made me a Sunday school teacher for ninth graders. The kids loved me. One day during class, a girl asked me, "Mr. Watts, should I square dance as part of the school curriculum or make a stand for Christ because dancing is sinful?"

I responded curiously, "Why would you want to look ridiculous in front of all your friends over square dancing? If I were you, I would just go ahead and do it. If you're going to make a stand, make it about something important—not something trivial."

That night I received a call from Rev. Simpson, the church pastor. "Jack," he said, "I want to ask you some questions about your position on some critical issues for teens." Sensing the underlying malice in his syrupy tone, I listened intently as he asked me my position on movies, dancing, cards, and numerous other things. Finally he said, "What's your position on mixed bathing?"

Without hesitation I responded, "I'm against it. I think it's okay for boys and girls to swim together, but I'm dead set against them taking a bath together!" Complete silence ensued. My attempt to interject a little humor actually made matters worse.

"I think we need to have lunch tomorrow. Can you meet me at twelve thirty?" It wasn't a request.

At 12:30 P.M. I met Rev. Simpson, a diminutive man in his midthirties with jet-black hair, pale white skin, and penetrating black eyes. As we sat down, I was very nervous and started to light a Marlboro. Rev. Simpson, in his most ingratiating tone, said, "Jack, it's all right if you smoke. I'll love you just as much if you light that cigarette as I will if you don't."

"I know. Thanks," I said and lit the cigarette. Enraged, he seethed with anger as I sat there speechless. He lit into me for smoking in the first place and went on from there with a tirade that would draw approbation from any prosecutor in the land.

Incredulously, I said, "Then why did you say it was all right to smoke?"

He refused to answer. At the end of the meal, he prayed and left with the self-satisfied confidence that he had set another sinner straight.

After he left, I was shaken to the core. I had been a born-again Christian for fewer than six months; but I knew I never wanted to be like this self-righteous, mean-spirited pastor. It bothered me so much that since then I have never been able to tolerate such misanthropy, especially by those who parade their Christianity as their prime asset. I went to that church less frequently and finally stopped going altogether. I became cautious and guarded around church people rather than open and transparent. I remember thinking that Christians shouldn't talk about loving people if they don't. That experience, along with several similar ones, made it easier several years later for me to join a group in California that eventually became a cult.

The Simpson episode, however, has a happy ending. My smoking, which was up to a pack a day, was becoming an increasing concern to me for a number of reasons. I tried to quit repeatedly, but with no lasting success. Finally, one of my Crusade roommates, Charlie Brown, said, "Jack, if you want to quit—*really want to quit*, I can tell you how. Do you want to?"

"Absolutely," I said, and I meant it.

"Okay, promise me you won't have another cigarette unless you check with me first." Promising, I actually threw a half-empty pack of Marlboros out the window—signifying the depth of my commitment.

I went to work the next day, and by noon, my body was screaming for nicotine. I wanted a cigarette desperately; but try as I may, I couldn't find Charlie anywhere to *check* with him. Having promised, I stuck it out. When I arrived at our apartment, Charlie was there. I said, "I can't make it. I'm going to the store to buy a pack."

"Okay, I'll go with you; but do you want to pray and ask the Lord to take your desire away just for now?"

That seemed reasonable, and I would never hear the end of it if I didn't; so I prayed, "Lord, please take the desire for cigarettes away from me." Nothing happened, but looking up at Charlie I said, "Maybe we can wait awhile. I don't think I need one right this minute." And I didn't.

The desire was gone, and although I waited for it to return, it never did. Not then, not the next day, not ever. I had been delivered from my addiction to cigarettes. That was a healing moment for me, which required a substantial commitment. I didn't know it at the time, but I would have to call upon God again years later to deliver me from my addiction to alcohol.

My dad was never able to quit smoking and remained addicted to nicotine his entire life. He eventually developed emphysema, which took decades from his life and made his final years a daily struggle to breathe.

With the Simpson incident freshly behind me, I began using my energy to start Campus Crusade for Christ at Georgia State University, my new school. Entering on strict academic probation, I took two classes the following winter quarter. I had to make a C or better in both, or I would flunk out. When it was time to take the final, I had a very low C in psychology.

Would I pass and go on, or would I flunk out and be forced to drive a Wonder Bread truck or worse? With my entire future on the line, I took the test—armed only with a pen and my knowledge of the subject.

I aced it—well, I got a 73, but all I needed was a 70. I was back in the game—off academic probation. I wouldn't have to drive a Wonder Bread truck after all. My grades improved steadily after that. When I graduated, my GPA was 3.25. Later I received an MA from Baylor University with a 3.85 GPA and all the course work for a PhD at Emory University with a 3.88.

By the time I started going back to school, my entire life was progressing well. I felt like I belonged, had wonderful friends, all with outstanding character qualities, and I was debt-free. My life had purpose, and my goal—to graduate and go on the Campus Crusade staff—seemed attainable and worthy. When I thought about the future, I smiled with deep satisfaction.

One day after class, I walked into the Crusade House on Peachtree Street, and Mary Jo walked straight up to me and said, "Mona just called. She's in town and is coming by to speak with Carl. She also said that she wants to see you—if you want to see her."

Chapter 11

The Enemy of the Best

I never expected to hear from Mona again, but I agreed to see her. When I did, I was stunned by how beautiful she looked. Once again, she took my breath away. If anything, she looked better than she did before having the baby. Her blue eyes sparkled with warmth and enthusiasm, and her figure showed no trace of having been pregnant. We talked superficially for a few minutes, each feeling a little awkward. She was in Atlanta to visit Emory where she had been accepted into a BS program for nursing. She also had been accepted into a similar nursing program at Georgia Medical College in Augusta and was planning to attend there. She just wanted to check out Emory first.

I had to go to Athens for the day and asked if she wanted to accompany me. I was surprised when she agreed. Frankly, I was surprised by everything—her wanting to see me in the first place and being interested in what I was doing. When we were at UGA, her major interest in me was that I was always interested in her and what she was doing. Her agenda was always our agenda, never the other way around. That's what surprised me the most. She was interested—genuinely interested—in me.

We went to Athens just like two old friends. I did what I needed to do, and we headed back to the Crusade house in Atlanta. We ate somewhere, and when we got back in the car, we looked at each other and then kissed—deeply and passionately. It was brief, but when we stopped, it was like nothing had ever happened between us. We were once more a nice, young couple without a care in the world. Within a week, Mona changed her mind about going to nursing school in Augusta, choosing instead to come to Atlanta for Emory and for me.

We picked up right where we left off. I kept waiting for her to tell me all about what happened—her labor, her feelings about giving up the baby, and, above all else, whether the baby was a boy or a girl. But she wouldn't talk about it—not then, not ever. Every once in a while I would gingerly broach the subject, but the visible pain on her face let me know she couldn't revisit what had happened. So a "no-talk rule" evolved between us. The baby and everything about those months were off-limits.

I told my mom that Mona and I were seeing each other again, and Murph pressed me hard for details. "Jacky," she said, "I pray for that baby every day, and I want to know whether it's a boy or a girl." Mom actually wanted to adopt the baby, but Dad was steadfastly opposed to it. So all Murph could do was pray, and pray she did—every day for the rest of her life. Reluctantly, Mona said one day she thought the baby was a boy, but she wasn't absolutely sure. That's all I ever learned.

To anyone who looked, Mona and I seemed like an ideal couple. She was beautiful, warm, and gracious, and I was funny and gregarious. But all was not what it seemed. I still loved Mona deeply and wanted us to spend the rest of our lives together. I was working full-time, going to school full-time, and devoting countless hours to my passion in life: Campus Crusade for Christ. As an unpaid volunteer, I not only started the work at Georgia State but I also raised all the money for fifty kids to attend biblical training at Arrowhead Springs in California three summers in a row. It was easy because of my fervent belief in the cause. I was a very busy young man, but I loved everything I was doing.

Mona, on the other hand, went to school, came to meetings, and spent time with me. But she was very careful not to let her family know we were seeing each other. I was her *secret*. I didn't like it, but she insisted that it be this way.

After six months, Mona came by one Friday afternoon and broke up with me again. I was devastated. That Sunday evening, she showed up at the Crusade meeting with a date. Carl was upset, and Mary Jo was furious—particularly because the meeting was always at the Crusade House where I lived. To Mary Jo, it was beyond tacky; it was inappropriate.

This went on for quite a while. Mona would come with her new beau, Monty Sawyer, a student at Columbia Seminary. Mary Jo would say, "She's just doing this to stick it in your face, Jack. I know what she's doing. I can see how she maneuvers to make sure you can see her put her hands on Monty." I didn't understand anything except how much pain I was in.

After six months of this, however, I'd had enough. One morning, I got up and decided to move on with my life. Shortly thereafter, I got a girl-friend—a really cute girl named Susan, who was a junior at Emory. The following Sunday night, Mona came to the meeting with Monty, playing her games; but I ignored her completely. I was done with her, and she could tell.

Susan and I had a beautiful spiritual relationship but with little passion to it. One week in March 1966 I got a terrible case of strep throat and missed the Sunday night meeting. The next day Mona came by with some chicken soup from a deli. She talked to Mary Jo and told her how foolish she had been to let me get away.

Mary Jo, who always wanted what was best for me, came into my room and said, "Jack, I have to be honest with you. You don't love Susan. You still love Mona, and after talking to her, I can tell that she loves you, too. You need to break it off with Susan and get back with Mona."

I was pierced to the core—exactly the way anybody would be when he discovers that he is in a serious relationship with the wrong person. "But, Mary Jo," I protested, "Susan and I have such a great Christian relation-ship."

"I know. But there's no passion to it, and that's not you. The good is always the enemy of the best. Susan may be a good choice, but Mona's the best for you. Remember that." This profound but simple truth stopped me cold in my tracks. She was right, and I recognized it as soon as she said it.

"All right, will you call Mona for me and ask her to stop by?" I talked to Susan immediately and was surprised by the enormous relief I experienced when that relationship was terminated. When Mona came, I was still sick in bed, so she came to my room to talk. I looked at her and asked, "Mary Jo says you have something you want to say to me. What is it?"

Chapter 12

"There's No Way"

Sheepishly, Mona sat down on the chair beside my bed and told me she loved me and was sorry she had let me go. She apologized and asked for my forgiveness, which I granted eagerly. She was humble, very humble—the humblest I had ever seen her or would ever see her. I was deeply touched and realized how much I still loved her, but I was reluctant to let my guard down. For one thing, I was still uncomfortable about our relationship being a secret. This started bothering me a great deal; it just wasn't right. Regardless, we were back together again.

Not long after this—no more than a week—my dad took his annual golf trip with several of his buddies to Pinehurst, North Carolina. I called and asked if I could drive up and have dinner with him. I told him I would bring Mona, and it would be a good opportunity for him to meet her. He readily agreed.

I knew what I was doing. Dad, on his worst day, would be very charming to a pretty girl, and I wanted Mona's first exposure to my family to be positive. Murph, on the other hand, was never handicapped by social pleasantries. I could just hear her say, "If you love him now, why didn't you love him before you sent my grandchild out in the world to live with strangers?" She also would have spiced her first inquiry with the f-word—carefully interspersed for effect. Murph was a master with the f-word.

My plan worked to perfection. We made the long drive to North Carolina and had a very pleasant dinner with Dad, who was mellowing with age, and had begun—for the first time—to show some genuine interest in my life. He even picked up the check. Mona thought he was charming, which was exactly what I expected her to think. We left to make the long trip back to Atlanta at about 10:00 P.M.

During the journey, we both had difficulty keeping our eyes open. Finally, I pulled into a rest area, turned off the car, and promptly fell asleep. A loud clap of thunder from a passing storm startled us. Suddenly we were wide awake with our emotional defenses completely down. As soon as we realized we were safe, we fell into each other's arms, and before you know it, we were having sex for the second time. It couldn't have been more spontaneous, and because it wasn't planned or expected, no precautions were taken.

Within a week, Mona announced she was pregnant again. "There's no way you could be certain this soon, is there?" I replied with puzzlement.

"I know what my body feels like, and *I know I'm pregnant.*"

And she was. I couldn't believe it. We had been together for three years, had sex twice, and she became pregnant both times. She was furious with me—absolutely furious. Repeatedly, she said, "This is all your fault"—like I did it single-handedly. "We're getting married next weekend. I'm not going through this again. Next weekend. Do you hear me? Next weekend!"

After she announced this, the following day I went into the kitchen, where Mary Jo was reading a magazine. Looking at her, I said, "Mary Jo, I've got to talk to you."

My tone obviously alerted her to the fact that something serious was about to be said. Instantly she gave me her undivided attention. All I had to do was look at her and she said, "Oh, my God. Mona's pregnant again, isn't she?"

I can't imagine how she figured that out so quickly, but she did. She did more than that, however. She immediately came to my aid and rescue. She told Carl, who offered to marry us, and she planned a very nice, intimate wedding at the Crusade House.

She made the whole experience wonderful, and I will never forget the depth of her generosity and kindness—never. If I have ever seen Christlikeness in a person, I saw it in Mary Jo as she poured out unconditional love when I needed it the most. There were no recriminations—only compassion and acceptance. Recognizing how uncommon this kind of love was, I have cherished it in my heart ever since as a model of how Christians should respond in a crisis—but rarely do.

After the wedding, Mona and I went on a three-day honeymoon to Chattanooga—the "mecca" for rednecks. We saw Rock City and Ruby Falls and stayed at a cheap motel where they sold Skoal at the front desk. It was quite an experience, but it was all we could afford. That Sunday night, when we returned to Atlanta, Mona went back to Emory, and I went back to the Crusade House.

No one knew we were married—especially her parents. Mona wanted to finish the second year of her three-year nursing program, and I needed to take finals. I also had to finish raising the money for another fifty kids to go to Arrowhead Springs, including Mona and me. Mona always studied hard, but I was a little surprised that I didn't hear from her for days at a time. I asked her why she was so distant, but she assured me she wasn't. Still, I was bothered by it, but I wasn't certain why. When finals were over, we started living together, and my uneasiness evaporated.

Ten years later, I learned Mona wasn't studying the whole time she was staying at Emory. She was back with Monty for one last fling before settling down to married life. Monty had now become *her little secret.* We had been married fewer than two weeks, and she was already sneaking around. I figured it out inadvertently. Mona had been talking about how unwise it was for couples to talk about past history, and all of a sudden, I knew. Don't ask me how; I just did. When I asked her about it, Mona was straightforward, admitting the truth.

Chapter 13

Fixing a Pound Cake

When school ended, we went to California and checked into Campus Crusade headquarters as a married couple. We told everyone that we were married on January 22, but it actually had been one month later. Because we learned so much from fabulous teachers such as Hal Lindsey, we enjoyed the entire time at Crusade headquarters. Our stay was for six weeks, but as our time there was coming to an end, Mona became increasingly apprehensive because she still had not informed her parents that we were married. As far as they knew, Mona had not seen me for nearly two years.

The day we arrived back in Atlanta, Mona wrote a letter telling them she had married me. Then we waited and waited and waited for what seemed like a month but was only a week. Finally Rose called and said, "Mona, when are you going to come home and bring Jack with you?" I was listening right next to her, and we both just looked at each other in stark amazement.

"When do you want us, Mama?" Mona asked eagerly.

"Come on down this weekend. I'll fix a pound cake." I didn't realize it, but "fixing a pound cake" was a big deal, signaling I would be welcomed. I was grateful it wasn't the slimy relish. That Friday we drove to Colquitt, and Rose greeted us both with open arms. She was a simple countrywoman with strong Christian values; she told me she would never be part of "putting asunder what God had joined in holy marriage," and she never did.

I grew to love that old woman, and she definitely loved me. She was kind, generous, giving, and though uneducated, wise in matters that really counted. She made sure to include me in everything—especially work around the yard. She asked us to come back three weeks later, and we said we would.

Mr. Lucian was taciturn by nature. It was much harder to read him, but he began to warm up to me over time. Mona's sisters, who reminded me of Cinderella's stepsisters, were always two-faced. Charles, her brother, remained sexually interested in me for years, which always made me feel uncomfortable.

Three weeks later, we went back, and Rose looked at Mona and said, "Mona, am I going to be a grandma?" Nothing passed her keen eye. Mona denied it but came clean the next time we came to visit. That's the funny thing about pregnancy: Mona couldn't lie for long—she had started to show.

On October 10, 1966, Constance was born at Crawford Long Hospital in Atlanta; we called her Connie. She was beautiful and healthy, and neither of us could have loved her more. I was in school full-time and worked full-time, but I always found opportunities to play with Connie. I would pick her up and hold her for hours. Occasionally I would wonder about our lost child, but I had to put those thoughts out of my mind. Mona was an excellent mother—caring, gentle, and completely attentive. We didn't have two nickels to rub together, but we were very happy.

Rose came to help Mona often and stayed for long periods of time. That got old, but she always brought tons of great food—everything but relish. As soon as Connie was born, Rose became Granny and, to my knowledge, was never called Rose again by anybody except her husband.

In the spring of 1968, a month after Dr. King was assassinated, our second daughter, Victoria, was born. Mona's birth control had failed, so Victoria was a surprise. But she was definitely wanted. Her features and coloring were more Watts than Everett, and she was a daddy's girl and has remained so throughout most of her life. With two, it was a little harder; but we managed. Earlier that year, the McMurrays were transferred to California, where Carl and some other senior staff members had a conflict with Bill Bright, the founder of Campus Crusade. Carl and several other key men chose to resign from the staff.

The primary reason for me going back to school was to join the Crusade staff, but now that all of my friends and heroes had left, I dropped the idea of joining. I started to feel lost and without direction. I graduated that May, but I didn't have a clue what I would do next. I was completely adrift—like Ben in *The Graduate*. Not knowing what else to do, I went to graduate school, but my heart wasn't in it.

I didn't drink much back then because we couldn't afford it. When the opportunity for free booze presented itself, however, I was always first in line. In the spring of 1969, Dick got married in Boston, and the liquor flowed freely. I went, and Dick's wedding day proved to be a pivotal one—impacting the rest of my life.

Chapter 14

The Rage and Fury

With the burden of caring for two small children, we decided that I should go to Dick's wedding alone. Not having Mona with me proved to be a big mistake. After the wedding, which was very nice, the reception began, and my other brother, Danny, and I started partying hard. We had a blast.

Danny's wife, Erica, left early. By now they had three children, and she left to bathe them, feed them something other than hors d'oeuvres, and get them to bed. Danny stayed, and we drank with the newlyweds late into the evening. By 11:00 P.M. the party was over, but Danny was not finished drinking. He said, "Jacky, let's go to downtown Boston!" So we went, finally arriving back at his house, where I was staying, at 3:00 A.M. Being as quiet as two drunks could be, Danny put the key in the door and opened it—only to be stopped by the chain lock. I was puzzled; he was furious.

Instantly, he flew into a rage, hitting the door with his shoulder. In one motion, he dislodged the frame, which secured the chain, right off the wall and gained access to the house. Their home was a split-level with the kitchen at the top of a short flight of stairs. Erica, in a teddy with exposed legs, raced into the kitchen and hissed, "Danny, you'll wake the children!"

Without hesitation, Danny grabbed a five-foot piece of framing from the door and threw it at Erica like a spear. It missed, but the protruding nails grazed her right thigh, ripping it open in two places. Looking at the blood pouring from the wounds, Erica immediately grabbed the wall phone and dialed 0 for the operator to connect her to the police. This was long before 911.

In a heartbeat, Danny was up the stairs, ripped the phone from her hands, and started hitting her on the head with it—once, twice, three times. He hit her with all the rage and fury he could muster. Erica staggered from the blows.

I stood at the threshold of the house in stunned horror. By the time Danny was using the phone as a weapon to hit her on the head, I was cold sober. Springing to action, I ran up the stairs into the kitchen, pulled the phone out of his hand, and pushed him away from her. Erica, seizing her opportunity, ran from the house in fear for her life. Danny, who was far more interested in Erica than in me, pushed me off and bolted from the house, sprinting after Erica, who had only a twenty-foot head start.

I remember thinking, *If he catches her, he could kill her.* I knew I couldn't allow that to happen—even if it meant that the former marine killed me instead. Without hesitation, I took off after him, still grateful for my gymnastics strength. I tackled him by a tree in their front yard. When I did, he turned all his rage on me. As we rolled in the grass in this violent encounter, he tried to gouge out my eyes. When I foiled this effort, he went for my balls, but once again I thwarted him. I finally got him in a half nelson and started to rip out his left shoulder.

I had him. He was defeated. As calmly as possible in these circumstances he said, "You win. You can let me go."

"No way," I said, but I eased up on the pressure a little.

"I'm okay, Jacky. Please let me go. Please."

"You won't go after Erica?"

"No, I promise. I won't," he assured me. I let him go, and that was the end of it.

The neighbors called the police, but Danny wasn't arrested. Erica was safe but had had enough of Danny. She filed for divorce the following week. Although I didn't realize it at the time, this incident irrevocably changed the dynamics in our family.

Chapter 15

"Come and Dine"

Back home in Atlanta, I was offered a job teaching high school in 1969 with a salary of $6,300 per year. With two kids and Mona not working outside the home, we were constantly broke. One month Mona paid all the bills and told me we had $4.00 left—with twenty-five days remaining in the month. So I took a second job, selling fashion shoes part-time, which generated more income than I made as a teacher.

Mr. Lucian's health declined, and he finally died of uremic poisoning, a painful way to go. He had fought in World War I, a "doughboy" under General Black Jack Pershing in France. He lived fewer than three years after Mona gave away our child. Looking back, it seems ironic that Mona was pressured mercilessly to abandon our baby because it "would kill Daddy" for her to marry me. So far, two generations have been dramatically impacted with familial dysfunction because of that decision. And what was accomplished? An old man's false sense of pride was protected—for a mere three years.

When she gave up our child, part of Mona also died, and I don't believe she's ever forgiven herself for her decision. The cost/reward ratio for that decision has been staggering for those of us left to pay the price, and yet there are those who still vehemently defend the wisdom of what she did, including Mona. I guess alcoholics aren't the only ones who live in complete denial of reality. Sadly, Mr. Lucian couldn't see—or didn't care—what impact this would have. He was too invested in his own perceived needs, regardless of the negative impact on others.

I was too young and far too busy to examine other people's motives back then, but I did know I wanted more for our lives than we were experiencing. Without Campus Crusade we languished, but no effort to rekindle that spiritual fire was successful.

One day I received a call from an old Crusade friend, Tom Weldon. He told me he had a real burden for me and asked me to come to California to "see what was happening" in Isla Vista, a radical hippie community adjacent to the campus at the University of California in Santa Barbara. Telling him I couldn't afford a plane ticket, I politely declined the invitation.

Two weeks later, he called a second time and said, "Jack, if I sell my scuba equipment and buy you a ticket, will you come?" To close the deal, he added, "And one more thing—Carl McMurray just moved here last week."

After talking to Mona to make sure she was okay with me leaving her with the girls, I called Tom and said, "Send me the ticket; I'm coming." Two weeks later, I flew to Los Angeles.

This was the first time I had ever flown into Los Angeles. It was February 1969 and very cold in Atlanta. I kept thinking—or should I say humming—*I'd be safe and warm if I was in L.A.* The plane landed, and when I walked into Delta's enormous rotunda terminal, there were more than two hundred smiling faces there to greet me. They were all singing:

"Come and dine," the Master calleth
"Come and dine."
You may feast at Jesus' table
All the time.

He who fed the multitude
Turned the water into wine.
To the hungry calleth now,
"Come and dine."

With song after song, the cavernous rotunda echoed with the joyous sounds of these energetic, exuberant young people, all of whom were there for one purpose: to welcome me to California and to their group. It took eighty cars for all of them to make the trip from Santa Barbara—ninety-nine miles each way, but they did it. They guided me to the middle of the circle, where I stood alone while they sat around me six deep. Everyone sang, and no one was embarrassed as people passed by staring in amazed curiosity.

I was not thrilled with so much attention; I was mortified. If you'll remember, I wouldn't even pray with anybody five years earlier, but here I was in the middle of a busy terminal, being stared at by everybody who passed by. I caught Carl McMurray's eye. He knew how difficult this was for me, but he just laughed and let it happen.

After collecting my bags for the weeklong stay, the caravan headed back to Isla Vista. Fortunately, I wasn't in a car that had Jesus graffiti written all over it—a humiliation I was grateful to avoid. I asked Tom Weldon why he hadn't prepared me for such an unusual reception, and he said, "I know it's a little different, Jack, but everybody has been praying every day for months to get you here." Since he paid for my ticket, I was his guest for a week. I was very uncomfortable and didn't feel like a guest at all. I felt like a hostage.

When we arrived in I.V. (Isla Vista), they had a potluck dinner. After that, there was singing, sharing, and teaching by the leader, Leonard Ravenhill. By the time I went to bed, my head was spinning, and I had never felt more out of place in my life. It was awful, truly awful.

This pattern continued day after day without change. I couldn't believe it. It seemed like all they did was sing, pray, sing, get together for meetings, and sing some more. I was drowning. One morning I was walking on the streets of I.V., which was a densely populated, isolated community—full of radical, anti–Vietnam War hippies. One of the "brothers" yelled out at the top of his voice nearly a block away, "Jack, Jesus lives, rules, and reigns forever." They loved to do stuff like that.

A hippie came out of his second-story apartment and yelled back, "Jesus wore a leather jockstrap!" Trying hard not to wince at what had just happened, I caught up to my demonstrative friend a minute later. He was seething with anger toward the hippie. Looking toward the scraggily guy who had returned to his apartment, my friend said, "I wanted to yell back, 'At least He had balls!'" This comment caught me by complete surprise, and I burst into laughter.

For me, that broke the ice. They were human after all—a little strange, to be sure—but human. From that moment forward, I started to like the people more and more. What I liked most was they had what was missing in my life: a shared purpose, a vision, and loving camaraderie. They had it. I wanted and needed it desperately, so I decided right then and there to pack up our family and move twenty-three hundred miles from Georgia to California. Once I had made the decision, I never deviated from it. At the end of the week, I said a reluctant good-bye to a place where I now knew our family belonged.

When I flew back to Atlanta, I told Mona everything that happened, and she was supportive and interested. She could tell how excited I was and shared my enthusiasm—until I said, "We're going to pack up and move to California." She was aghast, but being a Taurus, she gritted her teeth defiantly. With her hands on her hips, she said, "I'm not moving to California—and neither are the girls!"

"Yeah, you are," I said; but there was absolutely no hint of insistence in the way I said it. I added, "I'm so sure this is what the Lord wants us to do that we'll wait until you agree with the decision." A week or two later, she said she would go, adding, "I knew we were going the second you said you would wait for me to agree with you."

One week later, I came home from school and Mona announced, "I'm pregnant," in that tone that let me know it was entirely my fault—again.

This meant we couldn't leave right away. Brenn Watts, our third daughter and fourth child, was born July 28—just as I began my second year of teaching. She was beautiful and the sweetest child you could ever want, but we now had three children under five and one lost to the world. One of our friends remarked, "Mona's popping out kids like a PEZ dispenser." Not at all amused but knowing it was true, Mona informed me, "we are not going to have any more children—and that's final." She used two forms of birth control—an IUD and almost total abstinence.

At the end of the school year, I put everything we owned in a U-Haul truck—with a tow bar for our 1964 Plymouth Valiant—and headed for California. I had two friends accompany me in the cab of the truck, which had no air-conditioning. One flew in from I.V.; the other was a PhD chemist from Tech in Atlanta. He decided to join the group once he got there, just as I had. I not only talked him into relocating, I also talked another twenty people into moving from Georgia to California—and several more from Texas. We were all ex–Campus Crusaders and wanted to regain that sense of purpose and shared destiny.

Chapter 16

A Higher Calling

I arrived in I.V. in early June 1971. The Vietnam War was in full swing, as were the antiwar protesters. Like Berkeley, I.V. was an epicenter for thousands of hippies, all of whom were antiwar activists and none of whom worked. Instead, they chose to smoke dope constantly. A wealthy hippie was one who owned two pairs of jeans. Girls wore no makeup, didn't shave their legs, but were quite willing to open their legs for just about anybody. This was the era of "free love," and our communal church was right in the middle of it to raise the banner for Christ. It was exciting, really exciting—by far the best time of my life.

When I arrived, I had a wife, three kids, and no job; I neither cared nor worried. God would take care of us; I knew it. Everybody back home thought I was crazy, but they all wanted what I had—a higher calling than just grinding out my days in ignominy with no higher purpose than buying a bigger home or a nicer car. I received my teacher's salary through August, so I had nearly three months to find work.

Jobs were hard to find in California in the early seventies, but I found one—a really good one for people in our church. I was a pharmaceutical salesman. I received a new Chevy Impala and started at $16,000 a year—a huge increase for us.

Mona stayed at Granny's while I moved and set us up. She flew in with the girls on a Sunday afternoon, and nearly three hundred people from the church welcomed her at the Delta rotunda. It was the largest number ever to greet a newcomer. Mona got off the plane, knowing what to expect, but the enormity of the reception was still overwhelming. She said, "Do I need to give a speech?"

I roared with laughter and said, "No." I was thrilled to see her and the girls. We were back together as a family. It was a powerful time, and we were never more focused or happier. Life in I.V. was wonderful for the girls because there were a hundred kids from all of the ex-Crusaders now living there as a part of our semicommunal congregation.

We were going to change the world for Christ, starting with the politically radical hippies in I.V. As it turned out, they probably had more impact on us than we had on them. For nearly a year, our numbers grew, and people nationwide were talking about what "the church in I.V. was doing." It was great.

Our church society was far more than a spiritual community; it was filled with dozens of strong, fit, athletic young men who played basketball and softball, biked, or jogged several times a week. I was a good softball player, so I became the second baseman on the church team, which we named the I.V. Dogs because every self-respecting hippie had a dog. It was a part of the uniform for hippies, and I.V. had thousands of unkempt dogs running around. In I.V. you always had to watch your step—if you know what I mean.

Throughout Santa Barbara, people from other teams in the city league thought the I.V. Dogs would be a bunch of wild, dope-smoking hippies. Instead they were surprised when they saw we were clean-cut, sharp, and wholesome. We also had a basketball team. I had never played basketball, but as soon as I did, I fell in love with the sport and played full-court basketball three or four times a week for the next thirty years.

Not only was it excellent exercise but it was also therapeutic. By now, Mona was interested in being intimate only three or four times a year, and playing sports was my only legitimate outlet for excess energy. I kept hoping that our sexual problem would rectify, but it never did. Still in my midtwenties, this forced abstinence kept me in a constant state of frustrated sexual deprivation. Not being desired by my wife took a substantial toll on my self-worth. Consequently, I had serial flirtations for years—none of which progressed into adultery. I kept the letter of the law while violating its spirit repeatedly, which made me feel good about myself short-term and horribly guilty long-term. Because this conflicted with my core Christian values, I felt defeated, helpless, hopeless, and trapped—with no legitimate way out.

In the spring of our first year in I.V., my brother Danny visited. I brought him to several meetings, but he showed no interest in the spiritual dimension of our group. In late summer my dad, mom, and sister came for a weeklong visit. They had never come to Georgia, but they were curious about what was going on in I.V. It was always pleasantly cool in I.V. and only hot when the Santa Ana winds came once or twice a year. Unfortunately, those winds blew in during their visit. Nobody had air-conditioning, so it was miserably hot for these three Bostonians. Already in his late fifties and suffering from emphysema, my dad found the weather particularly difficult.

The night before they were to leave, Dad offered to take Mona and me, along with four other couples, to dinner wherever I chose. The Chart House was Mona's favorite restaurant, so we went there. Dad sat at the head of a huge table. When the plates were served, he picked up a sprig of parsley and bellowed to all, "Can any of you tell me the difference between parsley and pussy?" Dead silence followed for several seconds. Finally someone laughed, and then everybody followed suit. Not content to leave his faux pas alone, my dad finished the punch line: "Nobody eats parsley."

I could have died and my sister wanted to strangle him, but Dad never realized how inappropriate this was. To their credit, everyone let it go, and we actually had a delightful time. That's what happens when everything is in sync and going well. You don't have to take offense at every little thing, and you can enjoy people for who they are.

In the fall of 1972, however, things changed dramatically and overnight. Carl McMurray and a few others went to see Leonard Ravenhill about some of the things Leonard was teaching that they considered heretical. I won't bore you with theological details. Suffice it to say, Carl "broke fellowship" with Leonard. One day they were comrades in arms; the next day they were bitter enemies. Leonard, a soft-spoken, gentle, and slightly effeminate man, was, by far, the more gracious. Strong and handsome with exceptional verbal skills, Carl never missed a chance to "ream Leonard a new one."

I tried to act as a peacemaker between the bickering factions, but my efforts were futile. A third followed Leonard Ravenhill; a third, including me, followed Carl McMurray; and one-third moved on with the I.V. hippies. One day we were all in one accord with one hope and one vision; the next day, enmity and strife reigned supreme. Our cohesiveness was completely destroyed—without hope of reconciliation or restoration. The love and joy that radiated from the faces of these wonderful people were replaced with looks of anguish, pain, and despair. The disappointment was palpable.

There is a verse in the Bible that states, "Where there is no vision, the people perish" (Proverbs 29:18, KJV). It also can mean "the people are unrestrained." That's what happened to us; we became unrestrained. There we were in I.V., a den of iniquity, without purpose and disillusioned but with all the energy that comes with youth. Mixing all these ingredients together produced one thing: trouble.

Chapter 17

Lying on the Couch

For the next two years, people moved away from I.V. back to their home-towns—at first, just a few, but then they left in droves. The vacuum left by their absence was impossible to fill. Some of those who remained became involved in drugs, others in promiscuity, still others in both. Marriages failed. In fact, nearly all the marriages in the group loyal to Leonard Ravenhill failed within a few years. A couple of guys from the original group even ended up in prison.

Drinking had not been a problem for me when we came to I.V., but after the split, I got drunk—knee-walking drunk—every time my company had a district sales meeting. The guys I worked with were pretty wild, and I joined them in their dissipation once every couple of months. I thought of it as a healthy release from all the stress and pressures at home, which I now realize was nothing more than an emerging pattern of alcoholic behavior. It wasn't a healthy escape; it was medicating my disillusionment and emotional pain rather than dealing with it. At the time, however, I lacked the wisdom to understand this simple truth. I didn't really enjoy it, but I didn't have the strength to decline participation either. My sense of purpose was gone, and I couldn't retrieve it. Neither could anyone else.

Once we had a company golf tournament in Santa Maria, sixty miles north of I.V. The banquet following the round of golf was served very late, so the cocktail party was extended by an hour. I don't even remember if I ate. Driving home, I was pulled over and failed a field sobriety test. I was arrested for driving under the influence—a DUI. When they took me to jail, the police were physically abusive while I was handcuffed, but I was so embarrassed when I sobered up that I didn't even lodge a complaint. For any sane person, a DUI would serve as a red light—stop drinking, and never drive again when you've been drinking! For me, I chose to view it as a warning light instead. Because I was discouraged, without purpose, and lost, I viewed life for the first time through the lenses of an emerging alcoholic, which I was genetically predisposed to do.

While I was away for a weeklong sales conference in San Francisco in the spring of 1974, my brother Danny paid a surprise visit to Mona and the girls in I.V. He was still there when I returned. As I walked to the backyard to greet him, he was sunbathing and wearing only workout shorts with a pillow on his lap. As I came closer, I noticed he wasn't wearing underwear, and he was almost completely exposed. Before saying hello, I said, "Danny, cover yourself. The girls are playing right behind you."

"Okay, sure," he said, seemingly unaware that he wasn't decent. He covered himself immediately.

He spent the weekend with us before heading back to Boston. I had a great time with him, and I was sure the incident with Erica several years earlier had healed and was no longer an issue between us. His surprise visit was evidence of this, I thought. When I left him at the airport, I smiled as I dropped him off, blissfully unaware that my life would never be the same. In fact, it started changing the following week.

Mona became seriously depressed and started spending her days lying on the couch. She had always been a dynamo of energy, devoting hours each day to taking care of the girls, cooking, and keeping the house immaculate. Because depressive behavior was completely out of character for her, I thought she would snap out of it quickly, but she didn't. I would come home from work and ask, "What's for dinner?"

"Why bother?" she would whine plaintively.

"Because we have three girls and they're hungry. So am I."

This scenario became the routine for us. Not knowing what else to do, I started cooking myself. I thought, *This has to get better*, but she stayed on that couch, consumed with depression, for two years—*two years*. I did everything I could think of to help her. We went to counselors, doctors, nutritionists; nothing worked. She wouldn't even wash her hair regularly.

I would ask, "Mona, why don't you take a shower and wash your hair?"

"It will only get dirty again," she moaned.

"I know, but that's why we buy shampoo." At first I was frustrated, which quickly turned to anger; but it went on for so long that I became deeply concerned. I wanted my wife back from the dark place she went to every day, but I was powerless to make it happen. She wouldn't talk about what was troubling her—not to me, not to a counselor, and not to anybody in our church. She was alone in her depression—month after month.

Within a short period, I became the cook, the housekeeper, and the breadwinner. Mona stopped participating in our family life just as completely as she had stopped participating in our sexual relationship. She left it all up to me; *everything* became my responsibility. After a while the girls would run up to me when I came home from work and ask, "Daddy, what's for dinner?" We had meat loaf so often that none of them will eat it to this day.

I was so consumed with the day-to-day issues of a family of five and the desire for Mona to get out of her depression that I honestly never connected the origin of these events with Danny's surprise visit. Several decades later, I finally figured out that his visit is when it all started. She retreated to the couch shortly afterward—within a few weeks at the most. Something had happened while he was there—while I was out of town—that was so disturbing it plummeted Mona into a two-year-long, life-altering depression. The devastation wasn't explosive in nature; it was more subtle and insidious. It was like a crack in the foundation of a building that ensured it would crumble over time. In this case, the building was each of our lives—Mona's, Connie's, Victoria's, Brenn's, and mine.

Chapter 18

The Elders

Life in I.V. was like a soap opera. Several of my friends and I actually joked about it, saying, "This is just another day in *As the Stomach Turns*."

By 1975, the Vietnam War was over, President Nixon had resigned, and Mona finally got off the sofa. Several years earlier, Elrod Sunstrom and Carl McMurray started Grace Catholic Church for those of us who were left. It was more like a "cult of personality" than a church, because the leaders, who were called "The Elders," took on Elrod's personality—particularly the angry, confrontational, profane aspects of it.

By this time, Carl was no longer the enthusiastic Campus Crusader who mentored me for years. His personality had changed—he had become petty, vindictive, and cruel. His tongue was acerbic, and he took particular delight in criticizing Mary Jo, who became a shell of what she had once been. As the mother of his children, she would never divorce him, I knew. But the confident, capable woman who helped me put a wedding together in three days no longer existed.

Instead of the love and joy that typified our earlier group, Grace Catholic was characterized by fear, anger, intimidation, condemnation, and verbal abuse. To counteract the licentiousness that had become a part of our lives, The Elders had to "deal with sin in the camp." They did this by paying a visit—usually without warning—to an unsuspecting person who needed straightening out. They would sit the person down and shout at him or her, demanding change and compliance. They would start the meeting by saying something like this: "Mike, you know what you are? You're a worthless piece of crap; that's what you are. I wonder why the hell we even bother with you." From there, it would only get worse. By the time they left, the person was an emotional basket case—ready to do whatever he or she was told.

Those of us who remained tolerated this for two reasons. First, we had lived in such bizarre circumstances for so long that it didn't seem as weird or abusive as it actually was. Second, if you didn't submit to it, your entire family was excommunicated—shunned and treated with contempt, derision, and ridicule. This meant, for example, that your kids could no longer play with their friends from the church, and many other similar, petty acts of social cruelty. Most people complied. The social ostracizing of the others was truly painful to watch. I'm sure this was why Mona never wanted to confide in The Elders. I don't blame her for that.

Carl and Elrod Sunstrom started calling themselves Apostles and said that church tradition, particularly from orthodox churches, was as authoritative as the Scriptures. I couldn't understand this; it couldn't be happening. They had been Campus Crusaders, and now they wanted to wear collars like Catholic priests. What McMurray and Sunstrom were now teaching was the polar opposite of what they had insisted was true when I came to Christ a decade earlier.

The two of them kept talking about getting back to true church traditions. For me, that's what I left behind to have a personal relationship with Christ. If what they were now teaching was true, then I shouldn't have left Roman Catholicism in the first place. Ultimately, I chose to stick with the Scriptures as my authority rather than with men who arrogated God's authority, using it ruthlessly to beat the sheep. I stayed in the church, but I never accepted what they said at face value again.

I was disillusioned and badly confused. While in this state of bewilderment, I flew back to Boston—alone again—for my sister Jean's wedding to Tommy Malone. The song they chose for the wedding was one of Jim Croce's with the line "If I could save time in a bottle." I mused, *This could be the Watts theme song because we all loved the bottle.* This trip I stayed with Dick, thinking I would avoid needless drama with Danny.

Melissa, Dick's sister-in-law, took care of his young sons so we could stay at the reception longer. As usual, when we came back, I was intoxicated. Melissa had admitted to having a crush on me for a long time. After Dick and his wife, Julie, went to bed, she made her move. Well, you can guess what happened. We had a fourteen-second encounter—at the end of which I freaked out. I dressed, left the house, and walked for hours. My life was in shambles, and I knew it. I called Mona and told her exactly what had happened—all of it. I was desperate for help. She chose to call The Elders.

When I arrived back in I.V. the following day, The Elders were waiting for me—all of them. I wasn't allowed to go home until "they dealt with me." Upon my return, I had never felt so heartsick and remorseful in my life. I was willing to do anything to get back on track. The Elders could see this, but it didn't matter. They had only one method for handling every situation: verbal intimidation. After hours of enduring their malice, I actually started having suicidal ideations for the first time in my life. I was shattered.

Living under this oppressive cloud of condemnation for more than a year, my life was very difficult. But being isolated, which was my penance, afforded me an opportunity for intense soul-searching, which was new territory. I had always avoided being alone, but my solitude gave me an opportunity to be insightful.

In spite of all the chastisement, I was young and resilient, and I weathered the storm. Many aspects of our lives returned to normal.

Mona decided to go back to the local community college and finish nursing school. I was thrilled for her to do something constructive. She worked hard at her studies; and if anything, she did even less with the family. In addition to returning to nursing school, Mona also went to the YMCA religiously—three times a week—for aerobics. Within a few months, she was as trim and beautiful as the day I met her—even after having four children, which was quite an accomplishment. The transformation was truly amazing and quite rewarding, as Mona began to feel better and more energetic. Her days on the couch were finally behind her.

Several months later, I noticed that three quarters were missing from the table where I emptied my pockets each night. I had noticed this several times before, so I went into the girls' room and this time discovered the quarters hidden in Connie's drawer. I left them there but told all the girls they were missing and that I was going to look for them after breakfast.

With all three girls following me an hour later, I found the quarters, which were now in Victoria's drawer. Victoria cried and said she hadn't taken them; Connie never said a word. Comforting Victoria, I told her I knew she hadn't taken them. I gave Connie every opportunity to come forward, but she never did.

Later that morning, I had coffee with a friend I had brought into the church who was a PhD psychologist. After listening to me relate the incident with the quarters, he said, "Jack, you're going to have a lot of trouble with Connie later on. She needs help—serious help." His prediction seemed over the top, so I changed the subject and never returned to it. *She was only nine*, I thought; and we couldn't afford therapy for her. Besides, it was only three quarters. Nevertheless, I never forgot what he said.

While I was at a regional sales meeting in San Francisco in 1976, I received a call from Mona at 2:30 A.M. As usual, I had had too much to drink at the meeting; so it took me a minute to become coherent.

"Jack, are you awake?" Mona questioned.

"Yeah, I'm awake. Is something wrong?"

"Yes, there is. I'm sorry, but your dad just died," she said. "You need to come home right away."

Instantly shocked, I don't remember anything else about the conversation, but I do remember crying for the remainder of the night in a hotel room shared with another salesman who wanted to console me but had no idea how. I was distraught and overwhelmed with grief for a man I didn't really know but had called Dad my entire life.

As far as I knew, he hadn't even been sick. He had retired at sixty-four and was headed to Arizona with Murph, where they had bought a retirement home. We had planned to drive over the following weekend to see them. He got sick in Amarillo, was hospitalized, and died a few days later. When I asked Mom why she hadn't called me when he was hospitalized, she said, "I didn't want to spend the money for a long-distance call."

She grew up in the Great Depression. That's how people from her generation thought; nothing was as important as saving a few bucks. I was stunned and devastated because I never had the opportunity to say good-bye. While he was dying, I was drinking at a bar in San Francisco, unaware that his life was ending.

Feeling ashamed that I had been carousing while my dad was spending his last night on Earth, I flew to Boston for the funeral and was very reflective. Everyone in the family was visibly sad—except for Danny, whom I hadn't seen since his last surprise visit several years earlier. His behavior was erratic, disjointed, disruptive, and bizarre—especially toward me. I attributed it to grief, mixed with unresolved anger toward Dad. My paternal aunt, whom we affectionately called Sweetie Pie, was there, which also saddened me because I was certain I would never see her again. I was mistaken about that. Although it would be thirty years before I would see her again, she was still to play a pivotal role in my life.

Dad had an Irish funeral, which meant everybody got drunk except for him. It was our tribute; at least we called it that. Knowing how destructive life in Boston was for me, I couldn't move my wife and kids back there, but I could no longer remain in I.V. either.

By the time I returned to California, I was ready for us to move away. I wanted to go to graduate school; I wanted to learn. Having realized we were in a very unhealthy environment with The Elders, I wanted to understand things for myself rather than blindly accept what people such as Carl McMurray or my janitor Elder pontificated. So, for the next year, I feigned compliance at Grace Catholic but used all of my spare time to prepare for the graduate record exam, further education, and escape.

Loving politics and religion as subjects, I applied to Baylor University for a degree in church-state studies, the only program of its kind in existence. I was accepted with full scholarship and all of my expenses paid, but I also wanted us to own our own home rather than rent for the rest of our lives. Working a second job to put a limited partnership together in real estate several years earlier, I used my commission to buy shares in the partnership. I sold these shares for nearly $10,000 so we could put a down payment on a house in Waco, Texas.

Once again, I was ready for a fresh start as I packed up a Ryder truck and headed out, with Mona and the girls in a car right behind me. My purpose was not as lofty as when we moved to I.V., but I was seven years older and much more circumspect than I had been. A new adventure awaited us as we headed east to the Lone Star State and freedom.

Chapter 19

My Offer Is Final

We left California on a Friday morning in the early summer of 1977 and arrived in Waco late the following evening. It was more than 100 degrees. My plan was to look at some houses, buy one, and move in by the time our weeklong truck rental was complete. No one told me this was completely unrealistic, if not impossible, so I proceeded as if I could make it happen—and I did.

Starting Sunday afternoon, Mona and I left the girls at the motel pool with some friends, and we began looking at houses. We settled on a small, three-bedroom, two-bath brick home with a fenced-in yard and a garage. To us, it was huge, after living for seven years in the back half of a small duplex.

Quickly thereafter, I started my classes at Baylor, where I suffered culture shock as severe as when I first arrived in I.V. Coeds wore cute dresses and makeup, styled their hair, and even shaved their legs. Guys also were groomed and, in fact, were quite preppy. It was like going back in time to when I first arrived at UGA. It was wonderful; everybody seemed sharp, motivated, and bright. I took to my studies like there had never been a break, including my job as an assistant editor for the *Journal of Church and State* where—for the first time in my life—I learned grammar and punctuation. To supplement our income, I started selling women's fashion shoes again. My daughters found friends easily, and Mona started working at a hospital on the three-to-eleven afternoon-to-evening shift.

Shortly after arriving, Tom Weldon, who had sponsored my trip to I.V. years earlier, came to visit. Having been one of the first to leave I.V., he went to seminary, where he received a master of divinity degree. He was looking for a place to start a nontraditional community church and picked

Waco. So once again, I invited everybody I knew to help start a church. We had remarkable success. Although neither Tom nor I have lived there in decades, the church is still thriving in that wonderful college town.

The year before we moved to Texas, Danny married a woman who looked like Erica but with features not nearly as striking. Both Danny and she worked for Wall Street firms in Boston, where they were quite successful.

By the time Mona and I moved to Waco seven months after Dad's death, Danny had talked Mom into loaning him the money for a down payment on a vacation house in a Vermont ski town. Had Dad been alive, Danny wouldn't have wasted his time asking, but Mom was much easier to bamboozle. As his selling point, he told Mom he would pick her up and take her with them when they drove up to the house on weekends. She "loaned" him $26,500 for the down payment, and he took her with them once.

Within a year, Danny and his second wife divorced, and Danny gave the woman the Vermont home, along with all the equity, as settlement. Mom, who had not been informed of this, started asking Danny when she was going to get her money back. Danny was consistently evasive. After that stopped working, he told her she would get it when his estranged wife sold the place. Nothing happened.

Finally, Murph had had enough and called an attorney—only to discover that Danny had been lying to her all along. The attorney drew up papers to sue Danny for the money, but Mom just let it go. Danny, once again, had used someone in our family to get his way—this time our mother, leaving her heartbroken, nearly broke, and with a deep sense of betrayal.

What amazed me was that this kind of behavior never seemed to bother Danny. He seemed neither embarrassed nor remorseful. He acted as if it was his money in the first place—to do with as he pleased. In his mind, he was entitled to it. Later he told Mom, "Nobody made money" on the house in Vermont, implying that all the equity was lost when the house was finally sold.

Murph was sixty-seven years old at the time and could not sustain such a financial loss, but Danny went on with his life as if nothing had ever happened. Mom was so upset that for years she couldn't talk about it without becoming tearful.

Her sense of justice, however, was unaffected. Once Danny became engaged for a few weeks to a cute young girl many years his junior. They drove to New York, and Danny bought her an engagement ring. It looked like it cost more than $25,000. Later we found out it was cubic zirconium and cost much less. But Murph, genuinely fooled by the value of the ring, looked at it on the girl's hand, turned to Danny, and said, "If you've got money to buy this whore a ring, why don't you have money to pay me back?" As you can imagine, we never saw that girl again.

I had hoped that moving to Texas would help return Mona to normal, but it didn't. She was still trim and looked good, but as far as her relationship with me was concerned, she remained as aloof and distant as when she first lay down on the sofa. If what was behind Mona's getting on the couch for two years was the first crack in the foundation of our family, her *secret life* with her "friends" from the hospital in Waco was the second. Since the girls had to be out the door for school at seven thirty in the morning with me right behind them, I was always asleep when Mona came home from the evening shift. Occasionally I would wake up and notice it was 3:00 A.M. or later; and it looked like she had just arrived.

When I asked, she would respond, "No, I've been here for hours. I'm just unwinding a little with a drink before coming to bed." Having no cause to doubt her, I would go right back to sleep. It happened often enough, however, that I started to wonder if something else was going on.

One night, Brenn had a bad dream and couldn't go back to sleep. It was after 2:00 A.M., and Mona still wasn't home from her three-to-eleven shift. After Brenn finally went back to sleep, I stayed awake and waited for Mona to arrive, becoming increasingly apprehensive as time passed. When she arrived at 3:30 A.M., she was glassy-eyed, stoic, and distant. "What in the world's wrong with you?" I asked accusatorially.

"Nothing."

"Don't give me that. I know there's something wrong," I challenged, not even trying to approach her gently. "What is it?"

"Nothing. Nothing at all," she said with a look of open defiance.

This exchange went on for quite a while, but I was relentless. I wanted to know what was going on, and I wouldn't let it slide. With much reluctance she finally confessed, "I've been out with some of my friends smoking pot, that's all. It's no big deal."

"No big deal!" I repeated. Like smoking marijuana in the middle of the night was as innocent as going to the store to buy a loaf of bread. Because my interrogation was relentless, she finally admitted that her friends were a couple of young guys from the hospital. This admission increased my agitation and anxiety significantly.

We had three kids in grade school, but it was "no big deal" for her to carouse with a couple of redneck orderlies until three or four in the morning! There was a huge disconnect here—a red flag that I couldn't ignore. The next day I called a marriage counselor, and we started going regularly, which I realized we should have done early in our marriage—years before she retreated to the couch.

I found counseling to be quite helpful; Mona didn't. The reason was simple: you have to tell the therapist the truth, and Mona wasn't willing to be forthright. Perhaps she was fearful about opening up what was going on inside her—even a little bit—lest the floodgates burst and she would tell all. Sadly, this made her a prisoner to a lifestyle of increasing secrecy and estrangement from the girls and me. Alcohol, marijuana, and her "friends" helped her feel normal. She used each to medicate the guilt she felt deep in her troubled heart from giving up her baby, her current behavior, and other things about which I was still unaware.

As for me, I was far from the loving husband she needed, which counseling revealed in spades. I was angry with her and let her know it, demeaning and belittling her often. Perhaps her secretiveness was because she was afraid to be open and honest about her behavior, knowing that I would explode if she did. We were both emotionally immature—trapped in a dance of destruction that made each member of our family miserable.

What I came to realize from the counseling was that Mona was becoming someone quite different from the person I married. She was no longer trustworthy or honest, choosing instead to act more like a rebellious teenager than a responsible wife and mother, and I was becoming my wife's tyrannical father, routinely criticizing her behavior and lifestyle.

I was so alarmed that I couldn't wait to get us out of Waco. Once again I thought a change of scenery and friends would improve everything. Geographical changes rarely cure anything, but I didn't know that at the time.

By May 1979—less than two years after our arrival in Texas—I received my MA in church-state studies; was inducted into the Omicron Delta Kappa Honorary, Academic, and Leadership Society; was published in two scholarly journals; and was accepted into a PhD program with a full scholarship and an $18,000-a-year stipend at Emory University in Atlanta. We were going home.

Thrilled and relieved, I wanted to get the most equity out of the house as possible, so we put up a "For Sale by Owner" sign in our front yard and an ad in the newspaper selling it for $36,000. Nobody came, and there were no offers. Running out of time, I planned to sell it to a broker for $28,500—exactly what we paid for it. Coming home the day before I planned to meet with the broker, Connie ran up to me and said, "Daddy, I sold the house to an old couple today for thirty-six thousand dollars."

"What?" I said, genuinely puzzled. "To begin with, you're not supposed to let anybody in the house without me here, but forget about that. Now tell me again what happened—*exactly* what happened."

Sure enough, she sold the house to a retired osteopath and his wife. We received full value for it, too. She showed it and told them they needed to buy it that day or lose their opportunity. Not yet thirteen, Connie had helped us keep $7,500 in much-needed equity. Connie had a keen interest in money—that was clear.

With nearly $18,000 in funds available when the house closed, I flew to Atlanta to purchase another before starting at Emory. Putting all the money down, I bought the largest house we could qualify for—a $52,500 two-level house with a huge foyer and a two-car garage in North Atlanta. It was a nice house in a nice subdivision, and the schools were excellent. We would thrive here; I was certain of it.

Chapter 20

"She's Seeing Someone Else"

By the fall of 1979, Dick's marriage had fallen apart. A devoted family man, Dick spent a lot of time with his wife and two sons; but he was a Watts, and the blood of Ireland flowed through his veins—he drank a lot. His wife terminated the marriage, citing Dick's excessive drinking as the reason. Dick was devastated, particularly because of his sons. He stopped drinking—cold turkey—and has not had anything to drink since the mideighties.

Seeing what had just happened to Dick and to Danny twice, I was determined not to allow our family to fall apart. In spite of all that had happened in our relationship, I loved Mona and wanted our marriage to work. Because we were both born-again Christians, I believed God would keep us together. As it turned out, Mona's desires were in opposition to mine.

When I started at Emory, Mona went back to work on another evening shift at a local hospital. The girls—now thirteen, eleven, and nine—were busy with gymnastics, doing handstands and cartwheels in the house, the yard, restaurants, the mall—anywhere there was even a tiny bit of room.

With Mona working as a nurse five nights a week, I continued my role of cooking, cleaning, and getting the girls to bed. By now I was used to it. To supplement our income from Mona's nursing and my stipend, I sold women's fashion shoes again. In many ways, our life was just like it had been in Texas. In other ways, it was not.

We didn't join a church. I went often and took the girls, but we didn't belong or commit. Mona didn't even bother to go, choosing instead to play in the A.L.T.A. (Atlanta Lawn Tennis Association). When she wasn't working, she was playing tennis. By now, the crack in the foundation of our marriage had become an unbridgeable chasm, which was apparent to everyone—except me. From the time I began graduate school, alcohol had become a significant part of both our lives. I felt lonely and overwhelmed, so when I drank, it was always to excess. Mona drank less—but more frequently—using it to medicate what was troubling her.

In the whirlwind of these problems, Mom, Dick, and Jean came to visit us during the winter of my second year at Emory. Mom smoked, so I made her go out on the porch to puff away. Once I looked out, and there was this little old lady, shivering in the cold, smoking her Winston. She looked so pathetically cute that I told her to come in and pollute us with her second-hand smoke.

When I did, Mom said warmly, "Thanks, Jacky." Thoughtfully, she added, "You know, I still pray for the baby every day."

"I know, Mom." By now, the *baby* was eighteen and driving, but Murph, in her simplicity, still thought of the child as a perpetual infant. It was endearing—what a gal.

For entertainment while my family was in town, we went to our favorite bar. We talked, drank, and laughed for hours. We had a ball, including the girls, who played Pac-Man for hours in the back room.

During one of our trips, Mr. Ghirardelli, whom we called "The Chocolate Man" because of his name, met us there for a drink. He lived in our neighborhood and loved to camp. When he did, he always had a carload of twelve-to-fourteen-year-old girls with him. Mona often included him in our family activities. The girls loved him, especially Victoria.

Within fifteen minutes of his arrival, Jean looked at Ghirardelli and said, "What are you doing with my nieces, Ghirardelli?"

Looking a bit uncomfortable, he said, "We go camping or to the movies. Sometimes I help Mona by taking the girls places when she has to work—things like that."

Jean just glared at him for several seconds, making all of us feel uncomfortable. Dick and I looked at each other, participating in a nonverbal exchange that let the other know we had no idea what Jean was thinking. We looked at Murph, but she was busy reading the label on her pack of cigarettes. Finally, with all eyes on her, Jean said, "I think you're a pervert, Ghirardelli, and I want to know what you're really doing with my nieces."

"I'm not a pervert," Ghirardelli stammered defensively—as everyone at the table tensed.

At that point I joined in his defense, saying, "Ghirardelli's a friend of the family, Jean. He's not a pervert."

Without taking her eyes off him, Jean said, "Let me handle this, Jacky.

Ghirardelli, you're in your forties. Why do you want to spend your time with my teenage nieces?"

Ghirardelli started to go into an elaborate explanation, but Jean cut him off by saying, "You're a pervert. I know you are, and I'm going to make sure that my brother, Mona, and the girls know to watch out for you. Now get out of my sight."

With that, Ghirardelli said a hasty good-bye and made his departure. When he was gone, Dick and I looked at each other and burst into laughter. Such behavior might seem a bit strange, but let me assure you, laughter is how a lot of Irish folks relieve tension. Mom laughed, too, but Jean was deadly serious.

Later, when Mona arrived, Jean quizzed her about Ghirardelli relentlessly. Mona finally said that Ghirardelli had been questioned by the police more than once for questionable behavior with girls in their early teens; and several mothers also had called Mona to caution her about Ghirardelli. Mona had never disclosed any of this to me, but Jean grilled her until the truth was revealed.

When all of this came to light, I was really curious and puzzled about Jean's insight and impressed by her incisive interrogation of Ghirardelli—Mona was impressed, too, for that matter. I also wondered how she recognized him for who he was with such speed and accuracy. I always knew "The Chocolate Man" was a little goofy, but I never thought there was anything deviant in his nature. Jean recognized it instantly. To me, it seemed like she was using more than good judgment and common sense.

Since I was the more present parent of the two, I wondered how I hadn't known what was going on. I hate to admit it, but I didn't suspect a thing. It was certainly my responsibility to protect my daughters—to keep them out of harm's way. But I guess I just trusted the guy. Despite all the hardships in my life, I am somehow a genuinely trusting person, to a fault. I fear that I had been negligent, for which there is no acceptable excuse.

During their weeklong stay, I had planned numerous activities, but Murph preferred to go to the bar every night and talk. Since we had so much fun when we were there, that's what we did.

Mona came, too; but she was noticeably distant and estranged from everybody. My family, who loved Mona, repeatedly asked what was wrong with her. Murph, noticing that Mona was petulant and even a little abrasive, questioned, "Do you think she's seeing someone else, Jacky?"

"She's not seeing anyone else, Mother," I responded in defense of my wife, but her question put that thought into my head. *Maybe Mom's right,* I mused for just an instant but quickly erased the thought from my mind. I couldn't think about that—not even for a minute. It was too painful. Besides, why would she see someone else? She hated sex; I knew that for a fact.

When they packed to leave, Jean searched the house for her white cashmere cardigan sweater. It was nowhere to be found. All of us joined the hunt—but with no success. Giving up, she left without it. Several months later, Mona sent Mom some pictures of the girls. Connie was wearing a broad smile—and Jean's sweater. It was years before Jean told me this, but it was the second episode of Connie taking things that didn't belong to her, carefully concealing her behavior.

———

In January 1981, Ronald Reagan took the presidential oath of office, Atlanta had a major ice storm, and Mona stayed away for three days because of the inclement weather. I was worried sick and didn't believe she couldn't get home from work. I accused her of being a liar. But she insisted that she couldn't get home. She said she was staying with a girlfriend who lived close to the hospital, but she refused to tell me the girl's name or address. After that, she frequently stayed out all night. I was scared and bordered on raging, but nothing I said—whether it was pleading or vitriolic—made any difference. She was now routinely absent most of the time. Her beautiful blue eyes were no longer warm and friendly. When she looked at me, her eyes were filled with guile, resentment, defiance, and open contempt.

Thus began a vicious cycle that precipitated the collapse of our marriage. She would stay out all night. When she finally came home, I was furious, pouncing on her the instant she walked in the door—just like Murph did to my dad so many years earlier. She wouldn't say where she had been or whom she was with. This would infuriate me, and I would scream in her face—inches from her nose—attacking her character and self-worth, profanely demeaning her with a verbal assault that exceeded the wrath of The Elders and the fury of my father. Seemingly impervious to anything I said, she would just smirk, openly contemptuous of me.

When I would finally leave the living room, which had become an emotional war zone, she would seize her chance and sneak out again. If I had seen her try to leave, I would have physically stopped her. That's how bad the situation had become. It wasn't what I wanted, of course, but by this time I had lost control of everything, displaying my volatile emotions routinely.

Once I realized she was gone, I would reach for the bourbon to help calm down, drinking alone until I passed out. By this time I was getting drunk three or four times a week. This destructive dance went on for nearly a year.

She would promise the girls to pick them up after school but leave them waiting for hours. When she would finally arrive, she would have a bucket of Kentucky Fried Chicken with her and tell the girls that buying the chicken was what made her so late. They believed this nonsense and defended her tardiness, which infuriated me more. Worst of all, the girls blamed me for Mona staying away. Who could blame them? I was the one who was angry all the time. Drinking more than ever, I was absolutely miserable.

By now, I was sure Mom was right: Mona had found someone else. She had the smell of another man on her regularly—his smell, stale cigarettes, the worst kind of smell. When she came to bed, she would reek of that smell—tobacco, spit, and alcohol—on her neck, her face, her arms, everywhere. It made me nauseous as fear, jealousy, and apprehension consumed me.

Changing tactics, I would implore her, "Mona, please tell me the truth. What's going on? Are you seeing someone else? Please answer me."

"I would never do that," she would protest with believable innocence. "I'm a Christian; it's not in my value system. No, I'm not seeing anyone else. I'm tired. Now go to sleep." With that, she would turn over, put her head on the pillow, and sleep soundly.

We went to marriage counseling once a week. It was the only time I could count on Mona's presence. She used each session to count, recount, and rerecount once again all of the grievances she had nurtured in her heart over the years, keeping perfect score of each of my real and perceived flaws. Asked point-blank by the counselor if she was having an affair, Mona rose in righteous indignation to deny and defend her moral purity. The counselor, Doug McIntyre, a minister and former center on John Wooden's first national champion basketball team at UCLA, believed her and said nearly all of the problems in our marriage originated with me. I was the one with anger issues and, according to our counselor, I had not displayed the leadership qualities necessary for the family to be healthy and stable. I was willing to take responsibility for all of it. I didn't care. I just wanted things to be normal and right, but I felt powerless to change anything.

I was so defeated and confused, I didn't know what to do. Like a visit to a medieval barber, this bloodletting went on each week for half a year—at the end of which there was little left of the adventurous kid who moved across the country on a whim to serve the Lord. I was shattered—a beaten, broken man who had a drinking problem.

Mona went to work one Saturday afternoon and didn't come home that night, which was now her well-established pattern. Starting early Sunday afternoon, I drove all over Atlanta, looking for her car. I had done this many times before but with no success. On this day, however, at 4:45 P.M., I saw it parked outside the Rusty Nail, a sleazy bar in Stone Mountain. Pulling up, I went inside, and there was Mona sitting at a booth with two drinks on the table.

"Hi, Mona," I said, slipping into the booth across from her. "Where's your boyfriend?"

She was hesitant and apprehensive, wanting to leave but unable to move. Finally taking a deep breath and smoothing her dress, she said, "I don't have a boyfriend. I've told you that a million times. Now go home. I'll be home later. Go!"

Not this time. There was a limit, and I had reached it. Looking around the nearly empty bar, I noticed a guy staring directly at us. Sliding out of the booth, I went straight up to him as our eyes locked on each other warily. "Are you screwing my wife?" I asked more like an indictment than a question.

"I'm not screwing your wife; I'm making love to your wife," he said, trying to make a distinction without a difference.

I was stunned and didn't know what to do. I thought of hitting him like in the movies, but this was far too serious—with way too much at stake— to settle with fists. I remember my first thought, *So she does like sex—just not with me.*

Then I took a good look at this ugly, foul-smelling, unkempt man. His eyes were crossed; his hair was long, greasy, and unwashed. He had a scraggily beard—mingled with hair growing out of his nostrils, smoked like a chimney, had a huge pot belly, dirty fingernails, used profanity in nearly every sentence, and was obviously close to illiterate. No woman in her right mind would pick him over me. Realizing this, I said to myself, *She's flipped out, and I need to help her get back to normal. I'm not going to divorce her.*

All of these codependent thoughts transpired in my racing mind in no more than a few seconds. I had made my decision to act as her rescuer and started behaving accordingly. This one moment in time sobered me literally and figuratively. Going back to the booth, I said authoritatively, "Mona, get in the car and come home with me right now."

"No, I'm going with Milton," she said defiantly. "I'll be home later."

I argued but with no success and watched Mona, the love of my life and mother of my children, get into an old, grimy pickup truck—long before they became fashionable—and drive off with another man. As they were pulling out of the parking lot, Milton looked directly at me and smirked.

Chapter 21

For More Than Two Years

When I got back home, I vomited, and all I could do was pace. My mouth was dry, and I couldn't eat. Surprisingly, I wasn't interested in numbing my pain or feeding my anger with bourbon. In fact, I knew alcohol would be my most dangerous enemy in my efforts to win back my wife and restore our family. I was particularly fearful of igniting my anger with booze. So I quit drinking—cold turkey—right then and there, and it lasted for more than a year. Part of my newfound self-control came from regaining focus and purpose, rather than feeling adrift, with no power to control anything—including my drinking. Incidentally, my ability to make this decision—and stick to it—was one of the things that kept me from believing that I was really an alcoholic.

When Mona finally came home, she walked into the living room, and we sat to talk. She said, matter-of-factly, "I'm in love with Milton. This isn't a casual affair. I love him, and we want to be together."

"But you're married to me," I said—numb from the pain these words would have caused even a day earlier.

"I know, but I hate being married to you. Milton and I have talked, and we want you to move out."

"What about the girls—*my girls*, not Milton's?"

"They'll get used to the change. In time, they'll grow to love him like I do," she said dreamily.

When I heard this, it was obvious to me that her perspective was completely detached from reality, so I said, "I don't believe that for one minute. What do you think we should tell them when I move out?"

"We'll tell them that we had a fight," she reasoned, "and we're separating for a while." When she said this, I could tell she had thought this through.

"But that's not true," I said firmly. "I don't want to lie to them and say it was because of a fight when it wasn't."

"Well, it could have been," she said in a poor attempt to justify a lie and make it the truth—her specialty. "Do you have a better idea?" she challenged.

"I need to think about it. I'm going to call Doug."

Excusing myself, I left the room and called our counselor. He listened intently, only interrupting to ask clarifying questions. I asked, "Mona wants to come and see you tomorrow if you have time. Do you?"

"I have time, but I don't want to see her, and I'll never be involved in counseling her again," he added.

"Why?" I questioned pleadingly. "We need your help more than ever."

"I know you do, Jack, and I'll help you but not her. She came in here every week for six months and never told the truth—not once—even when I asked her directly several times about having an affair. And it's been going on for more than two years! In my fifteen years of counseling and ministry, I've never seen anyone as deceitful as Mona." He added, "I can't help her. It's not that I don't want to. She needs more help than I'm trained to give. There's deep pathology here. I'm sorry, but I won't see her."

He said this not out of condemnation, but out of a crystal-clear understanding of who he thought Mona really was. I heard every word he said and was terrified about what the future might hold, but I refused to believe that Mona would never return to normal. Not giving up was ingrained in my nature; I was a rescuer and had been my entire life, starting with my alcoholic mother. As it turned out, his assessment was totally accurate, but I couldn't accept it. I wouldn't give up—not yet, not that soon. I wasn't ready to quit.

He added, "As far as what to tell Connie, Victoria, and Brenn, you tell them the truth. Say, 'I'm leaving because your mom is having sex with another man.' Don't lie to them under any circumstances," he exhorted. "Do you understand? Will you promise me that you will do this?"

I did understand and promised. Upon disconnecting, I went back into the living room and told Mona I was going to tell the girls the truth before I left.

"No, I don't want them to know the truth," she said fearfully.

"I'm sorry, but I'm not going to lie for you," I said.

"Then I don't want you to leave," she declared. "We'll just go on like we have been."

"While you're having sex with Milton? I don't think so," I stated.

She pushed hard for maintaining the status quo. In her distorted think-ing, she thought I would be okay with this if she resumed having sex with me, too. But I knew that wouldn't work. After hours of talking, we made a deal. Mona committed to stop seeing Milton for six months, work on restoring the marriage—including sex—and spend time at home. If, at the end of six months, she still wanted to be with Milton, I would leave and not tell the girls the real reason. I even wrote down the terms of our agreement and had her sign it. It would be difficult, but it might work. It was my last chance to save our family.

Chapter 22

"She Won't Leave Me Alone"

By the time I discovered Mona in the bar with Milton in the late fall of 1982, I had finished all the course work for my PhD, passed my comprehensive exams, had my dissertation proposal ready to submit to my doctoral committee, and had taught upper-level classes at Emory University for a year. I had worked very hard to get as far as I had, but with the disintegration of my family, I never went any further. There had been substantial sacrifice and hard work to get where I was—not just mine but Mona's and the girls' as well, but none of it seemed as important as keeping our family together. With the level of stress I was under, I don't believe I could have finished it anyway. I lost forty pounds and looked like a little boy wearing his father's clothes within two months of the discovery of Mona's adultery.

During the political campaign of 1982, I worked for a Republican running for Congress. He just happened to be a friend of the senator who chaired the Banking Committee, Jake Garn—the first U.S. elected official to fly in space. I was hired as the issues expert because of my educational background. I spent a significant amount of time researching the voting behavior of our opponent, but I also discovered I was talented at marketing the candidate. I eventually abandoned academia for marketing—a decision I've never regretted.

During the campaign, I went to Washington, DC, in the spring of 1982 to see numerous political action committees (PACs) to raise money. Because of my candidate's lifelong friendship with Senator Garn, I quickly became an insider. One afternoon, I was in Lee Atwater's office. By title, he was a special assistant to the president, but he was far better known as the person responsible for "dirty tricks" in the 1980 presidential campaign.

During my hour in his office, he introduced me to two men whose job it had been in the 1980 presidential campaign to shadow Jimmy Carter and rattle him whenever possible. These men, who resembled characters from a John Grisham novel, believed Carter was having an affair during the 1980 presidential campaign, and they tried to catch him at every turn. They also believed the former president and his wife had once been part of a wife-swapping club in Americus, Georgia, years earlier—before Carter was governor of Georgia. I'll never forget how thrilled they were with their mischief, which they considered to be a high calling. They assumed they were talking to someone who would pat them on the back approvingly for their efforts, but they were wrong. I was appalled and didn't believe any of it—regardless of what they said. By the time I left the room and the presence of these odious miscreants, I was out of politics, never to return. I finished my job in the campaign, but my heart was no longer in it. I didn't want any part of it.

So there I was—educated for politics but repulsed by it at the same time. What I witnessed in real life was far from the sanitized perspective presented in the classroom, and I knew I didn't want to invest my life in such pettiness and malice. Consequently, I put in my résumé for a marketing and sales position at Walk Thru the Bible, a Christian ministry that taught seminars and published monthly magazines. The selection process was long and arduous, but I was finally hired shortly after discovering Mona's infidelity. I was thrilled to get the new job, thinking it would help us get back to where we needed to be spiritually. It did necessitate substantial travel, so I was absent for days at a time. By this time I was grateful for the break from all the familial discord.

Once, I had a meeting in Chicago that was canceled, so I came home a day early—only to discover that Mona was with Milton, which both surprised and discouraged me. Predictably, however, I became incensed, confronting her when she finally came home. With his smell all over her, which nauseated and infuriated me, she once again promised to stay away from him. I accepted this at face value, but my days of naively trusting her were over.

The following month, I said I was scheduled to be in Los Angeles from Monday through Friday, but I had planned all along to come back a day earlier. Sure enough, Mona was sneaking off again to be intimate with Milton. I didn't know where Milton lived, but I had a good idea about where to look. I drove through parking lot after parking lot until I discovered Mona's car sitting right in front of an apartment door.

I knocked on the door. There was no answer, but I could hear scurried activity inside. I knocked again . . . and again . . . and again. There was still no answer, so I beat on the door for nearly an hour. A neighbor challenged me about what I was doing. I replied, "My wife's in there having an affair. Do you have a problem with me knocking?" He apologized and went back to his apartment.

With people looking out of windows and doors all over the complex, I continued pounding on the door. Out of the corner of my eye, I finally noticed Milton sauntering around the corner from the back of his apartment building, rolling up his sleeves like he wanted to fight. I knew instantly what that meant and flew at him in a rage I'd rarely experienced before—a rage that surprised and frightened him. He was about ninety feet away, and by the time I reached him, he was actually on his knees, cowering like a dog. "Jack, I know you're trying to get back together with Mona. I want to help you," he whined, "but she won't leave me alone. She just comes over. I can't stop her. I've tried."

Not expecting this response and confused by it, my fury abated immediately, much to his relief—mine, too. He got up, and we talked for nearly an hour outside; while Mona, who had been exposed to the entire apartment complex as an adulteress, refused to show her brazen face. Milton said, "You think you know Mona, but you don't. You think she's a sweet Christian girl who just got mixed up with the wrong guy, but she's been lying to you for years. She's admitted to me that she's had five affairs before me, and a girl who'll admit to five has had fifteen."

Stunned by his words and that he would expose Mona so eagerly, I couldn't take it all in, but I could see he was telling the truth. Her fling with Monty Sawyer the first month we were married was not an isolated incident. There had been others—maybe many others. He knew things I had no idea about, so I listened—really listened to everything he had to say.

He continued, "One time last year, I went away for the weekend with another girl. That's okay, right? I'm single! I can do that, right? Okay, so Mona found out about it and came over," he said. "She has a key, so she came in and put all of my things in the commode and then crapped on them and didn't flush the toilet. She put shaving cream everywhere. Then she took the keys to my truck and put dog crap all over the keys, too."

Mona couldn't possibly have done these things, I thought. I had never seen her behave like this—never. But I could tell he was being as forthright as he knew how to be, so I listened. I couldn't move.

Pointing to her car, he said, "See those dents? She told you she had a little accident. She didn't. The other girl was over, and Mona came in and started a fistfight with her. I told them to take it outside, okay. They started fighting in the parking lot—punching, scratching, biting, and pulling hair. Then the other girl had had enough and got in her car. Mona got in her car, too, and rammed the other car," he explained with a self-satisfied smile. "Then the other girl rammed Mona. This happened three times," he said with a smirk. Concluding, he added, "And it was all about who was going to be with me."

He was actually proud of this—unbelievable. I was no longer mad nor was I committed to doing everything in my power to save our marriage. I had had enough. I didn't know Mona; I probably never did. Frankly, after listening to what Milton had to say, I didn't want to know her—at least not this version. Looking directly at him, I simply turned and walked away without uttering a word. I got in my car and quietly drove off without the least bit of anger. The beautiful girl I met at Chi Omega years earlier had become someone who would participate in a two-car demolition derby— with Milton as the victor's prize. She wasn't going to "snap out of it." This is who she was, and I finally realized she didn't want to be rescued. This is where she belonged—with Milton, not with me.

Recognizing that Milton had ulterior motives, I checked out what he had told me with Mona who, for once, admitted the truth. It was all true— completely true. From that point forward, I no longer looked for ways to save our marriage. Instead I detached from Mona and looked for ways to stay away from her and her redneck boyfriend.

Interestingly, our nonexistent sexual life took a bizarre twist after this. I no longer sought intimacy, so Mona became the initiator—not because she desired me, I realized, but more likely to use sex with me to punish Milton. For the first time in our seventeen-year marriage, I wasn't inter- ested. Our marriage counselor was right; there was deep pathology here, and I didn't want anything further to do with it.

Not long after discovering the enormity of Mona's perfidious secret life, I came to my senses and sat down with her. "Mona, I'm not going to leave the girls with you under any circumstances," I declared. "You're the one who will have to leave. I'm not involved in adultery—you are." She protested vehemently but acquiesced within a few days. By this time, she openly came and went as she pleased with no interference from me. I was still angry—no doubt about it—but I didn't try to keep her from seeing Milton. Remaining abstinent also kept my anger from becoming too explosive.

When this happened, Connie was nearly sixteen, Victoria fifteen, and Brenn twelve. Mona was now absent nearly all the time, spending more time than ever with Milton. I reluctantly continued to keep her secret from the girls—concerned about the damage it would cause them if revealed. By doing this, however, I realized later that I had actually became Mona's enabler in her adulterous lifestyle. The insane situation was intolerable for everybody in the family, so it's not entirely surprising that it took only one little incident to bring everything crashing to the ground. That incident occurred on a Sunday afternoon, nearly a year after I discovered Mona and Milton at the bar.

Chapter 23

Removed from Life Support

One weekend, Mona decided not to come home at all. Victoria stopped me in the bathroom and asked, "Dad, where's Mom? Do you know? I want to talk to her. Tell me where she is. Dad, do you know where she is?"

Victoria badgered me relentlessly for an hour. Finally, her persistence wore me down. "Okay . . . okay . . . okay!" I snapped, "Yes, I know where she is."

"Take me there. I want to see my mother right now," Victoria insisted. So I did, knowing that the secret would finally be revealed. Looking back, I think taking Victoria over to Milton's was one of the worst parental mistakes I ever made, but by that point my emotional judgment was impaired and I couldn't maintain my resolve to say no. What she discovered hurt Victoria for years, but my own pain was so acute that I couldn't think beyond the immediacy of the situation.

When we arrived, Mona's car was out front, just as I knew it would be. Victoria, without hesitation, started knocking gently on the door. "Mom, it's Victoria. Open the door. Please open the door." She whimpered her request brokenheartedly time after time—with no response. It took twenty minutes for Mona to open the door. By that time, Victoria was sobbing and nearly frantic.

Looking as nonchalant as possible, Mona smiled as she invited us in. I could see that every hair on her head was in place and her makeup was flawless, which explained why it took her twenty minutes to respond. At least Victoria was spared the devastation of seeing her mother disheveled from her salacious behavior. "Mom, what are you doing? Come home please," Victoria implored.

"I'm just visiting a friend, Victoria," Mona said innocently and then introduced Victoria to Milton. He tried to be charming and engaging; but Victoria would have none of it, dismissing him without looking at him directly or saying a word.

"Mom, what are you doing here—*with him?*" she said with obvious contempt and a look that burst any hope of Milton being warmly received by her daughters. For the first time, reality was obvious on Mona's adulterous face. Her illusions were shattered; her daughters would not love Milton as much as she did. This part of her self-deception evaporated before my eyes, which was gratifying.

Shortly thereafter, I drove home alone—with Victoria in Mona's car, following behind. When we arrived, Connie and Brenn saw that something was amiss, so they followed Mona and Victoria into the master bedroom. I walked in, too.

"What's wrong?" Connie inquired.

"Mona, you tell them," I said, allowing her to choose her own way to disclose such devastating news.

"I have a boyfriend. His name is Milton. I love him, and he loves me. We want to be together, and it doesn't matter because this marriage is over anyway."

With insight and conviction, Connie replied, "Both of you destroyed your marriage, Mom. But you destroyed our family—not Dad."

"Well, he's committed adultery, too," Mona said to deflect culpability from her own egregious behavior.

All eyes immediately turned to me. Mona was referring to my brief indiscretion at Jean's wedding nearly six years earlier. I couldn't believe it. I had tried for nearly a year to spare our daughters from the pain of Mona's unrepentant three-year adulterous affair, but she felt no similar restraint. All she was concerned about was shifting blame so she wouldn't have to admit how wrong she had been—regardless of the consequences to our children.

Nevertheless, I couldn't deny that my past behavior—where alcohol played a decisive role—was something that put me on the same level with Mona. Both of us had committed adultery. Although I admitted my mistake immediately, it cost me a huge price in the eyes of our daughters when they needed me the most. This, of course, made us equally guilty in their eyes. To me, it seemed totally unfair, but that's how Mona played. At that moment, I lost the last bit of respect I had for her and now saw her for exactly who she was—a self-serving, deceitful, manipulative woman who cared about nobody but herself.

Looking back decades later, I see things a little differently. I now view Mona as a tragic figure. She couldn't be the person she wanted to be, and she was tired of pretending to be someone she was not. With Milton, she was free to be herself. It's what she needed at the time, and I believe that's what drove her to him.

———

Our marriage was now removed from life support. The end was imminent. Neither of us wanted to deal with that reality, however, so we just drifted along like this for a month or two. Coming home from work one day, Mona was at the top of the stairs in the foyer—surrounded by Connie, Victoria, and Brenn. Looking up at them, Connie stepped out, as the chosen spokesperson, and said to me, "Dad, we've talked and decided: if someone has to leave, we want it to be you and not Mom."

I was crushed—so crushed that I not only accepted this decision but simply turned and walked out of the house to go "off the wagon" after more than a year of abstinence. That was the precise moment when I lost my family—when it ceased to exist, leaving me with the feeling that my role of being a husband and father had been ripped from my life. Although I didn't realize it at the time, I was destined to try to re-create a family with other women and their kids—with about as much success as all the "king's men" had at putting Humpty Dumpty back together again.

Connie took charge of the situation, but it was my responsibility to set her straight, and I didn't. I believed she made her choice because she thought she could control her mother and bully and badger her younger sisters—something she had begun to do frequently.

I should have replied, "I don't care what you want. I'm the father and the responsible parent. She's the one having an affair, and she's the one leaving." Instead, I just accepted their decision—as if they were the adults and I was the child. It never occurred to me to do anything different. By that time, I didn't own enough of myself to stand firm. From that day forward, all of our lives changed—and not for the better.

Chapter 24

They Didn't Like Him

I was a naive and trusting young man, particularly where Mona was concerned, and it cost me dearly. My brother Dick has always been equally as gullible. We can trace this character trait back through Murph's side of the family to our great-grandfather Paddy, who arrived on Ellis Island as an immigrant in the early 1890s. He arrived on a boat from Ireland with his older cousin Frank; and both walked through the streets of New York mesmerized by the enormity of the city. They were determined to acclimate to America from the moment they arrived. This included the food Americans ate.

Noticing a street vendor on one corner, Frank said to Paddy, who was only twelve, "Will you look at that, Paddy. They eat dogs in America."

Paddy looked at the HOT DOGS sign where the vendor was busy serving several customers. Paddy's heart sank, and he felt nauseous. Frank interrupted Paddy's reverie by saying, "We're going to be Americans, Paddy. You go sit on that bench over there, while I go and get us some dog to eat for lunch."

Paddy obeyed—grateful to sit down because his legs felt a little weak. A few minutes later, Frank came over with their lunch and gave Paddy his. My great-grandfather carefully opened his sack, looked at his hot dog for a long moment, and with trembling hands, carefully wrapped it back up. Looking at his cousin, he said, "Frankie, what part of the dog did you get?"

Throughout this entire situation with Mona, I had been as naive as my maternal ancestor ninety years earlier. Beginning my new life as a single parent, I found an inexpensive apartment where many nice, older people lived. I moved out shortly before Thanksgiving 1983. I couldn't afford a telephone, so I had to walk two blocks to an outside pay phone to call the girls. Call-waiting was not yet available in North Atlanta, so I would get a busy signal nearly every time I tried. Such was my dilemma, trying to call three teenage girls who were constantly on the phone with their friends. I would stand in the cold for an hour or more every night that entire winter, trying to get in touch with them while Mona would tell them I didn't call because I didn't care. She knew this wasn't true, but I guess it better served her purpose to twist it that way—not considering the emotional impact to our daughters. Many divorced people behave this way.

With me out of the way, Mona was free to bring Milton over to the house to "get to know" the girls. Both he and Mona hoped that he could simply take my place and they would be a happy family. Neither Connie, Victoria, nor Brenn saw Milton as Mona did. Perhaps it was because Mona had chosen to spend every afternoon with Milton—just as soon as she would leave work, while Connie, Victoria, and Brenn waited hours for their mother to pick them up from high school. Because this happened so often, they learned they couldn't depend on their mom.

Yet, somehow, all three girls still seemed to defend and protect their mom fiercely, blaming either Milton or me for every displeasing situation. They refused to take an honest look at their mother's behavior. Often this was frustrating, but how could I fault them? I still did the same thing with Murph—with the same passion and intensity, knowing that she was a hopeless alcoholic and nearly always wrong. Perhaps it's human nature to defend your mother, no matter what.

The girls hated Milton, and not just for the affair. Once, when he was mad at Mona, he defecated in a bucket. Then he left it at the front door of their North Atlanta house for all of them to find when they came home. He would also frequently show up—unannounced, drunk, and screaming obscenities at them because they wouldn't allow him entrance. He hit Mona often and Brenn once—slapped her right across the face. He carried a gun, occasionally revealing it to intimidate them, but above all else, he was verbally abusive. He smoked pot daily, had relationships with other women, which caused Mona constant anxiety, never had a real job, and took her to Small Claims Court numerous times to work out their petty grievances.

Milton was a piece of work, but Mona loved him very much. When the Olympics came to Atlanta years later, people were encouraged to buy commemorative bricks for loved ones to pave Centennial Park, the same park that was bombed during the Olympics. Mona bought a brick for several people, including Milton. It said *Milton Bingham: My One True Love.*

This is how she thought of him. In spite of the obvious pathology, they found something in each other that neither found in anyone else. This is what kept them together for many years after our divorce. Mona wouldn't marry him, however, because none of her daughters would even consider accepting him as part of the family. So he never became more than a constant and perpetual outsider. Sadly, this just caused more frustration and problems. Mona was forced to continue seeing him on the sly, having a tawdry affair for another decade instead of something more permanent and honorable. Having loved Mona from the first time I saw her, it's sad for me to think that her life never got any better than this, but it didn't. For Mona, Milton was her high point—as good as it would ever get.

———

I left in November, and on December 23, 1983, Mona filed for divorce. It brought a crushing sense of finality and failure to our long and tumultuous relationship. Since I worked for a Christian ministry, Walk Thru the Bible, I had to tell them what was happening. My supervisor arranged an immediate appointment with Bruce Wilkinson, the president. Expecting to be fired, I went in to see Bruce. He knew what I was going to say, and I could see cold detachment in his eyes—which let me know I was right. Coming right to the point, he said, "Jack, tell me what's going on."

With a broken heart and tremulous voice, I started telling him the story. Instantly, his demeanor—even his posture—changed. He became a pastor to me instead of a businessman. I'll never forget it. He didn't fire me. Instead he offered a hand to help.

Once, toward the end of winter, he came to me and said, "My wife and I have been praying for you and want to give you five hundred dollars to take your girls for a long weekend at Hilton Head. It will do all of you some good. But you have to use it for that. You can't pay bills with it." We went and had a wonderful time. Bruce and his wife really couldn't afford it, but they did it anyway. Years later, Bruce made a fortune by selling more than ten million copies of *The Prayer of Jabez*, but Bruce's gesture of much-needed kindness, when he was nearly penniless himself, made me fiercely loyal to him and a very fruitful salesman for the ministry.

The day I was served, I called my mom and told her the news. She sent me an airplane ticket—not a bus ticket—to fly to Boston for Christmas. She said, "Jacky, I don't want you to be alone for the holidays. Come home." So I got on a plane and flew to Boston, where it was below zero with windchill. The weather was miserable and so was I. At least I wasn't alone.

While there, Mona called and asked me to pay for her car repair. Murph, overhearing the conversation, picked up the extension and said, "Mona, this is Mary. If you want that money, why don't you go out and turn a trick for it like all the other whores do?" That was Murph; she always could shoot straight to the heart of the matter or, in this case, a little lower.

By this time, Mom was living in a mother-in-law suite at Dick's house and had been for several years. After Danny took her money, leaving her nearly broke, this alternative was best for her, and Dick was glad to have her. Not long after my Christmas visit, Mom's abuse of alcohol finally took its toll on her body. She was diagnosed with cirrhosis of the liver. The doctors told her she had three months to live.

This news finally got her attention. She stopped drinking right then and there—no slips, no excuses, no AA, just no more drinking. Frankly, I didn't think she could do it; but she did—just like I did when I discovered Mona's infidelity.

She was sick for many months but recovered remarkably and lived alcohol-free for the next ten years. We like to call these the "wonder years" because it was wonderful to finally have the mother we always wanted. Her personality was sweet from then on—that is, except for when someone crossed her and she would respond with "the finger." Some things never change.

When I returned to Atlanta after Christmas, I couldn't bring myself to retain a divorce lawyer—I just couldn't. Not until the day before our first hearing did I get one. So when I went into court, I was ordered to make a onetime payment of nearly $6,000, which was thousands more than I earned each month. And all I had was ninety days to do it. When my lawyer informed the judge how much more it was than I made, the judge said, "He got them into this mess, not me. Let him figure a way to get them out."

This was my first experience with being a part of the legal process, and it was a costly lesson. Within thirty days, Mona filed contempt of court charges because I couldn't pay off the accumulated bills fast enough. I felt like I was drowning, but I also knew the Lord would take care of me—and He did. I received an unexpected refund from the IRS and one from Georgia Power as well. I made an out-of-the-blue $1,500 bonus from Walk Thru, and Mom sent me another $1,500. She had a windfall and asked Dick what to do with it. Dick said, "Send it to Jacky. You don't need it; he does." To my surprise—and Dick's—she did. The "extra money" I received was within $5.00 of what I was required to pay. So I paid off everything I was required to pay, avoiding a contempt of court penalty by one day.

Our divorce progressed very slowly. I learned quickly not to use my lawyer as a therapist because the meter was always running. I told him not to pray for me because I would be charged for it, and I doubted God would listen to a divorce lawyer anyway. He laughed; so did I. One day, Mona called and said, "I found a Christian mediation group that's not expensive. Do you want to use them to finalize our divorce?"

"Absolutely," I said. "Great idea, Mona. When can we get started?"

Soon thereafter, when I met with the mediating attorney, I told him I would love for them to help. I was also crystal clear that I didn't want to "get back together" with Mona. Our marriage was over, and all we needed was help with the property settlement. He was equally clear that this was acceptable with the mediation team.

Mona and I had already been separated for nearly sixteen months, and I wanted the divorce finalized so I could get on with my life. Nevertheless, the process dragged on for another year. When I arrived at one of our final meetings, the Christian lawyer triumphantly said, "We've been meeting with Mona for several months now, and she's ready to put your marriage back together again. She hasn't seen Milton for over two weeks, and we believe the two of you should get back together. Will you take her back?"

I was stunned when I heard what he had to say. I didn't want this and had made it clear this wasn't an option and hadn't been an option from day one of the process. Looking at him intensely, I said, "Do you remember what I said before we started this—that I didn't want to get back with her?"

"Yes, I remember, but Mona has made some tremendous strides here."

"I don't believe her," I said. "I've been down this road before. She says she's done with Milton, and then she goes right back to him. I'm sorry, but I don't buy it." Then I added, "And one more thing: I don't love her anymore."

Without dispute or defense, Mona looked at me and said, "Tell me to my face that you don't love me."

"Mona," I said, looking straight at her with no acrimony in my tone, "I don't love you—sorry, but I don't."

With the room dead silent, Mona responded, "I don't love you either."

"Then what are we going through all of this for?" I pleaded.

At that, we began to finalize our divorce, once and for all. The final stumbling block was the house. Mona agreed to sell it when Victoria graduated from high school in three years. In the meantime, I would take out a second mortgage, pay off all of our debts, and make the monthly payments on the second. When the house sold, we would pay off the second and split the remaining equity equally. I would pay child support for Connie, Victoria, and Brenn until each was eighteen. Because I could prove adultery, Mona didn't qualify for alimony in Georgia, so I didn't have to pay anything for her.

When Mona left, she didn't go home; she went to Milton's apartment. It had been her hope that this would punish me, but it didn't. I had moved on emotionally.

What's worse, Mona began reinterpreting the events of our divorce. Since she was "willing" to give up Milton and had done so for two weeks, she reasoned she was no longer the one who wanted the divorce. *It was me! I divorced her.* Forgetting that she had been in a continuous adulterous affair for nearly four years by now, she would say, "In my heart, I know I was willing to get back together. Jack wasn't, so he divorced me."

The most amazing part is that she actually believed it—and still does. She exonerated herself, minimizing her adulterous lifestyle, while blaming me for everything. All of our mutual friends, who knew better, were shocked and outraged at Mona's perspective, openly mocking about how ridiculous she sounded. Not even Granny, her own mother, accepted what Mona said at face value. Only three people bought Mona's line—Connie, Victoria, and Brenn, the three who counted most to me. Her revisionist history found fertile ground in their impressionable young hearts, causing nothing but trouble, especially in their relationship with me.

The divorce became final one month after we signed the papers. I wasn't even required to go to court. Mona, being the plaintiff, was required to be there. She called me at work and said, "It's over. We're divorced." Without another word, she simply disconnected. That moment was hard for both of us. In spite of everything, even a poor marriage is difficult to end. I had been with her for nearly twenty years and married seventeen. It had been a long time—my entire adult life. My self-worth was shattered. Feeling like a failure, I wondered what the future would hold.

Mona must have felt like a failure, too. One time, nearly a year later, she called me on a Saturday night. Very upset, she was crying uncontrollably. Genuinely surprised and concerned, I asked what was wrong.

She said, "Jack, if anything happens to me—if I do something to myself, I want you to know there will be a letter for you explaining everything." Barely able to get her words out, she added, "I owe you that much."

Responding, I told her that I was fine and that I didn't want her to commit suicide, which I didn't. She finally calmed down and never made a call like that again. Many times since, I've thought about what that letter might have revealed, but the offer of an explanation was never proffered again.

In spite of Mona's behavior, I came to realize that I was equally responsible for the failure of our marriage. I always wanted it to work but didn't have a clue about how to achieve that goal. Not understanding what a good husband was, I did what my father did and what Carl McMurray did—my two role models. I demeaned my wife repeatedly and maintained an angry countenance more often than not. I had never shown her that I cherished her—which I had committed to do. But I didn't know how. I loved her as much as I was capable of loving her, but my capacity was minimal. As I look back, her desire for escape seems far less reprehensible than it did at the time.

When she was pregnant with our first child, she said, "I don't want to marry Jack. He's a little boy." She was right; that's all I was. Although I was in my late thirties when our divorce became final, I was still a little boy in more ways than not. Shattered by all that had happened, I wondered if God still cared about me. I know I didn't.

Chapter 25

A Problem I Couldn't Deny

Anyone who experiences a divorce knows that when you go through such an encounter, you make life-altering choices with predictable results. Most people don't realize that's what they're doing, but that doesn't alter the consequences of their choices. Many choose to deal with their pain and sense of failure by becoming bitter, retreating to a lonely world—comforted only by smoldering anger. Others choose to hit the singles bars to dance, talk, and drink with others who also choose to medicate their pain with alcohol and short-term sexual encounters—always hoping the next person will be "the right one." Many retreat to overeating, overworking, overspending, or overexercising to avoid dealing with their troubles. Some choose to go to church and self-righteously extol their troubles to other victims who commiserate and pray with them—with the unspoken assurance that they, too, were once bound in a dreadful marriage just like yours.

None of these strategies work—that's the predictable part. And they certainly won't help a person heal or grow, but that's what I wanted: healing and growth. Pursuing this goal, however, proved to be a daunting task.

This became crystal clear when I attended Dick's second wedding. After Julie divorced Dick, he floundered, being ill at ease and emotionally unprepared to be alone. Some people simply do better when they're in a relationship; Dick is one of them. So am I.

Dick had known Ellen Martin since high school—as did I. She was a beautiful woman with short, highlighted blond hair, beautiful blue eyes, and a mesmerizing smile accented by cute dimples. She and Dick worked together at the corporate office of Star Market, seeing each other daily for years. They were good friends.

After Dick's divorce, he asked Ellen out and proposed to her on the first date. At least that was Ellen's story. They became an item and Ellen finally moved in with Dick, but Dick abandoned his talk about marriage when she did. After living together for three years, Dick finally acquiesced to make it permanent, so they were married about the same time Mona and I were finalizing our divorce. With a heavy heart, I flew to Boston to attend Dick's wedding.

As always, the liquor flowed freely; and as always, I got knee-walkin' drunk. Dick had a nice, simple wedding in his backyard with a reception at the local Marriott. Toward the end of the festivities, I saw two great-looking girls who were not with our party, and I went over to talk to them.

The next thing I remember, a security guard was waking me up. It must have been hours later. Shaking my shoulder gently, he said, "Sir . . . sir. You can't sleep on the couch in the hotel lobby. I'm sorry. You'll have to leave."

I had no idea where I was or where I had been, but I had to go to the bathroom. Looking in the mirror when I got there, I could see I was fully dressed and looked normal. My relief was enormous until I reached into my pocket and found my underpants tucked inside. *What?* I thought. *How did this happen? What have I done? I can't remember a thing.*

I was terrified. Blacking out was the kind of alcoholic behavior I couldn't deny. I was scared to death; and just like Murph, I immediately stopped drinking—cold turkey—no slips, no relapses, no excuses. Also like Murph, I didn't go to AA, as I should have; so I didn't deal with any of the underlying causes for my acting-out behavior. I just stopped drinking—with surprising success—for years. But I was a "dry drunk," with all of the causal factors for medicating with alcohol still lurking just beneath the surface, itching to emerge again and destroy me.

Chapter 26

"I Think I Know You"

One Friday evening, I left my office at Walk Thru a little early to make sure I didn't miss any of my girls' gymnastic meet. Both Connie and Victoria were on the varsity team at Alpharetta High School; and our school was mounting a solid challenge to unseat Tucker High, the state champions. Brenn, who was an eighth-grade cheerleader, also was a gymnast.

On my way to the meet that Friday, I stopped by Piccadilly Cafeteria. It was inexpensive and all I could afford. Two tables over was a really cute, long-haired brunette with great legs, eating enough food to fill a hungry athlete. When she left to refill her coffee cup, a busboy started to clear her place, and I said to him, "Excuse me, but I think that lady is coming back to eat her apple pie."

"Uh, okay," said the busboy, moving on to the next table.

When she returned, I said, "I saved your pie for you. The busboy was going to take it."

Smiling—a very warm, inviting smile, I might add—she said, "I wasn't going to say anything, but I think I know you."

I perked right up. "Really?"

"Yes. Are you Guy Cassidy?"

"No, but I think I know you, too," and I did. As we talked, we discovered she had dated one of the young men in my Campus Crusade Action Group at Georgia State nearly twenty years earlier. Her name was Martha Wilson, but now it was Tennyson. She had a seven-year-old boy, Hugh, and had been divorced for five years.

We hit it off right away. Unlike Mona, Martha was very communicative, which I liked, and straightforward, which I liked even more. Her eyes were brown—like her hair. She was quite striking, even beautiful, with a nose that was slightly large. To me, she had a perfect figure. I would learn later that her best feature, however, was her fidelity. She told the truth and was always where she said she would be. We began dating shortly after we met at the café and continued to do so for the next year.

During this time, I quit working for Walk Thru to become the marketing vice president for Faith Money Management, a start-up company. It was risky, but I made only $27,000 a year at Walk Thru. Faith started me out at $50,000. Faith also provided me with a new 1985 Cadillac Sedan Deville—with leather seats—as a company car. After being broke since the late 1970s, I jumped at the chance. The girls loved riding in the Cadillac, which Mona resented.

Several months after we began dating, I brought Martha with me, in the new Cadillac, to a regional gymnastics meet at Alpharetta. As we entered, Mona spotted us and gave us a dark stare. The moment we sat down four rows away from her, she rose dramatically and stormed out of the gymnasium. Martha looked at me uncomfortably, but I shrugged it off. Thirty minutes later, however, I tensed, looked at Martha, and said, "The car!" I don't know what it was, but all of a sudden I became aware of how vulnerable my company car was—parked outside with Mona skulking around.

I got up and walked briskly outside to the parking lot with Martha trying hard to keep pace. When I got there, the Cadillac was keyed from one end to the other—four panels in all. Each had a deep scratch, making this beautiful car look ugly. Mona and I were divorced—had been for half a year—but I could infer that her behavior was out of anger that I would bring another woman to the meet. The hypocrisy of such anger obviously escaped her, and she keyed my car in retribution. She later denied this act of vandalism with all the wounded innocence to which I had become accustomed, but she did it.

Weeks later, Milton called and told me she had admitted to being the culprit. I could tell that he loved exposing her and enjoyed telling me about Mona's duplicity. He needn't have bothered to make the call; I knew what she had done before I ever reached the car. From then on, I started calling Mona "Scratch"—a nickname that seemed appropriate.

Sadly, as the years passed, Mona became increasingly resentful toward me, in similar proportion to my decreasing interest in her. I just didn't care anymore, and it bothered her. Milton was no longer a secret, which took much of the excitement out of their relationship. What she was left with was a pot-smoking handyman who couldn't hold a job and wasn't presentable in public. My life, by contrast, was just beginning, and I was very grateful that it was.

Unfortunately, at Faith Money Management, my damaged company car was the least of our problems. The president of the company, Jim Bob, had been systematically misappropriating funds, diverting them for his personal use. Worst of all, he had been taking the life savings of ministers and others, who could ill afford the loss, using the money to fund his opulent lifestyle. One investor became extremely suspicious and went to the FBI. It was a real mess, but in the end, Jim Bob admitted sole responsibility and went to prison for nearly three years. Watching the FBI investigation unfold was intense and intimidating, an experience I wouldn't recommend. Gratefully, I returned my Cadillac and returned to work for Walk Thru with a raise and added responsibility.

Chapter 27

She Needed Me

One evening after a year of dating, I was reading the paper and Martha was balancing her checkbook. Suddenly, and with no discernible premeditation, Martha said offhandedly, "I've given this a year. That's about all I'm going to give it."

My insides froze. For the first time, I felt pressure. We had had a delightful relationship, and being together was free and easy. Part of me wanted to run, but another part thought marriage to her was inevitable and would work out positively. After that, we talked about marriage numerous times, and I finally agreed. This made Martha peaceful and content, but as the days went by, I became increasingly apprehensive.

One day while riding together in my Fiat 2000—the Cadillac long gone—I told her exactly how I felt. I wasn't ready to get married again. It was too soon, and I was scared. On and on I went. Finally, Martha said she understood and agreed to call it off. My relief was instantaneous until she said, "Take me home, please."

I had assumed—incorrectly, I might add—that we would just go on as before, but she didn't want that. It was all or nothing, and as she got out of the car, she said a warm good-bye. I was stunned as I drove off. By the next week, she was dating someone else, and I was very unhappy about it.

It was painful to lose her, so I came up with a plan to salvage the relationship. I went by the school where she taught and proclaimed that we would get married the following Monday afternoon if she'd have me back. She smiled and agreed, but was still a little dubious. The ball was in my court to make everything happen.

So that's what I did. I got one of my best friends from Crusade, who had also been part of the church in I.V., to perform the ceremony. His name was John Fitts, and he had become the minister of a small church in Birmingham, Alabama. He was thrilled to be asked. Sending a FedEx with the money for the license, his wife, Patty, went to City Hall and secured all of the paperwork. She also arranged for flowers, a singer for the ceremony, and a dinner reception to follow—just like Mary Jo had done twenty years earlier. All this took one day. Sunday, the day before the wedding, Martha finally went shopping and bought a dress, reasoning she could always use a pretty dress. By now, she thought this really might happen and was warming up to the idea.

At 3:00 P.M. on Monday, I left Walk Thru—without telling anybody but the girls about my plans—and picked up Martha at school. By then she had informed all three of her siblings, and each dropped everything—as did my daughters—to drive to Birmingham for the wedding. We drove over, got married, had a nice dinner and reception, drove back to Atlanta, and consummated the marriage. Then she went to school the following morning to teach.

Martha made it clear that she didn't want any more children, and I had no problem with that. She planned to start taking the Pill as soon as her cycle would allow, which was two weeks after we were married. Toward the end of her cycle, however, she was spotting and went to see her gynecologist. After careful examination, the doctor told her that she was pregnant. She was in utter disbelief.

When they called me into the room to break the news, I wasn't nearly as surprised as she was. How could I be? This was now my fifth unplanned pregnancy. Because Martha was spotting, there was a chance she would miscarry. When she asked if I hoped she would, I responded, "I want what the Lord wants for us." And that's what happened. Martha's spotting stopped, and she had a normal pregnancy with a strong, healthy fetus.

"I hope it's a girl, Jack. I really want a little girl. You must want a boy, right?"

"Martha, I really don't care. Little girls always love their daddies; so a little girl would be just fine with me. Besides, girls are all I seem to be able to make," I said playfully. "But all my girls are lovely, and our little one will be, too." I knew the baby would be a girl.

Sure enough, Jordan was born on June 9, my fifth and final child. She arrived at the end of the school year. Martha had to grade papers between contractions to have her students' final grades ready for the last day of school. Martha radiated; and Jordan was the sweetest, most loving child any parent could ever want. Enough was enough, however. The following week I had a vasectomy—a humbling but necessary surgery.

Two weeks after we were married and before Martha was certain she was pregnant, Brenn—now a sophomore in high school—called and asked if she could live with Martha and me. I was surprised but delighted. I wanted to say yes right away, but I needed to discuss it with Martha first. After all, we were living at her house.

Much to my surprise, Martha was adamantly opposed to the idea. She felt it was too overwhelming in our first year of marriage. Plus, she argued, the house was too small for us, her nine-year-old son Hugh, and a new baby. I knew she had a point, but I wanted Brenn to move in, regardless of the inconvenience. I knew that living at Mona's—with Milton always skulking—wasn't good for anyone, and I'd always preferred to have my daughters with me.

Brenn's frequent appeals tore me to pieces. Brenn would plead, "Dad, I can't live over here with Mom. Milton is around all the time, and he scares me, Dad. Please, I want to come live with you." I was her father, and she needed me. Every fiber in my body wanted to drive over and pick her up immediately, but I had to get Martha on board first. This was causing conflict that needed resolution—and fast.

In America, if you can't resolve a situation, what do you do? You go to therapy, of course. And that's what we did. I brought all of them to therapy—Martha, Brenn, Hugh, and me. Hugh loved the idea of Brenn moving in; the more the merrier for him. He was a great kid. Martha's opposition mellowed a little because the therapist thought it would be in Brenn's best interests to come. But there really wasn't enough room in the house, and since I was still paying for the second mortgage on Mona's house and for child support, we couldn't afford a bigger house either. What we did have, however, was a large, unfinished basement—complete with a boarded-up fireplace.

The very next day, I called a neighbor, and we made a plan to build three rooms in the basement—a bedroom, a playroom, and an office. Scraping every cent I could find, we built the rooms—nearly 1,000 square feet.

Finally, the remodeling was ready, and Brenn came over to see her new accommodations. She beamed. This was the first time she had ever had a room entirely to herself.

Brenn thrived in this environment, and she settled down to the life of a normal teen. She was popular in her new high school, made the best grades of her life, was an All-American cheerleader, and was captain of the gymnastics team at Norcross High School, which finished third behind Alpharetta and Tucker during her senior year. Best of all, I loved having Brenn with us; to me, she made our family complete.

During this same period, Hugh's father, Junior, filed a lawsuit against Martha, accusing her of being an unfit mother. Junior had remarried a woman with two boys about Hugh's age, and Junior wanted Hugh to live with them. When Hugh would visit his dad's house, Hugh would have to undress in the foyer and put on clothes Junior and his wife had bought for him. The same procedure was performed when Hugh returned to Martha's house. It was weird, really weird—and sick, if you ask me. Nevertheless, we had to deal with this every other week and take Junior's lawsuit seriously.

The peculiar part of it was that Martha was an excellent mother—the best I have ever seen. The suit was groundless, but Junior had substantial resources and was determined to press the issue. Custody battles produce carnage with every person involved, and this baseless lawsuit was no different. It was heartbreaking to see all of the distress on Hugh's face, but the real destruction was between Martha and me. In a crisis, some couples pull together; others take out their stress on each other.

When we would go to court-ordered mediation, Junior would voice his position, and Martha would sweetly and politely do all she could do to refute it. When the meeting was finished, however, Martha was exhausted. In her frustration, she would vent her rage in a safe place and at a safe target—me. This legal process went on from shortly after we were married until Jordan was nearly two—with Martha raging at me as Junior's proxy, causing irreparable damage to the foundation of our marriage in the process. Her anger was so intense that I would do almost anything to avoid or appease it. I didn't want our relationship to deteriorate to a screaming match like mine had with Mona, so I began a cycle of keeping it all bottled up for long periods of time, then snapping and letting it out when it became too much to handle.

Martha wasn't always cross, however. There were long periods when she was delightful and easy to be around. But when she became angry, she became almost like a different person. I suspect she would say the same thing about me. To avoid conflict, I started keeping things to myself. As you can imagine, being bottled up caused significant problems as time passed.

The lawsuit was finally settled amicably among all parties; but by that time, the damage done to our relationship proved to be irreversible—at least as far as I was concerned. Often, Martha's cutting words reminded me of my dad and The Elders. In the year we had dated, I had never seen this side of Martha. I wanted to run, but I didn't—not for several years.

The irony is that Junior attacked Martha's strongest suit—her parenting. I knew from day one that no court would ever side with him and take Hugh away, but Martha couldn't rest in that truth. It afforded her no peace. She was terrified by the idiotic lawsuit and, once again, I began to feel alone in an increasingly loveless marriage.

If it had just been her anger, I think I could have handled it—especially for Jordan—but it was more than that. Martha's life had a set order of priorities—Hugh and Jordan first, then her mother and extended family, followed by her job and her friends, and then her husband, me. I felt like I was the least important part of her life, which her actions often validated—at least that's how I perceived it. She needed the slot filled to be a complete woman, but that's all I seemed to be—someone to fill a vacant role in her life. I was necessary to make the house payment, cook, and show up beside her so she was no longer a single mother. Being unimportant wasn't enough for me, so my commitment to our relationship declined appreciably.

Connie graduated from high school and received a gymnastics scholarship to Georgia Southern in Statesboro. The following year, Victoria graduated—as homecoming queen, I might add—and also went to Georgia Southern. She was supposed to have an athletic scholarship, but she tore her anterior cruciate ligament (ACL) during her senior year in high school, which effectively ended her gymnastics career.

When Victoria graduated from high school, I called Mona and asked when she planned to fulfill her end of our divorce settlement: to put the house on the market. She hung up. This happened repeatedly.

I tried to be nice, reminding Mona of her legally binding agreement, but she refused to comply. Connie and Victoria were now away at college, and Brenn was living with me, so it was time for Mona to sell. Because she continued to stall, I had my lawyer file a contempt of court charge against her for failure to comply with the terms of the divorce agreement.

The day before she was ordered to appear, she listed the house, averting a penalty. The listing remained, but Mona now refused to mow the grass, take out the trash, flush the toilets, or clean the kitchen. Potential buyers would drive up, take one look, and drive on. Mona was determined to stay put. Meanwhile, I was required to pay the second mortgage on the house every month, which was killing me financially—which seemed to delight Mona.

Finally, I came up with a solution that was acceptable to Mona. My plan would allow her to keep the house. She would refinance the mortgage, rolling the second into the first, pay the bill herself, and keep the house for as long as she wanted. When she sold it, she would split my accrued equity equally between Connie and Victoria, allowing them to pay off their student loans. In that way, I would pay for their education, but I would personally receive nothing, which was fine with me. Brenn wasn't included in this arrangement because she was already in my custody.

––––––

During Connie's second year of college, she called me one day and said, "Dad, I'm pregnant."

"Are you sure?" I asked.

"I'm sure," she said emphatically. "Keith and I are going to get married. Will you help me pay for the wedding, Dad?" Keith, who was Connie's long-standing boyfriend, was in the army. Evidently he stayed with Connie when he went up to see her on weekends.

I liked Keith and knew that he and Connie had been committed to each other for some time now. So I responded, "Of course. Let me talk to Martha, and I'll let you know what we're going to do, okay?"

"Thanks, Dad. I really need your help. I'm sorry it happened this way, but Keith and I were going to get married someday anyway."

"I know you were. I love you, Connie," I said, ending the call with a promise to get back to her quickly.

When Martha came home from school, I told her about Connie's situation. With a look as furious as I had ever seen, Martha exploded. "I can't believe she would do this." She refused to help or even to attend the wedding.

Stunned by her outrage, I was devastated. Once again, I was split right down the middle between Martha and my child. I could come to Connie's aid, which I desperately wanted to do, or I could keep peace in my new family and refuse to help. I chose neither. I stalled Connie and started working on Martha. When Connie would call, which was nearly every day, I put her off. I could tell she felt like I was abandoning her. Who could blame her? Worst of all, I couldn't be forthright because I didn't want to alienate her from Martha.

With just four days until the wedding, Martha relented and agreed to help. Why she changed her mind, I never discovered, but I called Connie immediately, telling her what we would do. Connie was very gracious throughout the entire process, which made me feel even worse about stalling her.

Martha and I hosted a lovely dinner for everybody the night before the wedding at a large Chinese restaurant. In Martha's eyes, we had done our part; in Connie's eyes, we were reluctant participants. In my eyes, I was ashamed that I didn't offer Connie unconditional love and acceptance immediately—just like the kind I experienced from Mary Jo McMurray nearly twenty years earlier when Mona was pregnant with Connie.

At the wedding dinner, which was very nice, everybody thanked Martha for making it so lovely, which she accepted graciously—as if she deserved it. This embittered me toward her, which I internalized. Right then and there I said to myself, *I will never let her do this again.*

Chapter 28

They Often Look Trustworthy

Not everything was difficult. Brenn was a delight—as were her friends. Teenage girls have so much energy that life is always exciting just being around them. Hugh was great, too. He was into every sport imaginable, and because he was so intelligent, he went to the magnet school for high achievers. I remember going to the first meeting of the PTA at the magnet school, remarking to Martha that it looked like the bar scene in *Star Wars*. There were a lot of strange-looking people with weird ideas, but it was fun. I was still teaching Sunday school at First Baptist, and I was developing my own marketing business after leaving Walk Thru to do similar work for ministries. Many things were looking up.

Best of all was Jordan, who was precious and the delight of my life. As I predicted, she was a daddy's girl. Martha was wonderful with her—patient, kind, attentive, and above all, loving. She was never cross with Jordan. She was, however, often cross with me.

Instead of holding my ground with Martha when she became angry, as I should have, most of the time I would do anything to mollify her. In an effort to keep the peace, I stopped taking care of myself, but I didn't just let things go. I kept my wounds bottled up instead, which proved to be very self-defeating. On other occasions I would overreact and explode in anger.

Martha continued teaching after she had Jordan, so we took Jordan to a babysitter each school day. Martha was thorough in her search for the best day-care situation possible, finally deciding on an older couple who kept no more than six children in their home at a time. It was a wonderful environment, and we felt lucky to leave Jordan with "Mamaw and

Papaw," a semiretired couple in their early sixties. Jordan stayed there for three years.

When she turned four, Jordan came into the living room one Saturday morning and asked me if she could watch TV.

She picked up the remote control, handed it to me, and climbed up on my lap. As I started going through the channels looking for something kid-friendly, there was one station where a teacher was talking to twenty children who were four or five, sitting at her feet in a classroom.

"That one, Daddy. I want to watch that."

"Okay," I said, and we both started watching the program.

The teacher on the TV show said, "Okay, boys and girls, today we are going to talk about touching. Some touching is good. Some touching is bad, and some touching can be confusing."

By the time she finished her paragraph, I said, "Jordan, this show isn't appropriate. Let's look for something else, all right?"

"No, Daddy. I don't want to watch TV." With that, she got down and walked into the bedroom where her mom was grading papers. Thinking little of it, I switched to the news.

Forty minutes later, Martha came in ashen-faced and said, "Jack, turn off the TV. You have to listen to what Jordan has just told me." I turned off the TV and looked directly at my precious four-year-old.

Jordan looked at me, mustering all the courage she could, and said, "Daddy, Papaw touches my vagina every day." Those were her exact words. I can remember it like it was yesterday. Martha wouldn't allow Jordan to use cute names for body parts. Jordan used correct names, which proved to be very important.

I was dumbfounded, but she had my complete attention—just like Bobby Marconi had all those years earlier when he told me about my sister Jean's molestation. As Jordan began her story, I was horrified and incredibly distressed, but I also knew that I had to keep my head on straight. I stopped her for a moment and retrieved the video camera. That way, Jordan wouldn't have to repeat her story as frequently to the police. For the next forty minutes, she told me—with the camera on—about Papaw's molestations. She went into vivid detail.

When she finished, Martha and I looked at each other, deeply disturbed, wondering what to do next. "Let's take her to the doctor," I said, so we got in the car and headed to the pediatrician for an examination. He had no openings, but when we told him the nature of the visit, he dropped everything and spent an hour with us. He assured us there had been no penetration, which gave us a measure of relief, because it meant that her reproductive organs wouldn't be damaged. He then said, "I have to call DFACS. It's the law."

"Good," I said. "I want Papaw to go to prison for this." Actually, I wanted to kill him and later told Martha this.

She said, "Then you would go to prison, and we need you."

This stopped my mounting anger and vengeful thoughts cold. She was right. I would be needed now more than ever. I wondered how we could have misjudged the situation with Papaw so badly, but that's the unique part of child molesters—they often look trustworthy and caring. They falsely lead you to believe that your child is in good, loving, and responsible hands. I was blindsided—no doubt about it. So was Martha.

We went straight from the doctor's office to the police station. Tears welled in my eyes as we discussed the situation with the police officers. I told them that I wanted Papaw to be punished for his terrible acts. Much to my relief, one officer reassured us: "We'll have his ass behind bars before dinner. He's not going to get away with this."

And he was true to his word, arresting Papaw that afternoon for child molestation.

Chapter 29

In Charge of the Courtroom

The police went to Mamaw and Papaw's house several hours after they watched the tape I'd filmed earlier in the day. Papaw surrendered quietly, and Mamaw called a family law attorney they knew to represent him and secure bail.

In the initial interview, with counsel present, Papaw said Jordan was a liar and had made up the whole thing. The police countered by saying four-year-olds have no sexual awareness and are incapable of making up a lurid tale like this one. With that, Papaw refused to continue the interview and at one point even had his lawyer point the finger at Hugh as the predator.

But the video evidence against Papaw was clear and compelling. His accusation of Hugh was baseless. Hugh was spared, but I was infuriated.

When Hugh finished high school, he went on to the Naval Academy, where he played football for the Midshipmen. After graduation, he was an officer aboard the USS *Cole*. While in Yemen in October 2000, the ship was attacked by Osama bin Laden's al-Qaeda terrorists. Hugh's quick actions, as reported by the press, saved several lives. None of this would have happened if Papaw and his sleazy lawyer had been successful in destroying his life before it began. And the video we took of Jordan that day was the prime evidence that Papaw could not refute.

Papaw was looking at doing hard time at a maximum-security prison, where a sixty-three-year-old white pedophile would probably not survive. His options were minimal.

To ensure that Papaw would go to prison, Jordan would have to testify. Martha and I agonized over the decision of whether to expose her to the emotional trauma of testifying, but ultimately Jordan made it clear she wanted to do it to bring Papaw to justice. He had already struck a plea bargain to stay out of prison so Jordan's testimony didn't impact the outcome, but she wanted to have her say in court.

Finally, the day arrived for Jordan to testify. She was brought to the witness stand at the beginning of the trial calendar, sworn in, and asked to tell her story in front of nearly two hundred people in the courtroom, including two rows of manacled prisoners in orange jumpsuits. As Jordan spoke, the busyness of the courtroom stopped, and all whispering ceased as every person listened intently to this beautiful little girl tell her story. People—dozens of them—began weeping openly.

Still a preschooler, Jordan was in charge of the courtroom. As she spoke, her words were clear and delivered with conviction.

Papaw never did time in prison, but he was discredited and humiliated. Papaw and Mamaw had planned to keep their day-care facility in operation for another ten years, but because of Jordan, they were forced to close it forever. Jordan's heroic behavior probably spared dozens of other preschool children from potential molestation by Papaw.

After the trial, with this ordeal finally behind us, I was mindlessly watching some inane TV show when the phone rang. I answered it. Mona was on the line. "Jack," she said cheerfully, "are you sitting down?"

"Yeah," I said. "What do you need?"

"Nothing. I just wanted to tell you that I got a call a few minutes ago from a young man—your son. He's found us and wants to come to Atlanta. I'm going to meet him tomorrow afternoon. After he sees me, do you want to meet him?"

Chapter 30

"He Looks Just Like You"

So the baby was a boy! Of course I wanted to meet him. I'd wanted that, prayed for it, and at my deepest level, believed for years that it would happen.

When I finished the conversation with Mona, I went out on the deck and paused reflectively. I remembered giving my unborn child to the Lord twenty-five years earlier—when I had no choice but to do so. I also remembered the overwhelming sense of peace I felt when I did. In the deepest recesses of my heart, I knew God would bring my lost child back into my life someday. I knew it; that's what gave me peace. The Scriptures call it "the peace of God, which surpasses all comprehension" (Philippians 4:7 NASB). That's what I felt back then.

Over the years, I came to believe this must have been an emotional release of some kind and not a promise; but I was wrong. That's what it was: a promise—a promise that was about to be fulfilled by a God who loved me and didn't want me to spend the rest of my life with such a loss and deep pain in my heart. With tears streaming down my face, I simply said, "Thank You, Father." Nothing else was needed.

The following evening, I had a meeting at my office and came home late, knowing that my son was already at the house. When I opened my car door, my son's wife stepped out onto the porch and looked at me. Screaming with a mixture of shock and joy, this beautiful, black-haired Central American beauty said to her husband, waiting inside, "Oh, my God! He looks just like you, Hunter." With that, she ran back into the house.

When I opened the front door and walked in, a young man, who looked like a cross between Dick and me—with a mustache like my dad's—stood up to greet me. Smiling, he said, "Hi, I'm Hunter Martin, and you're my dad."

"That's right. I'm your dad."

After looking at him for a few seconds, I held out my hand and said, "I've wanted to meet you ever since you were born. And who is this lovely young lady with the magnificent eyes, Hunter?" I said, wanting to include her in the conversation.

"This is my wife, Maggie. We've been married for five years, and we own a small house in Jacksonville."

With that, we sat down and talked—Hunter, Maggie, Martha, and me. They had just come from Mona's, and I was anxious to share the story from my perspective. So I began. The first thing I told him was that I never wanted to give him up for adoption. I explained, as carefully as I could without disparaging Mona or her family, that life back then was complicated, and people had conflicting opinions. My main goal was to tell him that I never— not for one second—wanted to give him up for adoption.

Hunter said, "I always wondered why I was given away. I came up with all kinds of scenarios; but for some reason, I always felt like my dad didn't really want to." Looking me square in the eye, my long-lost son added, "And I was right." With that, he looked at Maggie, who nodded at him, kindly validating her husband.

That Hunter had a deep belief about what his dad really wanted shouldn't have surprised me, but it did. For me to hear him say it like this, however, was kind of a bonus, further affirming that God had, indeed, answered my prayer. I tried to fight back the tears, but I couldn't. I wept. Everybody sat there silently, with tears in their eyes, until I finished and regained my composure.

"All right, now that that's over," I said, smiling through glistening eyes, "let me tell you the second thing I want you to know. Now that you've found us, I want to have a relationship with you from now on. I don't want to lose you again. Is that okay with you?"

"Yeah, sure. I can't be a little boy again, but we can be friends. Is that all right?"

"Absolutely. Is that all right with you, Maggie?" She nodded and smiled at me tenderly.

After a long and immensely joyous meeting, they left. They stayed in town for another two days, but I saw them only once more during that time. They wanted to see Connie, Victoria, and Brenn and spend some time with them. By this time, Brenn was out of school and living with some friends in downtown Atlanta, so Hunter and Maggie couldn't get back to see me for a longer visit. It was fine with me. I knew that nurturing each relationship with his three full siblings was important.

In the years that have passed since that first meeting, my relationship with Hunter and Maggie has become the predominant one in the family. I've become a major player in their lives and they in mine. They now have three children, and each loves Grandpa Jack. The Martins have come to Atlanta half a dozen times or so, and I've gone to Jacksonville at least forty times. I'm the only grandpa the kids know on their father's side. I'm a normal and welcome part of their lives. I watch their ball games, fish with them, take them to dinner and the movies—everything grandfathers are supposed to do. They've never had any problems because of what happened decades before they were born. I'm their grandpa—just like I was always meant to be. That fact brings me immeasurable satisfaction.

Mona, unfortunately, has chosen to remain distant. Hunter has repeatedly reached out to her, but she has remained aloof. What she did do, however, was give him life, which she didn't have to. The price she has paid for this has been staggering, but the reward, for me, has been endlessly valuable. Regardless of all the difficult things that happened between Mona and me, I admire and respect her for her decision to give birth to Hunter.

What really has amazed me about Hunter is this: he is just like my dad—his facial expressions, his joviality—even the way he scolds his twin boys, Matt and Mark. But his kids are just as carefree and into mischief as Dicky and I ever were. Since Hunter never knew either my father or me in his formative years, it continues to amaze me how much he reminds me of my dad.

When they left after our initial meeting, Martha and I opened a bottle of wine and had a commemorative toast. I didn't get drunk; it was just a glass of wine. Because of the stress and pressure from the custody battle with Hugh, the molestation case, and everything else, I had started having a drink or two occasionally—just to unwind. After being abstinent for years, I came to believe that I wasn't really an alcoholic. I could control my drinking; I was certain of it.

Looking back at how I denied reality, medicating the anxiety and unresolved issues in my life with alcohol, all I can add are three little words: tick . . . tick . . . tick. My moment of truth was approaching.

Chapter 31

"Don't You Come Back"

Martha's house was dark and lugubrious—painted in deep, dingy browns and dark, aging yellows—inside and out. So I began to make significant improvements, including painting the ceilings white and the walls ivory. I painted everything, making it much brighter and more cheerful.

Nevertheless, there was always the unspoken reality that, although Martha and I had "become one" in marriage, the house was hers alone. One day, as I was about to put the second coat of paint on the baseboards in the family room, which was all that remained to complete the job, I stopped. Looking at my work, I thought, *Why am I doing this? This is Martha's house, not ours—and certainly not mine.* With that, I put the paintbrushes away and never touched them again.

Like the guy on the golf course who said I should go to the University of Georgia, which hugely influenced the trajectory of my life, putting the paintbrushes away did the same thing. So many incidents in my life seemed random at the time, but were actually pivotal. I now realize that this was the precise moment when I left the marriage emotionally. I just stopped trying, but I did so without informing Martha, which was cowardly and unfair. Instead of being transparent, I churned my anger inwardly. I started keeping score in a secret game of "Who does the most around here?"—a game she had no chance of winning, since she didn't know she was a participant. I embraced this role, never realizing that I was building a permanent wall between us.

When we first married, Martha changed her retirement plan, instructing the school system to withhold the maximum allowed from her check to build a large retirement nest egg for her. This action seriously decreased her take-home pay. Consequently, the monthly house payment and utilities were left up to me. She said this would benefit "us" in the long run, but my name wasn't on anything—not the house, not as a beneficiary on her insurance policy, not on her retirement package. At first, this didn't bother me; but as the years passed, it bothered me a great deal. I became embittered about building equity for her without being included. As I saw it, our marital partnership was entirely one-sided. When I would broach the subject, she dismissed it and refused to treat the problem as one that needed addressing. I accepted this on the outside, appearing to be satisfied, but on the inside—where it really mattered—my resentment intensified.

At the same time, she would complain that I didn't make as much money as the husbands of her three best friends. Once, she took my paycheck, looked at it, and simply dropped it on the table, walking off with a smirk. I was crushed. That hurt me deeply. Years later, when I mentioned the incident to her, she didn't even remember it.

For that and several other reasons, my wounds, which had never been aptly addressed from my first marriage, grew deeper, and I started drinking more frequently and in larger quantities.

Although I did my best to remain externally calm—with mixed results—internally, I was deeply wounded. It all came to a head one Sunday at 4:00 A.M.

The phone rang. Answering out of a deep sleep, I responded, "Hello."

"Dad, it's Brenn. I'm at Northside Hospital."

"Are you all right?" I asked—fully awake and sitting upright on the edge of the bed.

"No, I'm not," she answered. "Dad, I'm pregnant, but it's not normal. It's a tubal pregnancy, and they have to operate on me right away. I'm bleeding a lot, but they won't proceed without your consent because I'm not twenty-one. Please come right away and sign the papers." Beginning to cry, she added, "If you don't, they say I might die."

"Oh, my God," I said. "I understand. I'll be right there."

"Don't get a cup of coffee or anything, okay?" she pleaded. "You have to come right now. Please, Daddy, I'm scared," she said, bursting into tears like a little girl—my little girl.

"I'm on my way. I'll be there in twenty minutes." I was dressed and out the door in less than two minutes. While the garage door was opening, Martha came to the kitchen door, which opened into the garage, and said, "What are you doing? Where are you going at this time of night?"

"I have to go to Northside Hospital. Brenn has to have emergency surgery. She has a tubal pregnancy."

"She what!" Martha was instantly enraged. "I don't believe it," she continued—as her anger intensified. "This is terrible. Don't you leave here," she threatened. "I'm serious."

"Martha, maybe you don't understand. If I don't go sign the paperwork, she'll bleed to death."

"I don't care. If you go, don't you come back," she said with a sneer. "I mean it."

Looking at her in utter disbelief, I said, without raising my voice, "You did this to me once before, with Connie, and it hurt my relationship with her. You're not going to do it again. You're crazy if you think I'm going to let Brenn die. If that's the way you want it, I won't come back."

Martha slammed the door, symbolically ending our marriage—at least for me. I got into the car and drove off to take care of my daughter, who desperately needed me.

Upon arrival, I saw Brenn, who was pale white. I signed the papers, and they wheeled her into surgery immediately. John, her longtime boyfriend, was there in the waiting room, looking as guilty and deflated as anybody I had ever seen. Sitting next to him, I told him about how I "got Mona in trouble" years before, but I used the experience to come to Christ and change my life. He now had the same opportunity to use a life-altering event to initiate positive change. He hardly listened—probably because he was stoned.

Nevertheless, Brenn came through fine, but because they had to remove an ovary, they doubted she could ever have a child. When she told me this, I could see a deep sense of loss in her eyes. I held her hand for a long time and stayed with her at the hospital until she was released in the early afternoon. Then I drove her back to the house she rented downtown.

In the early evening, I went back to Martha's house. She was cold and hostile toward me, but I didn't care. I began to stand up to her, and it felt good—especially when I knew I was right. I had no alternative other than what I did. I couldn't allow Brenn to die because her predicament was an embarrassment to Martha.

Once again, I felt absolutely miserable. Drinking more than ever, I medicated the pain in my heart with alcohol and began flirtations with several women—my other medication. Both validated me, if only for a short time. In my neediness, I willingly abandoned any sense of self-restraint.

While married to Mona, I had numerous flirtations—none of which became serious. I wouldn't get involved physically, even though none of my sexual needs were being met at home. At the same time, I accepted validation outside of the marriage. Whenever I considered infidelity, I would see the faces of my daughters in front of me, and I just couldn't let them down by "getting strange" with another woman.

The same restraints kept me in check during my marriage to Martha until a woman from my office began to focus her attention on me. I was quite enamored with her. Our time together was filled with hurried passion, along with a promise of more to come, which I believed would happen but never did. I was convinced that her feelings for me were genuine, but they were not. In my desperate need for validation—despite the price to be paid for such a betrayal—I rushed headlong into a short but intense affair with this woman.

Martha didn't deserve this. Nobody deserves infidelity. I hurt her by my affair, but what really crushed me was that I had also betrayed Jordan—my precious daughter and the light of my life.

My shame and guilt from this episode have haunted me ever since, never resolving completely. Worst of all, I have no one to blame but myself. I was guilty of the same behavior that had wounded me so badly—behavior that I held self-righteously over Mona for years. The only difference between us was that I didn't get caught, like she did. Because I couldn't justify my behavior or get past the guilt, I continued to numb my pain with bourbon.

Like everybody engaged in adultery, I tried to justify my actions, but for me, it was a hopeless endeavor. I was wrong and couldn't manipulate the truth by blaming Martha. I was the one who cheated—not she. As I thought about it, I couldn't believe that I had fallen so far, but I had—eagerly.

By the time it ended, I had become a walking wound, which is how alcoholics feel when they spiral downward. While in that conflicted state of mind, I moved out of the house, ending my seven-year marriage with Martha. My leaving had a sobering effect on her. She wasn't serious about me never returning after I left to help Brenn, and she tried to get me back. If I had it to do over again, I think I might have returned—especially if I had any idea about what was to follow. I didn't know it at the time, but the problems resulting from two failed relationships were destined to resurface, exacting a terrible toll on me.

Karma is not exactly a Christian concept, but that doesn't mean it isn't

true. It is; I know it is. In the back of my mind, I wondered if my perfidy—
as brief as it had been—was destined to poison my future, never allowing
me to experience what I always wanted: a loving, mutually satisfying relationship with a woman. I hoped that it wouldn't but, in my heart I was
concerned that it would.

Chapter 32

"Your Grandson"

Once separated in 1991, I was relieved, but my guilt over leaving caught up with me quickly. I was drowning and knew it. To do something so contrary to my nature—like having an affair and walking out—really caused me severe emotional conflict, which lead to increased drinking. I just couldn't take any more and used a little Bud Light and a lot of Jack Daniel's to numb my pain. I felt absolutely worthless—unworthy of God's love or anyone else's.

My emotional state affected every area of my life, especially my relationship with the Lord. The positive part of being a Christian and having Christ in your life is that He never leaves you. The "negative" part is that He never leaves you alone—even when that's what you want. That was my experience, living alone again in an apartment. This time I didn't sit and pine away. I started hanging out at bars. I drank heavily and often. I couldn't drink enough to drown out the Lord. Heaven knows I tried.

Shortly after leaving—perhaps four or five months later—Martha once more tried to reunite. When she did, I had a long, heart-to-heart conversation with her, telling her everything, coupled with a genuine apology. Keeping her in the dark didn't seem fair.

A few days later, she called, informing me that it was probably best for us to proceed with our divorce. By coming to this conclusion, the decision to split was mutual, which made it easier for everybody. We agreed to raise Jordan well. Knowing how badly it would hurt Jordan to tell her about my infidelity, Martha never used it as a weapon against me, for which I always admired her. From that time forward, Martha and I have coparented amiably and become friends in the process. Unlike Mona, Martha always kept her end of the bargain—regardless of the situation. Because of that, we both developed respect for each other—a respect we didn't have while married. Since Martha's parenting skills have always been exemplary, I've never had real cause to complain. Over the years, we've had no more than two or three conflicts, all of which were resolved within a day or two. Neither of us speaks ill of or undermines the other, especially in front of our daughter. Jordan actually believes we were well suited for each other and never should have divorced. Since we couldn't make the marriage work, Martha and I decided to make the divorce work well. It's something I'm very proud of.

———

Shortly after I left, I received a call from my sister, Jean, saying that Mom was dying. She had lived nearly ten wonderful years without alcohol, but the cumulative effects of drinking for half a century had taken its toll. Murph had liver cancer and would die in three months or less. This time it really was going to happen.

I called Mom the next day—when I thought I could do so without crying. "Hey, Murph," I said like always. "How are you?"

"I'm fine, Jacky—really I am."

"Mom, I talked to Jean yesterday," I said cautiously, broaching the subject.

"I know. She told me. It's all right, Jacky. I've lived long enough anyway."

I couldn't help it; I started crying.

"Don't cry, Jacky. You'll make me cry, too," she said as she started crying.

After several minutes of disjointed sentences and much more crying, I said, "Mom, I'm coming up. I want to see you and say good-bye." With that, I started crying again and couldn't stop.

Because Mom needed special care, Victoria flew up to help, staying for a week or two. Victoria was a real trooper, although it was Jean who did most of the work. Mom was grateful for both of them, especially for keeping her company. We all were. Mom was still living with Dick, so Victoria stayed upstairs in Dick's part of the house.

Danny came by regularly, nearly always drunk, and caused conflict with everybody—even Mom. When he left, she was often in tears because of his caustic words and insensitive actions.

He also had a particularly nasty conflict with Jean, who was nursing her infant son while being the primary caretaker for our dying mother. In their confrontation, Danny threatened to do Jean bodily harm—as well as to her husband, Endicott. It was so serious and heated that Jean and Danny stopped speaking and have never spoken since.

When I went north, I brought Jordan and Hunter with me. When Jordan saw Murph, she said, "Hi, Grandmama Mary. I'm glad you didn't die before I came."

Laughing that sweet Irish way, Murph said, "I'm glad I didn't die before you came either. You're so big, Jordan. Come here and let me hug you." With that Jordan hugged her.

"Mom," I said, barely able to get the words out, "I have someone who wants to meet you. You remember the baby you prayed for—for twenty-five years? Here he is—your grandson Hunter."

Mom looked up and started crying tears of joy for a long-lost grandchild who had finally been recovered. Reaching out for Hunter, she hugged the poor kid so tightly I thought she would hurt herself. To his credit, Hunter was not uncomfortable with this display of affection by his grandmother. I was grateful he came. It was Mom's dying wish to meet him, and it was being fulfilled. They talked for a long time, and Mom even commented about how much he reminded her of Dad.

"Hunter," she said, "a harsh word never crossed your grandfather's lips. That's what your grandfather was like. God rest his soul."

Unfortunately, Mom suffered from Irish Alzheimer's. That's where you forget everything other than your grudges. Dying or not, neither Jean, Dick, nor I would allow Murph to get by with that nonsense. Each of us laughed and gave Hunter a much more accurate picture of what Bill Watts, his biological grandfather, was really like.

Unfortunately, Mom was in no condition to entertain. Two days later, Hunter, Jordan, and I left to return home. Before we walked out, I said my last good-bye. When I did, I hugged her, kissed her, and then asked, "Is that alcohol I smell on your breath?"

"Just a little, Jacky. What harm can it do now?"

I was shocked, but she was right. It couldn't hurt now. I've thought about that moment a thousand times since, and it helped me understand how cunning, baffling, and powerful alcohol really is. Mom was never sober—not really. She just quit drinking—a big difference. It has also made me realize that once you're an alcoholic you're never free from its influence. No matter how long you've been sober, you can never let your guard down. You can achieve great things through sobriety, but alcohol remains your constant enemy. You can never drink again.

Chapter 33

Money without Earning It

Mom died two weeks later, and I flew up for the funeral. While I was there, Dick pulled me aside for a private conversation. He told me something that, for me, was earth-shattering.

He explained that shortly before her death, Mom confessed something to him. When he had his accident on the bike with the cab when he was seventeen, Dad claimed that he had never received any settlement money from the insurance company.

On her deathbed, Murph told Dick that wasn't true. In fact, my dad received $50,000, which he and Murph secretly kept.

This was a huge sum of money. In 1962, $50,000 would buy what more than $300,000 would buy half a century later, so this wasn't chump change—it was serious money.

I was surprised and offended by the avaricious duplicity—still am offended by it, in fact. What kind of a man would do this and never own up to it?

After Dick told me the story, he said, "I asked Mom why she was telling me now." I looked at him intently for what was coming next.

"She said, 'I don't want to go see Jesus with this on my conscience.'"

Flying back, I wondered how many families have parents who steal from their kids. Mona cheated me out of my part of the house. Danny stole from Mom—Dick's money, as it turned out. But for parents to steal from their kids! It didn't compute.

I thought about my children. Could there be any scenario where I would steal from them? Could any of them ever justify stealing from me? I couldn't imagine it.

My anger toward Dad had abated over the years to the point where I actually sought out his company in the latter years of his life. He had mellowed significantly, was a wonderful grandfather, and I had come to think of his fables as cute rather than malicious.

Murph's deathbed confession, however, changed that. The animosity I had for Dad when I was young resurfaced. I became deeply angry, which seemed appropriate. He had betrayed us—all of us—and I couldn't forgive him, and I didn't, not for a long time. Not only had he deceived his family, especially Dick, but he also never used the money for anybody other than himself. His selfishness was exposed to all of us, and he seemed singularly unworthy of either love or respect.

At first, my anger was directed toward Dad alone, but he had been dead for fifteen years and Murph had remained silent about what had happened. She shared responsibility for this, too.

Still, I knew it was unhealthy to nurture this bitterness in my heart. I had to release it. I didn't need to look any further than my brother Danny to see the consequences of a lifetime of resentment toward Dad. Danny started hating Dad in the 1940s and has never stopped. Dad died in 1976, but Danny's deep-seated hostility has continued to consume him ever since. It's produced anger in Danny, which is his most dominant characteristic. Danny has always been consumed with bitterness.

In my musing about what he had done, I remembered thinking about Dad's goal: *how to get money without earning it.* As I thought about it, envisioning the plaque above the clothes hamper in my boyhood home, I laughed with contempt. This was my state of mind when I left Boston after Mom's funeral.

This was too much. I needed help to sort it all out.

Chapter 34

A Game of Self-Deception

When I returned to Atlanta, I kept busy. I played basketball nearly every day; spent more time developing my new business, Watts & Associates, which did creative and marketing work for large Christian ministries and publishers; started seeing a counselor as well as attending group therapy; and went to a Bible study. There I met Eleanor Benedict, the MD I dated, the one who bit Jordan.

The business helped distract me from my distress; but by now I was drinking excessively at least three times a week—*not like an alcoholic*, but just to release the pressure. My life was stressful, and I needed the release that alcohol provided. That's all. It wasn't a problem, I reasoned.

Obviously I was playing a game of self-deception, but that's what alcoholics do. They put on a happy face and say "Everything's fine"—especially when it isn't. They use alcohol to numb pain and blur reality. Once this destructive cycle begins, it's as hard to stop as a roller coaster going downhill. Worst of all, they end up plunging toward a certain crash, which they rarely see coming. Everyone else sees it—but not the alcoholic.

It was at about this time that Eleanor gave me the ultimatum to stop drinking. Even though I was surprised by it, I also was ready for it. My time had come. I was sick and tired of being hung over several times a week, and I still wanted to make something of my life. I had a purpose; I knew it deep inside. I hoped that God still had plans for me—in spite of everything. So I went to an Alcoholics Anonymous meeting and picked up a white chip. Surprisingly, it wasn't difficult to admit that I was *one of them, an alcoholic.* Maybe it's because I knew things were going to get much worse if I didn't. My mother and Danny had always been prime examples of that.

Unlike most alcoholics, I didn't hit rock bottom because of my drinking. I never lost a job or anything like that; but I thought like an alcoholic, and recovery from alcoholic thinking has taken a long time—years, in fact. It's an ongoing process that requires consistent work and probably will for the rest of my life.

People who have trouble with addiction—any addiction—understand what alcoholic thinking is; they live it every day. It's thinking you're not okay the way you are, but you would be okay, if you had something to give you a little confidence, a little edge, a little courage. Your addiction validates who you are and makes you feel like you are okay—after you've had a drink or two. In the AA club I attend most frequently, there's a poster that describes it well. Here's what it says:

> *We drank for happiness . . . but became unhappy.*
> *We drank for joy . . . but became miserable.*
> *We drank to be sociable . . . but became argumentative.*
> *We drank for sophistication . . . but became obnoxious.*
> *We drank for friendship . . . but made enemies instead.*
> *We drank so we could sleep . . . but woke up tired.*
> *We drank to gain strength . . . but ended up feeling weak.*
> *We drank for relaxation . . . but ended up with the shakes.*
> *We drank to get courage . . . but we became afraid.*
> *We drank to be confident . . . but became doubtful instead.*
> *We drank to make conversation easier . . . but we slurred our speech.*
> *We drank to feel heavenly . . . and ended up feeling like hell.*

I believe that admitting my alcoholism and making a conscious decision to "run against the wind" was the actual beginning of my adulthood. That's when a divine measure of wisdom—God's wisdom—entered my life and began to truly transform me. I had been a Christian for years, but when the going got tough, I relied on alcohol, not God. No more. When I made this conscious decision, which involved going back to where the problems began, I was fifty years old, but about eighteen emotionally—maybe even younger. It was time to grow up.

Chapter 35

My Moment of Truth

One day, after my relationship with Eleanor ended and after I began AA, I went on a date with a woman who was more than twenty years younger than I. Her name was Mitzi, and she was a knockout. She radiated such a sensuous demeanor that men's eyes followed her from the instant she entered a room until she exited. When I went out with her, I felt a little self-conscious, but because being with her was so flattering to my ego, I grew to enjoy it. When I was with Mitzi, guys always gave me a nod of approval.

We had a lovely dinner, talking well into the night. I was pleasantly surprised by how knowledgeable and insightful Mitzi was. Shortly before we left the restaurant, she told me that she liked me and that she was attracted to me. I told her that I felt the same.

Pausing for a minute, she asked nervously, "Jack, I'm traveling to the Virgin Islands next week for a vacation. I'm going by myself, and I wonder if you would consider joining me." Looking at me warmly with those big blue eyes, she added, "Would you? I'd really love it if you would."

I was stunned by the invitation, but I also could tell that she was serious. I was as flattered as I can ever remember being. Within a few minutes, I couldn't seem to think of one good reason to decline the invitation, so I agreed to go on the trip. She smiled longingly, and I was captivated.

Less than a week later, we boarded a Delta flight headed for St. Thomas, followed by a short ferry ride to St. John, which was the final destination for our weeklong stay. Before going, we established some ground rules. We mutually agreed to stay in the same room but in different beds, which we did—Scout's honor.

The first morning, Mitzi went out to the beach in a thong bathing suit, which was not a common choice at the time. One woman—looking at Mitzi as she walked to the water—actually said to me, "That's not the first time that cute little fanny has seen sunshine, is it?"

It wasn't a compliment, and I felt mortified. The woman was right. Mitzi wasn't sporting any tan lines. Just one day into the trip and I realized how foolish I was for placing myself in such a situation, and there were six more days to go.

That evening, Mitzi said, "I'm going to the park for a few minutes to score some drugs. Do you want to come?" That's when I began to realize my sobriety would be severely tested while in her company.

My test came the following day. I rented a boat, and Mitzi and I went from one small island to the next, exploring. The sun was hot and by 2:00 P.M. we were both thirsty and hungry. Mooring the boat in Cruz Bay, Mitzi went to a restaurant to buy each of us a sandwich and a Coke. I had to stay on the boat while she was gone. We weren't allowed to leave the boat unattended; our allotted time for mooring was just twenty minutes.

When she returned, she had two sandwiches and two bottles of beer—no Coke, no water, just beer. Because my mooring time had expired, the attendant insisted we return to sea. When I did, Mitzi handed me the beer and said, "Here, Jack. Go ahead and drink it. I promise I won't tell anybody."

As I looked at the beer, which was a Bud Light—my brand—I never wanted anything more in my life. The beer was so cold the bottle was sweating, just like it does in commercials. The day was hot, I was thirsty, and all I had to do was reach out and take it. Mitzi might as well have been Eve handing me forbidden fruit. In her alluring eyes, she urged me to take it and anything else I might desire.

My moment of truth had arrived.

Mustering all the courage I could, I refused; I was emphatic—not because I was strong, but because I was weak, terribly weak. I wanted that beer so much my insides ached. My mouth was so dry I could taste it; I still can. My hands also were shaking from another desire as well, and she knew it. If she had pressed the point, I'm sure I would have succumbed. My entire life might have been different, but she didn't. She accepted my decision and ended up drinking both beers herself, much to my relief.

If what doesn't kill you makes you stronger, then this incident empowered me, making me stronger than I had been before. It turned the corner for me. Because of that experience, I've learned to control my desire for alcohol and not allow it to control me.

By the time the trip was over, so was my relationship with Mitzi. When I told her good-bye, I was finished with her and with the lifestyle she represented. I had put myself in harm's way, narrowly avoiding disaster.

Gratefully I walked away, relieved that I didn't have to pick up another white chip at an AA meeting for relapsing. At the end of my first year of sobriety, Jordan, who was still quite young, came to a meeting and gave me a blue chip, marking my one-year anniversary.

As part of my recovery, I needed to solidify my relationship with my daughters, starting with Connie. She was the linchpin for her sisters; at least I thought she was at the time. If I could reconnect with Connie at as deep a level as I had with Jordan, I could make a substantial step toward developing the type of relationship I always wanted with her and her sisters. I decided to hire her as my administrative assistant for Watts & Associates and give her responsibility for accounts receivable and accounts payable. At the time she had just graduated from Georgia Southern, where Keith, her husband, was stationed in the army close by. He was a Ranger. They needed the second income and jumped at the chance when it was offered. Connie called and said, "If you let me do this, I'll do a good job, Dad."

"Then the job is yours," I said, trying to contain my emotions. What I didn't know and wouldn't realize for years, however, was that this decision would prove to be one of the costliest of my life.

Chapter 36

I Longed for a Soul Mate

In the early 1990s I bought a house in Buckhead, one of Atlanta's most fashionable areas. I paid only $128,000 for it, so you know it was a dump. Nobody recognized the jewel it could be but me. I knew right away and immediately started out to make it a beautiful home. I had it gutted and began renovations before I moved in. By the time I finished, it was beautiful outside and in. Jordan had her own room and loved to come to "our house in the city," which was peaceful and safe.

Watts & Associates was going well; Connie kept on top of everything. Because Keith was often gone for Ranger duties, Connie had to juggle numerous activities, but she was bright, competent, and energetic. Best of all, we talked constantly and developed a better relationship than we had ever had. I loved having her in the business; it made every day fun.

During that same time period, Brenn, now twenty-three, called one day with more than casual conversation on her mind. Coming right to the point, she said, "Dad, I'm pregnant. Willie's the father, so our baby will be half-black. I'm going to keep the baby, but Willie and I aren't going to get married. What are you going to do?"

Her question was straightforward, and I knew exactly what she meant. Without hesitation, I said, "I'll love your baby just like I love all my grandchildren. That's what I'm going to do."

"Promise?"

"Promise," and I meant it.

Six months later, Brenn gave birth to Christopher, who was absolutely beautiful. He was healthy, and because of her earlier tubal pregnancy and the threat it posed to her reproductive system, the birth was an even more joyful blessing for Brenn and the family. At nearly the same time, Maggie, my son's wife, gave birth to a daughter who was half–Central American and equally as good-looking as Christopher. I began calling myself "an equal-opportunity grandpa." Not yet fifty-one, and I already had four grandchildren.

I may have had five children and four grandchildren, but I also had two failed marriages and longed for a soul mate. But I wanted immediate gratification, which is a recipe for disaster. Her name was Jesse DeNapoli.

I joined a dating service where I went to a clubhouse and looked at pictures and videos of various women. Online dating services didn't exist. Occasionally, Jordan went with me and was always willing to give her opinion. I saw Jesse and picked her. We went out and hit it off right away.

Jesse and I dated for several months and began talking about marriage. She had three children, all of whom lived with their father in Cleveland. I saw this as a plus, which was a big mistake, but I didn't realize it at the time. When young children don't live with their mother, this is a huge red flag; but all I saw was green.

At the same time, Dick called me one evening and said Ellen was having some medical problems, and they were doing some tests. Ellen was a beautiful woman, but she was a chain-smoker and drank wine to excess daily. Six weeks later, I received a call from my sister, Jean, telling me that Ellen had died thirty minutes earlier. I couldn't believe it. I had just been to Boston, and Ellen was fine. Now she was dead. I flew immediately to Boston to be there for my brother.

The funeral brought my mortality into perspective. With those thoughts in mind, I decided to marry Jesse, which was not smart. Nor was it how I should have made such an important decision, but that's how it happened. It's like going to the grocery store hungry; you buy what you don't want and don't need simply because you're hungry and anything looks better than being without food. Once again, I made an impulsive decision—a decision I would live to regret.

Jesse had a sweet, attractive face. Her smile was genuine and pleasant, and it was accented with freckled cheeks and a narrow, aristocratic nose. Her eyes were brown, as was her long hair, which was always held together by a large bow, the kind little girls wear. Her figure was nice, but she always complained that she held more weight in her hips and thighs than she wanted. Her coyness and coquettish demeanor were enchanting. Although she graduated from a Big East university, Jesse really wasn't as bright as most of the women I had dated.

Nevertheless, I made the commitment to marry her, and she moved in with me soon after the funeral. Several weeks later, we went on a cruise of the Greek Isles—perhaps the most beautiful region of the world. We went to Ephesus, where the Apostle Paul preached in biblical times. We also went into the cave on the Isle of Patmos where the Apostle John purportedly wrote the Book of Revelation. I loved it. Jesse, however, saw nothing profound in any of these sights, preferring to spend most of her time drinking heavily on the trip.

By the time we returned home, I told her we might have made a mistake in talking about marriage so hastily. It was not healthy for me to spend the rest of my life with someone who drank. She had never had that much to drink before we went on the trip, but I didn't really know her that well, which made me appear very foolish.

Within six weeks of moving in with me, Jesse was laid off from her job and started lying on the couch all day. No kidding—there she was, lying on the couch just like Mona did years earlier. It sent shivers up my spine. She took Prozac daily, chasing the pills down with wine, which is contraindicated while taking antidepressants. The combination made her behavior bizarre. She slurred her speech and stumbled routinely. From my perspective, the situation was intolerable. Something had to give, and it did give soon thereafter.

Eleanor Benedict's best friend, Sarah Remington, also was a doctor, and she was getting married to Adam, who had become one of my better friends. When Eleanor and I broke up, I got custody of all the friends. I was a groomsman in Adam and Sarah's wedding, which was a lavish affair. Jordan also was in the wedding party. I told Jesse she could come—if she promised not to have anything to drink. For me, her alcohol consumption had already reached the breaking point. I also told her she could stay home, and that would be fine, too. All I wanted—and I was crystal clear—was for her not to get drunk at the wedding and embarrass me in front of my friends. She wanted to come and repeatedly promised not to drink. With trepidation, I agreed for her to attend.

After the wedding ceremony, I stood next to the bride's father in the reception line for nearly an hour. During that time, I saw Jesse go over to the bar at least six times to fill her glass with wine. By the time my reception duties were complete, Jesse was a staggering drunk. I went over to confront her immediately, but in response she slurred, "I haven't had a drop. I haven't." She was on the edge and I knew it. At this point there was nothing I could do that wouldn't jeopardize Sarah's wedding.

Looking at Jesse, I wondered how many times I had done the same thing. Drunks always think they're charming and the life of the party, but all I saw was an obnoxious woman nearly out of control. For once in my life, I saw things clearly and abandoned any thoughts of being a rescuer. Her drinking was a hindrance to my sobriety. I knew it, and I wasn't going to allow that to happen—again.

As the band began to play, Jesse took a shine to one of Adam's friends and danced with him for hours. He was a black guy named Antoine. Jordan, who was just ten, was my greatest concern. I didn't want her involved in Jesse's drunken drama, so I kept away from Jesse and just let her do her thing with Antoine. Her behavior didn't make me jealous; it repulsed me.

As the evening progressed and the party atmosphere intensified, I decided to take Jordan home. Jesse had driven herself, but she was too drunk to drive home, so I asked her if she wanted to come with us, promising to get her car early the next morning. She wouldn't come, saying she was perfectly capable of driving herself later. Sarah's father, who also was a doctor, told Jesse he would call the police if she got behind the wheel, but this did nothing but infuriate her. As the drama intensified, I was not willing to allow Jordan to be exposed to any more of Jesse's escalating drama, so I departed, leaving Jesse to find her own way home.

I took Jordan back to her mom's house early in the morning—hours before Jesse got up. When I returned to the house, Jesse was in the bathroom, vomiting. She was sick the entire day, and I carefully avoided her. On the following day, Monday morning, I went on a three-day business trip and told Jesse I wanted to talk to her when I returned. I didn't want anger to cloud my judgment. I needed time to think.

On the trip, I did nothing but think about the future and what the rest of my life would be like if I went through with my promise to marry Jesse. By the time I returned to Atlanta, I had decided to break it off with her.

"That's not an option," she casually replied to my declaration.

"It is for me. I'm sorry, but I'm not going to spend the rest of my life with an alcoholic."

"I'm not an alcoholic, Jack," she said defensively. "Just because you are doesn't make everyone else one, too."

Without another word, she turned on her heels and left the house. I didn't see her for another week.

Chapter 37

"You Are under Arrest"

The next time I saw Jesse was one week later, when she pulled up to the house, banging on the front door, demanding entrance at 1:00 A.M. The noise startled me awake. Her hostility was so apparent I refused to open the door.

She called the police, and a squad car came and parked in my driveway. Jesse raged to the police about how I had physically thrown her out of the house, and she had bruises to prove it. She raised her sleeve and showed a small bruise—the kind someone gets from bumping into a door. The policeman paid no attention to it, saying it was old, but the officer told me that because she lived there, I had to let her back in. It was the law. She had a legal right to come back in, and I couldn't prevent it. When I let her in, she took one bedroom; I took another.

The next morning, I called my lawyer. He warned, "Jack, someone is coaching Jesse. Ever since the O. J. Simpson trial a couple of years ago, lawyers for women have been trying to provoke domestic violence to extract more money out of men like you. They call it 'palimony.'"

"But I've never hit her. I've never even considered it," I said, thoroughly alarmed.

"I know, but it doesn't make any difference. This is their strategy," he continued. "Make sure you're never alone with her again."

"How can I do that," I asked, "when she's staying at my house?"

"I don't know," he admitted. "The best way you can. Be careful around her, or you could end up in jail."

That seemed unlikely, but her behavior ended any thoughts I had about going ahead with my plans to marry her. I wanted Jesse out of my house and my life as quickly as possible. That same week, she called the police twice more, saying I had hit her. In my entire life, the police had never been called because of my behavior. Now they had been summoned three times in one week. It was awful.

The third time the police were called, Jesse pulled up her skirt and showed fresh bruises on the inside of both thighs near the vagina. The cop looked at me and said, "Mr. Watts, you are under arrest." With that, he handcuffed me, put me in the back of the patrol car, and drove me off to jail. As we were leaving, I saw Jesse smiling the smile of the wicked when their schemes succeed. She now had complete control of my house, and I wasn't allowed to come near it.

I knew I was innocent, but I also knew being innocent didn't mean I would be cleared from the charge. I spent the night in jail with some of the scariest people I had ever seen.

One week later, in civil court, the judge returned sole possession of my house to me until the final hearing was held. I had my house back. Her lawyer, working with the district attorney's office, sent over one palimony offer after the other, but I wouldn't consider accepting any because each was based on my admitting some measure of guilt in the domestic violence case. I wasn't guilty, and I wouldn't negotiate in this area—not for any reason, period.

Consequently, the case dragged on and on. We were together less than six months, but it took more than a year to have all of the issues resolved between us.

I had to wonder how I could have been so blind in the first place with Jesse. How had I allowed a woman to come into my life who was capable of such deception? I realized that it was my own selfishness and impulsiveness that had blinded me. My ability to discern a woman's character and motives was deeply flawed.

Let me set the record straight: I am keenly aware that most women are not like the women I have dated and married. Most women are lovely, caring, and intelligent—*not crazy*. I genuinely respect women, but over time I have come to realize that there is something deep-seated in me that attracts me to severely troubled women. Perhaps the truth is that I look for women who are just like me—angry, addictive, and volatile.

Chapter 38

She Needed Rescuing

Within a few months of Ellen's death, Dick met a wonderful woman named Nancy at a health club. They have been together ever since and have forged a strong, mutually satisfying relationship. Nancy has a lovely face and a sweet, guileless smile. She is smart and emotionally strong, which is perfect for Dick.

Things were looking up for me as well. All in all, I had much to be grateful for. Billings for Watts & Associates were strong. I had never made more money in my life, but for some reason, there was never enough of it. To help Connie and to audit the books, I hired a CPA named Buford Billings. Yes, Billings. The perfect name for an accountant.

He and Connie worked particularly well together. I wasn't always pleased with Buford's work and wanted to make a change several times, but Connie always talked me out of it. It was gratifying to see this kind of loyalty coming from Connie.

During this time, I started producing a catalog to sell Christian CDs and videos for Bill Gaither, a well-known Christian artist, producer, and an honest man. We started out with a digest-size, sixteen-page catalog, mailed twice a year to 85,000 homes. We ended up five years later producing and mailing a full-size, sixty-four-page catalog to 650,000 homes four times a year. We were doing well. I was busy, sober, and the prospects ahead signaled more prosperity.

One Sunday, nearly two years after breaking it off with Jesse, I went to an AA meeting in the morning and saw one of the most beautiful women I had ever seen. I wanted to talk to her after the meeting, but she was busy with several other people. I left, hoping I would run into her again. Later that day, I didn't have anything else to do, so I went to another meeting across town in the early evening. I rarely went twice in one day, but for some reason, I did. Arriving late, I squeezed into a seat in the second row. A few minutes later, I turned to the right to listen to the woman sitting next to me who had just been called on to speak. It was the same woman, Judy Tremont. My world was about to be turned upside down again—and quickly.

All eyes at the meeting fell upon this gorgeous woman as she said, "Hi, my name is Judy. I'm an alcoholic and a drug addict."

"Hi, Judy," nearly a hundred people replied in unison.

Continuing, Judy explained in a charming, cultured voice, "I'm just visiting Atlanta and needed to come to a meeting after what I've just been through. I live in Monks Corner, South Carolina, with my daughter Shannon. I'm here today because she is in a lockdown facility for kids who have serious addictions to alcohol and drugs. Going through this with her has been very hard for me. I'm a single mom, and this is a lot to handle by myself."

My antenna went up the moment I heard she was single. My prayer was answered. Plus, both she and her daughter needed rescuing—my specialty! It was like she was the perfect answer for my deep-seated need to finish the job of being a husband and father that had been taken from me so many years earlier.

She went on to describe how she had just been informed that an older, trusted friend had taken advantage of Shannon, who was just sixteen, and how violated and angry Judy felt because of it. My heart ached for her. Judy continued talking for several minutes, and I learned that she had been sober for ten years. She worked for a sophisticated, upscale recovery facility in the North Georgia mountains—the Sanctuary. She owned her own home and had been doing quite well with her recovery until Shannon became addicted to cocaine. By the time she was finished speaking, Judy was clearly shaken. There was dead silence in the room—a rarity for an AA meeting.

The moderator looked around to call on someone else, and I slowly raised my hand. As he recognized me, I said, "Hi, my name is Jack, and I'm an alcoholic."

"Hi, Jack," was the united response.

Continuing, I said, "I've never shared what I'm about to say, but my daughter Jordan was also molested by an older man we trusted completely." I talked for at least five minutes, relating how difficult it had been for me, like Judy, when I first heard the story. Somewhere in the middle of my cathartic soliloquy, when I started becoming emotional, Judy reached over and held my hand—firmly but gently—until I finished. She reached out and touched me physically and emotionally with an instant connection that was new territory for me. It made me feel empowered with a woman at a level I had rarely if ever experienced. It's what I had always been looking for—no doubt about it.

The meeting went on for another thirty minutes for everybody but Judy and me. It was like no one else was there but the two of us. The moment had been electric for both—powerful and transformational. Energy radiated between us as others talked about their problems. Neither of us heard a word that was spoken for the remainder of the meeting. I was hooked—completely, totally, and irreversibly hooked. Not since Mona came down the stairs at Chi Omega sorority thirty-five years earlier had I felt anything as powerful as this. When the meeting was complete, I gave Judy my business card and told her I worked out of my home and would make myself available to her—regardless of what she might need.

I heard from Judy the following day, when she called and offered to buy me lunch. I had another commitment, but I wouldn't miss this opportunity—regardless of what I had planned. Making a call, I apologetically canceled my lunch engagement and met Judy instead.

When she came into the restaurant, she gracefully walked to the table. Judy had long, flowing brown hair that was perfect and natural for her petite figure. Later, I learned that much of her natural beauty came from several surgical procedures. She could have been a poster girl for Talbot clothes, where she shopped regularly. Her style was always preppy and understated elegance. Even her accent was low-country Charleston—enchanting and endearing.

As she walked to the table, I felt as if we were filming a movie and I was the leading man—eager to play my part in the drama that was about to unfold. When she sat down, our lunch was neither electric nor even romantic. We both had regained our composure and simply talked about our lives. She told me more about Shannon and the impact her daughter's drug addiction had on their relationship. Judy also told me about her son, Hamilton, his live-in girlfriend, and her granddaughter Hilary. We talked for hours—most of it about her life, but that was fine with me.

At one time Judy had her own catering business before she went to work for a large manufacturing firm. While there, one of the chief executives, a man named Stewart Black, and his wife sort of adopted Judy, mentoring her for years. She loved and respected them dearly and spoke of them and their kindness repeatedly. She still had lunch with Stewart every week. Obviously they saw what I saw in her—a quality woman with vast potential.

After lunch, Judy had several hours between appointments, so I invited her to wait at my house, which was nearby. She agreed, and we went there for several hours. When she left, I returned to work. Within fifteen minutes, however, Judy called, saying that she had left her sunglasses on the deck and would be back for them in an hour—if that would be all right. "Of course it would be all right," I said, trying not to sound as excited as I was.

When she returned, she walked onto the deck where I was, sat up on the railing, and waited for me to finish my business call. After hanging up, I walked over to her, and we kissed. It was another electric moment. She left shortly thereafter to keep her appointment before driving back to Monks Corner, several hours away.

Later that evening, when I returned home from running errands, I listened to my messages, and Judy had already called after arriving safely at home. We talked every day that week, and our burgeoning romance grew dramatically. When she came to Atlanta each weekend to see Shannon, she stayed at the house of a friend, a pilot named Jerry, whom she knew from the treatment center. She was quick to say they were just friends, and there was no romantic aspect to their relationship. This, of course, was precisely what I had hoped was the case.

By the next weekend, she suggested that she stay in my guest bedroom rather than at his house. This made me a little nervous, but I told her she was welcome. She came late that Friday evening, and early Saturday morning went to Safe Harbor, where Shannon was confined for treatment. When Judy arrived for the parental visit, Shannon was hostile and told her to leave within twenty minutes. With nowhere else to go, Judy came back to my house, and we spent the remainder of the day together. That night she came into my bedroom to sleep. I was surprised—really surprised—and not ready for it, but I allowed her to stay.

This intense weekend pattern continued for about six weeks, and our relationship became stronger and more serious each time. She was intelligent, sophisticated, passionate, urbane, and, best of all—sober. I felt as though I had finally found a good woman, someone without the deep pathology I had typically pursued.

Shannon began to respond favorably to treatment and to her mother. This turn of events both pleased and scared Judy. She was happy that Shannon was embracing sobriety but extremely apprehensive about what would happen when she left the treatment center. Would she stay sober or return to her drug habit? Judy didn't want to live in Monks Corner any longer—where Shannon's drug dealer also lived. Shannon's sobriety was too tenuous and fragile for that.

One day, when Judy was sitting on the porch, she got up and walked down the stairs to look at the utility space under the back of the house. She said, "We could build a bedroom and a bathroom in this space with a separate entrance for Shannon. What do you think?"

What I thought was that her idea was tantamount to a marriage proposal, but I simply replied, "It would be expensive."

She countered, "I could sell my house and use some of the equity to pay for it."

We were now at a crossroads. "Okay," I said, with a voice filled with nervous excitement, "I could call the guy who did my other renovations and get an estimate. Do you want me to do that?"

Without hesitation, she answered, "Absolutely."

After I discussed the possibility with my contractor, I called Judy. When I did, I was exuberant, hoping that this was real and the answer to my prayers. After telling her how much work and expense were involved, we decided that the plan made sense.

About three days later, she phoned and—with a quivering voice—said, "Safe Harbor is releasing Shannon in ten days." We both knew exactly what that meant: marriage.

The next day I phoned her and said, "I called Johnny, and he's starting to build the room first thing Monday morning. Do you agree?"

It was another electric moment; and after a significant pause, Judy said, "Yes, I do. Can you come up here for a few days and help me? I want to put the house on the market right away. We'll need the money."

"Certainly. I'll come tomorrow," I said, but my mouth was dry when I said it.

That's how we decided to get married. We just drifted into it like it was inevitable and meant to be. Granted, it was quick, but that was out of necessity more than anything else. Within a week I presented her with an $18,000 diamond ring, which obviously pleased her.

Progress on the renovation was slow. When Shannon was released, she and Judy stayed in my guest room. I liked Shannon, and we got along quite well. The girl needed stability, and I hoped to help provide that for her. She was strong-willed, but I always found her to be reasonable. When the work was complete, she moved into her room downstairs. To her credit, Shannon was always genuinely grateful for all the effort made to nurture her sobriety.

When I met Judy on that fateful Sunday, it was late winter 1998. Fewer than two months later, we were selling a house in South Carolina and busy with a major house renovation in Atlanta to prepare for what looked like a bright future. If you've ever done a major renovation, you know how stressful it can be—even to very solid relationships. Ours was no different.

When we had our first disagreement, Judy sent me a card on her personalized stationery, telling me how she felt about me. It said:

Dear Jack,

You are the love of my life. You challenge me to test my belief system daily. Our struggles, I know, will become our strengths.

My commitment to you is to never quit. To search deeply for the highest truth. To surrender my fears and release all outcomes to God. . . .

Your generous spirit is authentic, and your capacity for love is endless.

Your playfulness is such a delightful reminder of how much fun life can be. Thank you.

I love you,

Judy

Receiving this letter was exhilarating, validating, and empowering. At last, someone truly understood and appreciated me for who I was—and not for what I could do for them. The letter strengthened every fiber of my being.

We married in June. All my girls were there, as well as Judy's family. It was a wonderful, magical day, and I was the happiest I could ever remember being. I was sober and married to a beautiful woman who had more than ten years of continuous sobriety. The future appeared to be very bright.

We married on a Saturday evening, and we took all the kids and grand-kids to Six Flags the following day, which was fine with me. In fact, it was more than fine; it was a statement of what we were all about and what the future would be like.

Finally, I had made the right decision and found my soul mate. I couldn't have been happier or more content and secure. I was in love—deeply in love—and this love was reciprocated. This was the happiest day of my life, and I was certain it would last.

But it didn't. It changed, starting the very next day. Little did I know it at the time, but I wouldn't have another truly happy day for at least four years. My life was about to come crashing down again. I felt like Job; every aspect of my being was about to be tried, sifted, and, for the most part, found wanting.

Chapter 39

She Was Entitled to More

After we had been at Six Flags for several hours, Jordan wanted me to take her for a ride on one of the roller coasters. Because we had three toddlers with us—my kids' children—we had not ventured beyond the small children's section of the park. Jordan, now eleven, wanted to ride on something more exciting than the swings. So off we went together. But it was that moment—when Jordan and I ventured off by ourselves—that brought to light something I had never seen in Judy: a simmering resentment. It must have been there all along, just below the surface, but she had hidden it well.

On our wedding day, Judy began to show her true colors. And at first, her resentment was singularly directed at my eleven-year-old child, much to my utter dismay.

Each passing day, Judy's irrational anger toward Jordan intensified rather than diminished. Because this seemed so trivial, and so unlike the mature woman I had married, I didn't take it seriously for a while—for too long. Judy, who had been loving and accepting toward Jordan before we married, transformed overnight.

Routinely, Judy would treat Jordan with petty cruelties, such as buying presents for all of the kids and leaving Jordan conspicuously out. She also made Jordan feel unwelcome in our house, going so far as to lock her out of her room several times.

At first I tried to reason with Judy, explaining it was painful and destructive for Jordan to be the object of such cruelty, but that accomplished nothing. Then I pleaded with her, telling her that it was breaking my heart, but all this did was make Judy look at me with condescension and contempt. Finally I became angry, and that made it much worse. I was at a loss and didn't know what to do. Even marriage counseling didn't help.

Judy's misanthropy toward Jordan was constant. It never subsided or diminished—not ever.

Once again I was blindsided—and torn: but I knew Jordan was not at fault; so I started spending my time with her away from the house—far from Judy's anger. It was the only way I could protect Jordan from Judy's venomous behavior. Having failed in the past, I did not want another failed relationship under any circumstances, so I did everything I could to accommodate Judy while protecting Jordan at the same time.

I wasn't very successful. Judy's malice hurt my daughter deeply, and it required years for all the poison to work its way out of both Jordan's system and mine. This problem was substantial, but it was just one of many issues. Another surfaced at nearly the same time that was even more devastating.

Within two months of our marriage, Judy opened my MasterCard bill and noticed there was a substantial charge for Mary Kay Cosmetics. Connie was a Mary Kay distributor, requiring her to buy supplies regularly— but certainly not with my credit card. Because she was also in charge of all the Watts & Associates finances, Judy was immediately alarmed by the charge. I looked at the bill and then called Connie.

Getting straight to the point, I said, "Connie, I just opened my MasterCard statement, and there's a charge on it from Mary Kay. How did it get there?" Before she could respond, I added, "And *why* is it there?"

With trepidation in her voice, Connie replied, "I put that on there until Keith gets his paycheck. I was going to put it back."

"But you didn't ask me if it was all right to do this, Connie," I said, pointing out how inappropriate it was.

"I didn't think it was that important, Dad. You were out of town, and I couldn't get ahold of you anyway," she continued.

I considered this. Then I asked, "Have you ever done this before, or is this the first time?"

"I may have, Dad. I'll have to check."

That didn't make sense. Either she had taken money from me before, or she hadn't. Her answer—coupled with her history of stealing—unsettled me. "Connie, this is serious. Please check the records and get back with me right away," I said.

Before we disconnected, Judy looked at me and whispered, "Have her send over all the MasterCard statements. I want to see for myself."

Nodding, I told Connie to send them over. She responded, "I don't have them all together right now. Some may be at Buford's office. It will take me awhile to get everything together."

"Just make sure I get them soon."

"Okay," she said, and we ended the conversation shortly thereafter.

I looked at Judy, and we were both troubled. "Jack," she said, "let me see your credit card. I'm going to call MasterCard and get our own copies of the statements."

"Good idea," I said, handing her my card. She called, and within twenty minutes, we arranged for copies to be sent to the house. They arrived within a week.

Connie never did come up with all of the statements, but when the copies came from MasterCard, Judy and I sat down to pore over them in detail. It took an entire weekend, but we discovered there were more than $12,000 in charges that had nothing to do with Watts & Associates; and that number accounted for only seven months of the current year. This happened in late August—less than three months into our marriage.

Calling Connie, I told her what we had discovered and asked her how much money she had taken. Coming clean just a little, she answered, "Some here and there. I don't know exactly, Dad. Sorry, but I don't."

"Then you need to find out. If you haven't been keeping track, how would you know how much to pay back? I need some answers, Connie."

"I know," Connie said, clearly dejected.

"How long has this been going on?" I insisted.

By now my concern was substantial. Connie had been in charge of the books for more than five years—my best and most productive years. Because this was the busiest I had ever been—or ever would be—I spent all of my time taking care of the clients, leaving Connie, with the help of Buford Billings, to handle all the financial matters. Why we were behind in our finances genuinely puzzled me, and I asked Connie about it numerous times. But she always had an answer. Millions had gone through the company, and she was in charge of all of it. Instead of digging deeper, as I should have, I worked on generating more income, knowing that increased sales could offset the shortcomings.

By the time we reached this point, however, I insisted on specific, detailed answers from Connie. I said to her, "How much money are we talking about? Is it twenty thousand dollars, or more?"

"Something like that—twenty thousand dollars," she said.

"Okay," I said, "but I need to know the exact amount. No stalling, Connie. This is important. You have one week to find out—no more. Do you understand?"

"Yes, I'll get started right away, Dad."

Judy wanted to press the matter further with Connie, but I told her I was going to give Connie a chance to put it all together and come forward with the truth. At the end of the week, Connie gave me a total of $49,000 that she had taken with a plan for repayment, which I had insisted upon. It was a great deal of money but not enough to destabilize the company financially.

I was going to allow that to be the end of it, but Judy said, "You're not going to take her at her word, are you?" She continued, "Hello, Jack. Is there anybody home? She's stolen from you. You need to look into this further. You can't just let this go away. You have to dig into it and find out for yourself."

She was right, so we began a thorough investigation of Connie's activities. We ordered copies of the yearly summaries from American Express; and sure enough, the problem was much larger than Connie had admitted. She had not been forthright when confronted with her "borrowing," which I could see was a pattern of theft. I was forced to address the issue and fire her. I had to do it. As her father, it broke my heart, but I had a fiduciary responsibility to Watts & Associates as well.

I called Connie again and said, "We've just been through the American Express charges, and you've taken more than one hundred thousand dollars from there alone. I can't find one statement since you began working for me five years ago without some sort of financial irregularity. Connie, this problem is much more extensive than you acknowledged."

"Dad, you only gave me a week to figure it all out," she interrupted defensively. "That wasn't enough time."

"That's no excuse, Connie. How could you *borrow* that much money without asking?" I demanded. "You never asked me directly to borrow anything; you never kept track of how much you took; you never paid back anything; and you've tried to hide what you've done for five years—five years. That's stealing, Connie, not borrowing."

"It's not stealing, Dad. I may have borrowed more than I thought, but I've always intended to pay you back. I will pay you back," she said—clearly in denial of her capacity to do so.

"How, Connie? You've stolen at least one hundred thousand dollars from American Express, and there may be more—a lot more. How could you ever pay that much money back?"

She replied, "I don't know, Dad, but I will."

I could tell she had deceived herself and actually believed what she was saying. Changing direction, I asked, "And where was Buford Billings in all this? He's a CPA. How could this 'slip through the cracks'? Buford must have known what was happening. Did he?"

"Not really."

After a significant silence, I said, "I'm not going to take anything you say at face value again. I can't. You've stolen a lot of money from me and tried to cover it up. Send me over the checkbook, the files, everything. I'm sorry, Connie, but you can't work for me anymore." When we hung up, the lines were clearly drawn with a permanent chasm between Connie and me—a gulf that has yet to be bridged.

There wasn't much emotion involved in that conversation. It came, but much later. It grieved me deeply, but I was in too much shock to be emotional. Connie had been stealing from me for years, and I had absolutely no idea that she had been doing it or how much she had taken.

It never occurred to me that Connie would steal from me—never. I was her dad, and I trusted her completely. And besides, I had a CPA to account for everything. My heart pounded and my hands sweated. I was completely blindsided by this. As her father, I also was hurt. I thought our relationship was becoming stronger each day, which I wanted very much, but that was just an illusion.

I remember asking Victoria and Brenn, in separate conversations, if they ever thought it would be possible for Connie to steal from me. Without hesitation, both answered, "Yes." Victoria said she had to hide her clothes from Connie routinely when they were teenagers, and Brenn remembered similar instances of Connie stealing as well. I thought back to Jean's white sweater and to the stolen quarters Connie had taken and tried to conceal by blaming Victoria years earlier. My psychologist friend said Connie's behavior would foreshadow more serious problems later in life, which, obviously, it had.

Nearly everybody recognized Connie's character flaws much better than I, but there is a big difference between stealing quarters as a kid and stealing six figures from your dad as a full-grown adult. I couldn't believe she really did it.

I wondered, *Was there something wrong with me for trusting her so com-*

pletely? I used my AA tools to examine my part in it, but I couldn't come up with anything. I paid Connie nearly $40,000 a year throughout the 1990s for a part-time job. I overpaid her, but I wanted it to be a blessing to her and her family. But it wasn't enough; she must have believed that she was entitled to more.

Judy began spending nearly all of her time trying to discover precisely how much Connie had embezzled from Watts & Associates. Judy's work for the treatment center suffered as a result. Essentially, she stopped working, so we decided for her to take Connie's job and keep the books for Watts & Associates. She loved the idea, and by quitting, she severed her last ties with her life outside of Atlanta.

Judy was angry with me for not discovering Connie's stealing, so she no longer thought it was necessary to be civil with me. Every day—without exception—she told me how stupid, incompetent, and pathetic I was to have let this happen. Judy told me I was a fool, and that she was a bigger fool for getting involved with me in the first place.

Her constant, grinding criticism was debilitating. My confidence and self-worth suffered the most—followed closely by fear and apprehension about the future.

My ability to protect Jordan from Judy's cruelty also was affected. I was no longer capable of taking care of my own emotional needs—let alone Jordan's.

Regardless, the process of discovering the full extent of Connie's crimes was just beginning. I called Buford Billings, the CPA, and asked him to explain how this could have happened and how he could have missed it. When we met, he sat and tried to give an account. Judy listened intently to every word. When Buford was finished with his explanation, which was disjointed, unprofessional, and entirely unsatisfactory, he left. As soon as he was gone, Judy called her brother Arthur, a practicing CPA in South Carolina, and related everything Buford said with impressive detail.

Judy could take a sentence you carelessly uttered in the spring, tie it to another said in the fall, link it to an incident from the summer, and come up with an undeniable character flaw during the holidays, spoiling your Christmas dinner. I could never win with her and her vast file of my imperfections. But for once, this character trait was a benefit; she used it to nail Buford Billings.

During their lengthy conversation, Arthur asked many pointed questions, and Judy had answers for everything. In the end, Arthur found Buford's behavior to be so unusual that he suggested we call the Georgia State Board of Accountancy to find out if they had ever had any problems with Buford Billings. This seemed like a good idea. The next day Judy made the call with me standing right beside her. The State Board had indeed heard of Mr. Billings and had problems with him several times before. They told us he was not a CPA and had never been one. Because he had falsely represented himself as a CPA before and had been discovered, he avoided prosecution by signing a consent order, barring him from ever claiming to be a CPA again.

I was speechless. Buford wasn't a CPA. His business card said he was— as did his stationery and answering service. Every invoice he ever sent Watts & Associates had CPA on them, but it was all a con and a fraud. And I bought it.

I knew that I had been an idiot, but there was no time to be self-accusing. Judy was stockpiling ammunition of her own to tell me what a fool I was anyway. Instead I had to obtain legal help. The entire situation was becoming too complex, and I knew I was way over my head. I really didn't know how to proceed or what to do next. So I turned to a lawyer friend who was also my AA sponsor.

Chapter 40

A Pattern of Theft

The next morning, I went to the 7:30 A.M. meeting to unload and also to see my sponsor, a lawyer named Marcus C. He was a really nice guy and quite an interesting character. I chose him as a sponsor because he was bright, street smart, had seen a lot of life, and had many years of sobriety. When I told him about Connie and Buford, he agreed to come to my house, where all the evidence was, and discuss what needed to be done. After meeting for an entire day to bring him up to speed, I hired him.

For the next week, Judy, Marcus, and I met every day to go over records, documents, and bills. We also planned our next steps. I was needed to answer questions and to put everything into historical context. By Friday afternoon, however, Marcus suggested I leave the resolution of the fraud to Judy and him and return to running my business. I agreed—inwardly relieved to leave it in their hands.

For the next two months, I would come home to find Judy and Marcus poring over the records to unearth rampant embezzlement. It seemed like each day there was a new discovery. The total went from $49,000 to $100,000 to $200,000 and up. Every time they thought they were through, they would think of something else; and sure enough, Connie had thought of it, too. The final number was $340,000. That's how much Connie had stolen from me—her dad—and we could prove it in a court of law. It was actually closer to $400,000, but some of it wasn't provable in court, so we just let that go. There were so many acts of theft that it required ten separate three-ring binders to catalog all of it. Her embezzlement was massive.

At the same time, Judy assaulted me verbally with each revealed disclosure. I dreaded coming home. Finally, even Marcus had had enough. He told her he would quit the case if she didn't tone down her harsh vitriol; it was affecting his sobriety, he said. She didn't tone anything down, but she did restrain herself in front of him.

Not all days, however, were difficult; sometimes it was rewarding. One day, for instance, Judy came into my office with a look of triumph on her face.

Curious, I said, "What is it?"

"Jack, I was going through the canceled checks, and guess what I found?" She was positively beside herself with glee as she held a check out in front of her.

"I can't imagine," I said with piqued curiosity. "Let me see."

She handed me a canceled check that was paid to Buford Billings for $9,600. Buford had put his name on the "Pay to" line in his own handwriting. On the little line at the bottom of the check, where it tells what it's for, were the words "For IRS payment for Jack Watts" written by me. In Judy's other hand was an itemized statement from Buford Billings, CPA, stating that $9,600 had been paid to the IRS for me on the same day the check was written.

Looking at it, I realized that Connie had to have seen the canceled check made out to Buford and not the IRS in the monthly statement. They were in this together; they had to be. Despite their protestations to the contrary, they were coconspirators in this massive embezzlement. This discovery sickened me because it showed the true depths of their cunning and duplicity.

Buford had used funds I had authorized for taxes, appropriating them to himself. I remembered the incident vividly. He said I needed to send the IRS about $10,000 for quarterly taxes. He wasn't sure precisely how much to the penny, so he said he would fill it in for me and provide Connie with an e-mail with the exact amount. This seemed reasonable, so I signed it. He was my CPA. I had no reason to distrust him.

This sealed Buford's fate. Because of his fiduciary responsibility and the consent judgment against him, this would send Buford to prison, and both of us knew it.

A few weeks later, Judy came to find me with that same victorious smirk. Recognizing it, I immediately stopped what I was doing and said, "Oh, dear, what now?"

"You're *really not going to believe this*, Jack," Judy said with her beautiful, sparkling, malevolent eyes.

I responded, "At this point, nothing would surprise me. What's in your hand?"

"Three checks paid from Watts & Associates to Mona Watts."

"What!" I erupted and jumped right out of my seat. "I don't believe it," I said, grabbing the checks to see for myself. There it was in black and white—Pay to the order of Mona Watts.

I could be surprised after all. Connie had used my money to pay expenses for Mona. Looking at the checks, I thought Mona must have known what Connie was doing—she had to; no other explanation made any sense. I wasn't surprised that Mona hadn't told me about any of this, including the fact that the money came out of *my* business account. As I thought about it, I remembered how much Mona loved secrets.

As the discovery of financial irregularities finally wound down, Marcus's progress on the civil case began to diminish appreciably. I suspect that the case was becoming so large and complex—with substantial criminal implications against Connie and Buford—that it may have been beyond his legal training. But there were other problems brewing as well. He began to have medical problems. Also he and Judy started having conflicts of their own.

One day, he pulled me aside and said, "Jack, you're my client, not Judy. I have to be honest with you. I don't think Judy's really working for your best interests. There's something wrong with the way she's handling this entire situation." Pausing for a moment to take a deep breath, he continued, "I get the impression that she's not after the truth; it's almost as if she's relishing Connie's methods, like she's learning to do it better herself."

I didn't say a word, but by the surprised expression on my face, he could tell I had not expected to hear this.

He went on, "I know this might sound crazy to you, but when she doesn't think I'm looking, I can see the excitement in her eyes. I think she actually admires Connie."

"Marcus," I countered, rattled but determined not to believe that Marcus's assertion was accurate. "I love my wife. I know it's been hard, but when we're through with this, things will get better." It seemed so malicious. Judy may have been verbally unkind, but surely she wasn't capable of such villainous intent.

Musing, I reflected about Judy's card with her pledge "to never quit." In my heart, I still wanted to believe this was true.

Taking another deep breath, Marcus said, "I think you should divorce her."

"No way," I immediately retorted. I loved her, and I certainly didn't want to go through *another* divorce.

From that point forward, however, Judy and Marcus could no longer stand to work together. Marcus eventually quit, which probably was best. His biggest asset was his supportiveness, but what I really needed was a lawyer with a background in criminal law.

When I went home and told Judy that Marcus had resigned, she said, "Good. We need a shark, not a good old boy from AA." I nodded my agreement; she was right. Looking at the shelf behind me, she said, "Pass me the *Yellow Pages*." Within an hour, she had found a new lawyer, Michael Montgomery, a very savvy attorney—and a shark.

We went to see him the next day, and he quickly got the ball rolling. He went through the drill, explaining that it was both a civil and a criminal case and that we'd have to proceed with both cases simultaneously.

"There's one more thing," he said after he had explained the basics. "You don't have to pay taxes on income that has been stolen from you, but the amount of funds we're talking about will undoubtedly raise a red flag with the IRS. You could actually be entitled to a tax credit nearing six figures, but we will have to show them that you intend to prosecute Connie and Buford—not just say that you are. That's very important because, if you don't, they will disallow your tax credit and come after you for diverting funds."

"Come after me!" I said incredulously.

"That's right—unless you are relentless with your prosecutorial efforts. They will not accept such an enormous loss of tax revenue easily." He added, "I know what I'm talking about. I've seen it happen before."

He went on with his explanation for another five minutes—at the end of which I saw no alternative other than to prosecute. I was in a corner—put there by Connie and Buford, with only one alternative: to have both of them arrested and charged with embezzlement.

With my consent, he picked up the phone and called a defense attorney and former prosecutor, Steve Hennessy, to begin the process of putting pressure on the district attorney's office to arrest both Connie and Buford for embezzlement. I hoped it wouldn't come to that, but it probably would.

By now, we had been working on the embezzlement case for nine months and married for one year. On top of her increasingly oppressive attitude, Judy stopped any kind of physical relationship with me. This hurt, of course; it was painfully familiar territory.

I began to think more about what Marcus had said and how things just didn't add up. Once, when Judy was in South Carolina, visiting her son, she called and gave me a tongue-lashing that was devastating. I was surprised because there was no apparent reason for the tirade. After emoting for a while, I stopped to think about what was really going on with her. None of this made sense. I really didn't know who Judy was anymore; the wonderful, mature woman I married no longer existed.

Judy kept a detailed journal, and I decided to see if I could learn what was really going on inside her head. I opened it—with the purpose of gaining insight into my wife's character and behavior. I knew this was a breach of trust and I shouldn't have done it, but I was desperate, so I did.

Within fewer than five minutes, I was no longer distressed; I was enlightened. On the first page I opened, I was informed that Judy's relationship with her pilot friend, Jerry, had indeed been sexual, although she had insisted it wasn't, and her relationship with her "mentor" was not as innocent as what she described it to be. I was shaken and had to put the journal down. I couldn't handle it emotionally. She had lied to me from the beginning. I couldn't bear to read more, but I also was compelled to read it at the same time. Picking it back up, I read this:

> The thing that I have been unwilling to own is that I am being kept. I am compromising myself. Even though I do not have a sexual relationship with Stewart, I compromise myself every time I medicate with his credit card or his money. . . . I call him my mentor or "Grandfather." I refer to Muriel [his wife] as if she is part of all this. In reality, I know that she and their children would be completely appalled to learn of my relationship with Stewart. They would recognize . . . it as a very much younger woman completely taking advantage of a lovesick, older man. Now this is truly what this relationship is.

Judy's weekly lunches with Stewart, which continued the entire time we were married—and were encouraged by me—were a fraud. He came to grope her, and Judy let him because he was a steady source of income for her. Realizing the truth for the first time made me sick—literally sick.

I rushed to the bathroom and vomited. My wife had been deceiving me all along. She let a dirty old man grope her—for money.

But was it all a lie? What about the card telling me I was the "love of her life"? Was that true, or was that also a lie? In my heart, I knew the answer, but I had to see for myself. So I washed my face, brushed my teeth, and sat down to learn everything I could about Judy. I no longer felt guilty about invading her privacy; I wanted to know everything. She wrote:

- *I roped you [Jack] into my horror story and held you accountable for all the crimes ever committed against me. I tore you to shreds with my angry, toxic, cruel words; and I withheld my body from you because I never truly committed it to you. I crucified you with my spiritual self-righteousness.*

- *I believe women are far superior to men—men are pathetic and can be manipulated by sex . . . it is very easy to outsmart them.*

- *God, You are asking me to love the unlovable [Jack]. You are asking me to do something for which I have no reference point. I thought I had stretched so far already, surrendering my need to destroy. I was pretending; I have no reference point here. I find that I am very angry with You and with Jack. I've listed the reasons that I am angry with Jack so often that this has become my mantra. I have little, if any, respect for Jack. I see him as inferior, inadequate, insecure. He whines . . . and says childish, immature, and asinine things. He has no class.*

- *Jordan—"Jack's Little Princess," my superior—then my equal. Again, Jack refuses to see this relationship as "screwed up."*

- *I asked for the lesson: To learn commitment—to stay when I'd rather leave. And instead of embracing the lesson, creating a picture of acceptance, compromise, and communication—I have resisted the lesson, taking on my self-righteous cloak—rejecting, blaming, demanding, controlling, envying, being fearful and jealous. Making Jack pay a huge price for being imperfect—with the very same imperfections that have ruled my life.*

There was more—much more, including salacious sexual entries about numerous other men before me, but none of it is germane to my story, other than to inform me that Judy lied about practically everything.

My enlightenment, however, came at a heavy price. When she returned to Atlanta, I told her what I had learned and how I had learned it. She was enraged; I didn't care. She tried to browbeat and belittle me with her standard diatribe, but I was no longer susceptible. She tried to make it about me and how dishonorable I was for violating her privacy, instead of how wrong she had been for being so deceitful. My discovery changed everything.

She moved into the other bedroom and locked the door. The following day she scheduled plastic surgery for herself. She paid for the expensive procedures with my American Express—without my permission or knowledge, of course.

I stopped bringing Jordan to the house—completely stopped, and to my knowledge, Judy never saw her again.

One afternoon, Judy informed me that the pressure from the lawsuits, our impending issues from the IRS related to them, and our marital discord were getting to be too much for her. She was checking herself into the Sanctuary, the treatment center that had employed her when we met. She needed a two-week stay to sort things out. Her statement was an announcement of what she intended to do and not an issue for discussion. She left the following day, and—you guessed it—she paid for it with my money, without either my knowledge or consent. It simply didn't occur to me that she would do that, but of course it should have. I didn't discover it for months. It cost me nearly $10,000.

While she was gone, I went to see my two lawyers. Until now, Judy had been the point person, speaking with each of them nearly every day. Now I was going to take over. I told them everything that had happened.

"I wish you had copied that journal," Steve said. "It could come in handy during the divorce."

"I don't want a divorce," I said. "Maybe she'll come back from the Sanctuary ready to start over."

"You're kidding, right?" Steve queried. "Jack, she's a con artist. Cons don't change. You've got to divorce her. It's as simple as that."

Michael added, "We could get it annulled. If your spouse enters into marriage fraudulently, you can get an annulment. She's entered fraudulently to take your money, and I think we can prove it." Looking at me, he added, "Do you want to do that? We would have to go to court and it would be very expensive, but we can do it. Should we?"

"No," I said. The meeting ended soon thereafter. As I left, my heart was pounding, and I was nauseous. Should I stick it out and try to make the marriage work—or quit? I dismissed the idea of an annulment because when your lawyer says something is going to be very expensive, believe him. I didn't need another huge legal bill.

Everything in my life was unraveling, and I wondered what else could go wrong. I didn't have long to wait. The answer came the very next day.

Chapter 41

"I Want Out"

I received a call from the Gaithers, saying they had decided to produce their quarterly catalog in-house, starting immediately. They informed me of this without warning or notice. I was devastated, knowing that the economic consequences to Watts & Associates would be catastrophic. It took 60 percent away from our yearly billings, which would be nearly impossible to replace, especially as quickly as needed.

They came to this decision because they wanted complete control of the catalog from their home base in Indiana, not Atlanta. We did an outstanding job for them for years, and they were never dissatisfied with our work. Nevertheless, they had made their decision, and they were going to stick to it. It probably never occurred to them that this would be a colossal blow to my business. With this and Connie's embezzlement combined, would I be forced to declare bankruptcy? The fear of economic insecurity became overwhelming. The panic this caused was so severe that I would wake up in the middle of the every night and couldn't go back to sleep for hours. It was even hard to keep food down.

All this occurred in the winter of 2000. I was now in a desperate situation and had to take control of my circumstances and not allow them to deteriorate further. The following day, I went to the bank and changed accounts, making certain that Judy couldn't write any more checks. I also made sure she couldn't make further charges on any of my credit cards. By the time she returned from the Sanctuary, she was cut off completely.

Judy tried to circumvent my economic restraints several times but without success. I told the bank precisely what my situation was and directed them to prevent her from any access to Watts & Associates' funds. When Judy tried to make an end run, the woman at the bank stopped her cold in her tracks, flatly refusing to give her a dime. Judy came home that afternoon and announced, "Jack, I want out. I'm filing for divorce."

"I've been expecting this," I said.

Interrupting me, she added, "You'll have to find another place to live. I'm staying in the house. You'll have to move out."

"That's what you think," I said, offended by her audacity. "I'll give you a divorce, but not my house."

"You mean *our* house," she said. I had been so certain about the success of this marriage that I put her name on the deed, which I now deeply regretted.

"Judy, I've paid for everything in this house, and all you've done is steal from me."

"Then we'll just have to sell the house and split the equity," she said in her coldest, most calculating voice, which sent a chill through my body. I realized that being right might not mean anything in a court of law. There was a chance she could accomplish her purpose for marrying me: to steal my money, my house, and everything in it.

I thought, *Why didn't I copy her journal when I had the chance?* It might have saved me from being completely dismantled.

Several days later, I came home, and Judy was lying on the couch in the living room watching a rerun of an old *Law & Order* episode. I walked into the kitchen and saw the keys to her Volvo, which I was still paying for. Since filing for divorce, she always kept the keys protected in her pocketbook—which was close to her at all times. Having brought her suitcase into the house when she returned from the Sanctuary, I saw that her journals were in the trunk of the car, so I quietly picked up the keys and gingerly clicked on the trunk release twice, hoping it would work from inside the house. Saying good night, I went to bed. I set my alarm for 2:30 A.M.—Judy was always asleep at that time.

As it turned out, I didn't need an alarm. I woke up—filled with purpose and trepidation. Ever so quietly, I got dressed and left the house through the sliding door, crawled over the deck railing, and circled around the house to the driveway where the Volvo was parked. I was scared to death that either she would be up and see me through the window or that I had not been effective in triggering the release mechanism. I tried to open the trunk, and to my immense relief, it opened effortlessly. Looking in, I saw what I had come for—her journal. I took it—along with the new journal she had worked on at the Sanctuary—and headed for a twenty-four-hour Kinko's.

Each minute I was there, I was terrified of discovery. My hands shook like someone going through detox. My fear was irrational, but I was nervous each step of the way. I copied everything, never looking at a single word. When I was finished, I drove home, quietly putting her journals back in the trunk—which I had left ajar—closed the lid quietly, circled around the house, crept back inside, hid the copies in my closet, and went back to bed. I slept restlessly the remainder of the night. I was the Raskolnikov of spying. I couldn't wait for Judy to leave the next day so I could see what "treasures" awaited me.

Chapter 42

I Had to Outsmart Her

Judy left at 11:00 A.M. the next morning, looking preppy—without a care in the world—as usual. As I watched her move gracefully to the car in her haughty, imperious way, I felt a sense of victory of my own: I knew something she didn't know, and I hoped it would save my house and what was left of my shattered life.

As soon as I was certain she wouldn't return, I raced to the closet and started reading ravenously. I was no longer apologetic about invading her privacy. She had come into my life to destroy me, and I had to outsmart her to survive.

After reading for twenty minutes or more, I found exactly what I needed. In an entry dated just a few weeks earlier, while at the Sanctuary, she wrote:

> I married Jack under false pretenses, and I knew it. When he could not deliver his end of the deal, meaning security—and he expected me to help him, then I lost all willingness to even play the part. I felt duped. Beat at my own game. When men don't meet my expectations, I discard them.

There were many other damaging entries, but this one seemed particularly on target. With a sigh of relief, I took all the copies and brought them to a friend's house for safekeeping.

I didn't even tell my lawyers what I had until Judy left a week later to move into an apartment, taking, by the way, thousands of dollars of household items that were clearly my premarital property, including the $18,000 diamond ring, which she promised to return but never did. After she left, I went to see my attorneys.

Showing them what I had, Michael asked, "Jack, is this Judy's writing? Is this her penmanship?"

"Absolutely," I said. "She wrote it."

Puzzled, they looked at each other, and Michael asked, "How did you get it?"

I told them, and they sat there mesmerized. At one point, Michael said he wasn't going to charge me for the time it required to tell the story. It was too much fun, he'd said. Steve agreed, and both lawyers laughed heartily. The next month, I checked the bill, and each charged me for every minute—lawyers!

After I finished my story, Steve said, "In all the years I've been practicing law, this is the best piece of evidence for a divorce case I've ever seen."

"I agree," Michael interjected. "With this, you won't have to pay her a dime. She'll have to pay you. You don't have to worry about losing your house anymore; I guarantee it."

As I left the office, I felt empowered. I was fighting back. But I must admit that my happiness over legal vindication was tempered by my embarrassment. I was mortified to be in this situation in the first place. Once again, my impulsiveness had gotten me into a colossal mess.

A troubling thought from the past also began to resurface—one I couldn't shake or dismiss. I wondered if I had brought all of this on myself by my actions nearly ten years earlier. Was this some kind of cosmic consequence for the affair I had while married to Martha? People say, *What goes around, comes around*, and I wondered if this was my payback.

Judy had deceived me thoroughly, and I had bought her lies eagerly, pursuing, once again, an impulsive rush headlong to my own destruction—all brought on by my intense need to be loved. I believed her because I wanted to believe her, experiencing a negative consequence because I still hadn't learned my lesson, which was to wait for God's timing rather than impulsively taking matters into my own hands. I insisted that God bless my self-serving choices, which He steadfastly refused to do.

I am getting what I deserve, I thought. In the back of my mind, I was convinced that the tentacles from my earlier indiscretion were now reaching into my marriage with Judy, defeating any chance there might have been for our relationship to succeed.

As I took a spot inventory of my life, I could point to a few positive things, but most were negative. However, I had no alternative but to press forward, hoping for the best while resigning myself to expect the worst.

Chapter 43

"Under False Pretenses"

Judy left shortly before my fifty-sixth birthday. But that was not the last I heard of her.

Within a week of Judy's departure, Martha, my second wife, called and said that Jordan had just been diagnosed with a serious medical condition that required major surgery. My heart sank, and I was trembling just listening to her describe what the surgery entailed. We had to address Jordan's medical situation immediately.

The following day, I went with them to see the doctor, who explained that Jordan had a congenital problem with her back that could only be remedied by inserting six titanium screws in her spine. This was crushing news that made my legs weak, but it had to be done. The surgery was set for a few weeks later.

At the same time, my business was floundering with the loss of the income from the Gaither catalog. Because I had to spend so much time and energy taking care of delinquent bills, I couldn't focus on obtaining new business to replace what I had lost. I was in deep trouble. I desperately needed some help, and I received it from my daughter Victoria and my brother Dick.

By now, Victoria had delivered her first child—my eighth grandchild. As a stay-at-home mom, she had some spare time, so she assumed the job abandoned by Judy. It was a grueling assignment because creditors were calling every day, demanding payment. She would send them something and promise to send more when we could. The pressure was constant. We simply didn't have enough—not nearly enough—to satisfy the demand; Watts & Associates was close to bankruptcy.

One day, Victoria called and said, "Dad, we are out of money. We don't have anything. We can't go on. What are you going to do?" Her words paralyzed me with fear.

Not having any other choice, I called my brother Dick and told him how desperate the situation was. He sent me $20,000 the next day, but that barely made a dent. I called him again two days later and asked for another $30,000, which he sent within a week. This kept us afloat so we could go on for a while longer. Dick had to tap into his self-employed retirement funds, so the $50,000 I borrowed actually cost more than $69,000 because of IRS penalties for early withdrawal.

Earlier, I was forced to do the same thing—draining my IRA of $90,000 to repay bills from Connie's theft. My penalty for doing so was $24,000. By refinancing my house, I also liquidated most of my equity to pay off creditors. Consequently, my payments went from $1,800 a month to nearly $4,200. And the negative economic consequences just kept right on coming. It was like an unquenchable California firestorm in the dry summer months.

My situation was dire and my prospects bleak. I stopped taking vacations and quit buying clothes. I also stopped my bimonthly maid service. I deleted one expense after another to try to keep from going bankrupt, but regardless of how difficult it was, I was never tempted to start drinking again—not once.

I prayed and asked God why He had allowed all this to happen. I begged Him repeatedly to answer me. Finally, one day a voice—like thunder—seemed to come out of the heavens. "I don't know, Watts," the voice said. "Something about you just pisses me off!"

My sense of irony did me well in that moment, which was refreshing. I wasn't foolish enough to blame God for my predicament; however, He was the solution, not the problem.

Nevertheless, the pressure continued to mount from many fronts. Neither the case with Connie nor with Buford was close to resolution. My divorce from Judy was still in process. The IRS had challenged several years of returns in an effort to squeeze what little was left, and Jordan's surgery was imminent. But I knew that taking a drink wouldn't make my life better or change my situation; it would make it worse. Consequently, I remained sober. If I had started drinking again, I doubt I would have survived.

Dick decided to come down the day after Jordan's operation to be with both Jordan and me. We loved the idea because Dick always seemed to make things better. He brought Danny with him, too. I thought that was a great idea because I hadn't seen my older brother in years.

Jordan's operation went smoothly, and she was recovering in her room at Scottish Rite Children's Hospital when Dick and Danny arrived. I brought them in, and it seemed to cheer Jordan up quite a bit. They stayed at the house with me when we weren't with her at the hospital. After two days, Jordan was released, and she went home.

The following afternoon, however, Jordan developed a fever, and Martha called me immediately. As it turned out, her incision became infected, which resulted in a second surgery and a longer stint at the hospital for Jordan. It was a very dangerous infection. I was scared and so grateful to have Dick with me. Danny stayed in town, but he spent most of his time at the gym working out.

Danny's absence was all right with Jordan because she preferred not to be around him. She said, "He makes me feel uncomfortable, Daddy." I didn't ask her to explain what she meant by this. Danny has a difficult time feeling compassion for others and is uncomfortable doing so. He simply doesn't know how to react, and his attempts to feign empathy are pitiful. Over the years I've seen it many times, so I wasn't surprised by her response to him.

Jordan was even more specific with Martha, however, telling her that she didn't want to be left alone with Danny under any circumstances. She told her mom that she didn't like the way he touched her or the way he looked at her. Martha honored Jordan's wishes scrupulously, staying right by her side whenever Danny was present.

Jordan's surgery occurred fewer than six weeks after Judy left, but Judy never even asked about Jordan's condition. Why should she? She didn't care, and she no longer needed to pretend. Besides, she was far too busy trying to exploit her advantage over me economically. She had contributed greatly to my mounting debt, and I was staggering under the weight of it.

Finally, I had had enough and decided to put a stop to it once and for all. One Saturday afternoon, Judy and I were discussing some divorce-related details on the phone and she was being particularly spiteful. I was over it, so I cut her off cold, saying, "I know I never met your expectations, Judy. And when men don't meet your expectations, *you discard them.*"

There was dead silence on the other end. I didn't say a word for quite a while. She must have wondered if I knew something about her journal or had just made a lucky guess. I was nervous, but also emboldened. After what must have been a thirty-second pause, I added, "Besides, *you married me under false pretenses*, and you knew it."

She cut in. "You read my journal again."

"Yes, I did."

"That's just like you," she said with a sneer. "How dare you invade my privacy like that!"

She was just warming up, and I wasn't about to listen to another tirade, so I cut her off. "There's more. Do you want to hear it?"

Again, there was a long pause in the conversation. The power position between us had just shifted. Finally, I had shown her my cards; I had played the Ace of Trumps. Her power over me was finished; I now had power over her, and she knew it. She was terrified of being exposed to the world for who she really was, and I could do it.

"Jack, those are my private thoughts, and you have no right—no right to have read them," she said, her voice wavering ever so slightly.

I went on, "I made a copy of your journals. Everything you wrote. You're not going to get anything from me, Judy. Nothing! Nada! Not a dime." Then I repeated what Michael had said. "In fact, you'll be the one paying me."

"You son of a—" she hissed as I hung up the phone. But I didn't feel victorious—not even a little. Instead, I was shaken.

Judy, now exposed for exactly who she was and by her own words, never regained her momentum. Judy chose to cut her losses, settle, and move on, which was fine with me. She received precisely what she deserved from the divorce settlement: nothing.

———————

Because I was reeling from the aftereffects of several crimes committed against me, which felt staggering, I realized it was time to rekindle the relationship I had put on the back burner for several years—my relationship with the Lord. The following Sunday I got up, showered, dressed, and went to church. It was the first time I had done so since Judy and I were married. I longed to reestablish the strong relationship with Christ that had sustained me my entire adult life. Without it I felt adrift, and I knew I was an emotional wreck.

There was a church close to my house that looked interesting—the Church of the Faithful. So I went. It was undergoing massive construction, so the service was held in a long room with a low ceiling. I went in, and everybody was very friendly, which made me feel uncomfortable. I was too wounded to be friendly. When the service began, they all started singing. As I heard the songs that had been a part of my life for nearly forty years—songs of God's love and faithfulness—I started to cry, and I couldn't stop. I wept, and worst of all, I didn't have a tissue. The lyrics and melodies I knew so well began their soothing, relentless process of cleansing my soul of all the filth, bile, and pollutants that had made my life a wasteland. By the middle of the second hymn, I could sense that I was making people uncomfortable, so I got up and left.

Once outside, I regained my composure; but my brief experience demonstrated how far away from God I had actually drifted. My soul needed nourishment, and I knew where to go to get food. Once again, the Master was calling, *Come and dine.* I went home and took my Bible off the shelf and began to read. It was like finding manna in the desert. Every word provided life-giving sustenance to a soul depleted of nutrients. I knew I was back on the right path, getting stronger with each word I read.

The following week, I went back to church, with the same results. I didn't make it through the singing. The love and joy expressed in the corporate singing were simply too much for me to handle. My wounds were still too fresh and too deep. I did, however, bring a tissue this time, and tried to keep my weeping more private. This happened four more Sundays in a row. Heaven only knows what some of those people must have thought. I was embarrassed, but I couldn't help myself. It was like a cleansing tide, washing away decaying debris and leaving a clean, beautiful beach every time the music played.

Without Judy, the house was quiet. In the morning, I had time to drink several cups of coffee and read the Scriptures in peace. I also found my trusty copy of *My Utmost for His Highest* and started reading it daily, making notes in the margins as I meditated. I was in a deep valley, but that's where remorseful people heal and grow. During this time I also went to AA meetings nearly every day and cooked breakfast for a couple of hundred alcoholics every Saturday morning. My life was no less difficult, but I felt my character being enriched, which was what really mattered.

During this period of time, the stronghold of anger that had always been part of my life broke. I simply wasn't angry anymore. Joy returned to my life, mixed with sorrow and grief, to be sure, but I was able to have a measure of calmness in the midst of everything. My anxiety subsided ap-preciably, and I started sleeping through the night again.

Now that Judy was gone, I brought Jordan back to the house. Our lives started returning to normal—rich in love, acceptance, and peace. Life was taking on a measure of normalcy in the midst of chaos; and, like so many times before, I wondered what was going to happen next.

Chapter 44

Handcuffed and Taken to Jail

Buford Billings was the first one arrested. He was picked up, handcuffed, and taken to jail one afternoon in the fall of 2000. After I fired him, he found a job working in some office where the police showed up unannounced. I knew it was going to happen, but I had no idea when. Although anxiously awaiting his arrest for months, when it came, it was surprising to me and embarrassing for him. In court, he agreed to pay me an initial check of $5,000 along with a repayment plan with monthly payments of $453.50 until the debt was paid. Weeks later, when I went to criminal court, I asked that the felony charges be dropped, and they were.

It was nice to have one part of the problem resolved. Connie was still stalling the legal process, but I was moving forward. Unfortunately, there was more than enough stress on my plate to keep my anxiety piqued.

I was utterly unable to satisfy the constant flow of creditors and their insatiable demand for payments—they wanted money that I just didn't have. I had gone from being financially comfortable to being dead broke.

Eventually, the fear of economic uncertainty got the best of me. At one point, I didn't have a dime. There was nothing to eat in the house other than stale cereal and a little milk. I was hungry. My spirit was crushed, and I thought the world might be better off without me. At least my insurance would pay off all my debts with enough remaining to finish my child support for Jordan. I was worth more dead than alive.

Suicide seemed like the only way out. I was at absolute rock bottom—and it had nothing to do with alcohol. I had never felt sorrier for myself in my entire life. I had no desire to go on and wished I were dead. That's exactly how I felt, and I thought of how I would exit this world.

At the same time, I knew how destructive suicidal ideations were and somehow was able to reason that part of my self-destructive thoughts might have been from low blood sugar, so I decided to eat the stale cereal. That decision and subsequent action—getting up from my chair in the living room and going to the refrigerator—changed everything for me. In the twinkling of an eye, so to speak. From the living room to the refrigerator was thirty feet. In the time it took me to walk that distance, I realized, "I have something to eat." This may seem silly, but it was profound for me and proved to be a turning point. I realized that in the crucible of all my troubles, at the lowest point of my life, God did not leave me hungry. He was taking care of my most basic need. In that moment I began to shift my focus from my troubles to my solutions, which was a profound blessing.

I poured a bowl of stale cereal and thanked God for providing nourishment. I sat down and enjoyed my small meal, free from my suicidal thoughts.

I thought back to the meeting with Carl McMurray at my fraternity in 1964. He told me God loved me and had a wonderful plan for my life. In my nineteen-year-old mind, I thought God's plan would make me more successful and spare me from the problems that destroyed so many. I loved what I heard from Carl and embraced it. But it wasn't really true—at least not the way I interpreted it. God wanted me rich in character, and He would go to any lengths to accomplish His goal. I was a hard case; it took quite a bit of effort. It still does.

I also thought of AA and why God had delivered me from compulsive drinking. Perhaps it was so I could have a deeper understanding of what was important in life. Regardless, in all my difficulties, returning to alcohol never seemed like a worthwhile option, and I remained sober.

In the year that followed, while in the valley, I learned the value of joy, simplicity, and long-suffering. There was no other way for me to embrace positive character qualities than to learn from my many mistakes. But I did learn from them and became a better man as a result, enriching my relationship with the Lord in the process.

Going to church again became routine for me, and I joined the Church of the Faithful. Some things were looking up, and Connie's time of stalling was about to end.

Chapter 45

End Up in Prison

Business started to improve, and I began slowly paying off some major creditors. Soon enough, I had paid all my vendors in full. I had never achieved anything so difficult in my life, but I couldn't take time to savor the victory because there was still so much left to do.

My legal expenses were staggering, and problems with the IRS loomed, but progress was being made on all fronts. Victoria was a real help with her consistent encouragement and hard work in helping me regain my solvency. Resolving the legal issues with Connie, however, remained a huge hurdle to overcome.

Connie may have stolen nearly $400,000—with $340,000 of it provable in court—but she didn't have a penny of it left. Nothing, not a red cent. She had spent it on trips to Las Vegas, clothes and toys for her kids, furniture, booze, meals out, and who knows what else. Now completely broke and without her "extra income from borrowing," she couldn't afford a lawyer. Mona came to her rescue and gave her some money. Interestingly, Mona used the money that had been from my part of the house—the money that had been legally Connie's from the beginning—and it wasn't nearly equivalent to Connie's actual share, but it was money nonetheless.

Ironically, this meant I actually paid for Connie's lawyer to defend her from stealing from me. To top it all off, Mona refused to give Victoria her portion because Victoria was helping me, which both hurt and infuriated Victoria at the same time. Once more, Mona had moved to the middle of my life. Some days, her enmity toward me saddened me, on other days it was infuriating.

In the fall of 2000, Connie met with me in Michael's office to try to work out an agreement that would satisfy all parties. Connie was willing to sign a promissory note for the embezzled money, but that wasn't good enough, according to my lawyers. They wouldn't allow me to accept Connie's offer. After the meeting, we discussed my options.

Michael reasoned, "Jack, I know she's your daughter, but it's clear that she has no intention of repaying the money. She'll sign the note and then file for bankruptcy a few months later. That means you'll get nothing. She will walk away with a clean slate, and you'll lose everything. And the IRS may yet accuse you of diverting funds."

He continued, saying that we would simply need more leverage to make sure she'd be required to pay the money back. He reasoned, "That's why we must push for the criminal prosecution, as hard as it will be for you."

"I just wish there were another way," I lamented, knowing Michael was right and that ultimately I couldn't protect Connie from the consequences of her actions. She had backed me into a corner. I left that day knowing that my oldest daughter might end up in prison.

Chapter 46

Lies Increase Your Bondage

Nearly two months later, the police drove out to the Johnsons' house unannounced and arrested Connie while she was cooking dinner for Keith and her children. She knew it might happen, but there's a huge difference between the possibility and the reality of being arrested. Like Buford, she was handcuffed, put in the back of a police car, and hauled off to jail. It's hard to express how agonizing this was for me.

Connie and her husband, Keith, remained in denial that she had acted criminally, and they were furious at me that I had followed through with the charges. Connie also resented Victoria because she wouldn't join their cabal. Because she was intimately acquainted with every aspect of Connie's embezzlement and her attempts to circumvent the truth, Victoria simply couldn't deny reality and embrace a lie. As a longtime member of ALA-NON, she knew the importance of looking at life realistically. Victoria's refusal to participate in their denial, however, cost her a huge price—her relationship with Connie and her mother.

Brenn was the battleground in this war. Recognizing this, she moved to Nevada with Willie and Christopher. By leaving, she escaped much of the drama at home.

After Connie's arrest, the litigation issues came to a head quickly. Connie and Keith signed our agreement—which asked for only half of the money to be repaid to me, in installments of $300 a month for three years; followed by $500 for the next two; and $750 thereafter until the entire amount was paid. My attorneys then informed the state that we didn't want to proceed with the criminal prosecution. Reluctantly, they agreed to allow Connie to plead out with no jail time—not even probation. She walked away from the criminal charges without a blemish, which was a relief to her, and to me as well.

The following year, after Connie had already filed for bankruptcy, her husband filed, too. Connie was devastated, and asked for their monthly payments to remain at the $300 level from then on. She said, "Dad, we just can't afford to pay any more than that. Is there any way you could keep it at three hundred dollars?"

It broke my heart to see her like this, so I said, "Sure, just pay me three hundred dollars from now on."

"Thanks, Dad," was all she said. I've seen her only a few times since, and she's still adamant that she didn't steal the money but "borrowed it."

When I left the hearing and returned home, I got out my calculator and did the math. By my calculations, I will have to live until I'm nearly 120 just to receive half of the principal from the money she stole—with no interest.

Shortly after the trial, my divorce with Judy was settled, and I was ready to move on. God had something new for me; I was sure of it. Maybe even true love, which had remained elusive my entire life.

One Sunday when I went to church, a friend recommended that I attend a new singles Bible study. He gave me the relevant contact information, and that afternoon I made arrangements to go the following Sunday evening. It sounded interesting.

The next Sunday, which was mid-fall 2001, I arrived sharply at 5:00 P.M. and entered a mansion on Tuxedo Road, where the upper crust of Atlanta society resides. When I walked into the living room, I saw a beautiful blond woman in her midforties. She looked at me and smiled. Her name was Alexia Erickson—and I knew immediately that a new adventure was about to begin.

Chapter 47

Confused and Adrift

Jade Middleton, the hostess and owner of the impressive home, introduced herself as well as her boyfriend Sterling Squire, who was soon to become her fiancé. They had been high school sweethearts and met again at a class reunion, where they picked up their long-dormant romance. Jade was the daughter of a couple I knew through Campus Crusade when I first became a believer in 1964—small world.

I was then introduced to everybody in the room, including Alexia Erickson. She was a tall, slender blonde of Germanic descent on both sides of her family. To me, she was beautiful but also looked a little sad and lost.

Everybody sat down, and Sterling proceeded with the Bible study. Actually, it was more like group therapy with a Christian slant than a real Bible study. The Scriptures were never brought into the conversation. But this was the South, and people were far more likely to attend a Bible study than group therapy.

After several weeks, the Bible study was in full swing, and people really started to open up. It was engaging and quite enjoyable. Alexia wasn't there as often as I had hoped, but I enjoyed the group even when she wasn't there. During this time, Sterling and I started to become good friends.

Alexia worked as a lobbyist at the Georgia Capitol and was dating an elected official who had aspirations to become Georgia's first Republican governor since Reconstruction. He was a very bright man—nearly ten years her junior and one of the ugliest men you could possibly imagine. When you saw them together, they looked like a real-life beauty-and-the-beast couple.

I had hoped Alexia was available, but this politician was her boyfriend and there was nothing I could do about it. Her background, still, was very interesting to me. She was the daughter of a missionary couple. She was born in Costa Rica; lived most of her formative years in Panama; went to high school in Quito, Ecuador; and went to college at Central Michigan, where she graduated with a degree in fashion merchandising.

She met her husband in Michigan, where they dated for several years before marrying. When she had been married for twenty-one years, her husband was killed in an accident involving an eighteen-wheel truck, leaving her a widow with a daughter and an adopted son—all of whom were devastated.

When I met her, she was in substantial emotional turmoil because of the sudden death of her husband fewer than two years earlier. My heart went out to her immediately, and I befriended her. She needed a friend desperately—one who wouldn't hit on her or exploit her vulnerability. Since she was romantically unavailable, I was able to be that person. So I talked to her after each meeting, sometimes for an hour or more. Her story was tragic, and I could see how confused and adrift she was.

Eventually, when her relationship with the politician ended, she and I became good friends and began going out to eat together. After a while, we were seeing each other nearly every day—sometimes for hours at a time. Often she would just come by to do nothing more than make telephone calls from my house. She obviously felt better with me near her.

During this entire period, I never pushed myself on her and never attempted to become romantic. I didn't even make a suggestive comment; I just tried to be a friend—a good one. Our relationship went on like this for months. In the recesses of my heart, however, I wondered if I was destined to rescue her, which I earnestly wanted to do. Always the optimist, I had never abandoned my dream of having a wife and a family once again—of putting my Humpty Dumpty back together again.

One day, when she was in my living room, I noticed her looking at me differently. I'd never seen that look before. As I stopped and turned to ask her what she was thinking about, she stood up, walked over, and kissed me. It wasn't a peck. It was a real kiss. I was really surprised, but I kissed her back with equal fervor.

That afternoon we went out on a real date—as a couple and not as friends. That's how it happened. We changed from friends to a couple in one afternoon—a very special afternoon.

The next evening, on our second date, Alexia came to my house, and I could tell she had something on her mind. She said, "Jacky, let's have a trial marriage. Do you want to?"

"What?" I exclaimed. I couldn't have been more surprised. It came from out of the blue, but it was out there—the "m-word." Looking at her in curious disbelief, I queried, "What's a trial marriage?"

"Well," she started to explain, "we get married but don't tell anyone, and we don't change our names or anything."

"Okay," I said—not in agreement but in comprehension of her interesting but unusual idea.

"We also keep our finances separate," she lectured, like a math instructor teaching algebra. "Then if it doesn't work out, we can go our separate ways, and nobody gets hurt." She said the last part like it was an idea that had never occurred to me. "Doesn't this sound like a great idea, Jacky?"

I couldn't help it; I laughed out loud. It seemed so preposterous, especially for the daughter of missionaries, but her offer was quite serious, and she pushed for it. From then on, the topic of marriage was on the agenda regularly—after only two dates. To be fair, we had known each other for a while, but this was quick—even by my impetuous standards. Two dates!

From past experience, I knew that once the "m-word" was out there, you couldn't take it back. It was there to stay; there was no going back. Once again, marriage had become an option with a beautiful, troubled woman. On one level, I knew that I should have been far more circumspect, but my impulsive nature was still too strong.

Chapter 48

Distressed and Confused

Part of being a good friend was listening to her story, which was fascinating. Her situation was unusual, and it was easy to see why she was so distressed and confused. Long after she and her husband, Reed, married, they had one daughter, Tiffany—after nearly six years of trying. Tiffany was quite a handful and remained so throughout her childhood. Because they never had other children—try as they may—they adopted a ten-year-old boy named Blake. He was a problem child from the beginning and never adjusted to their family. When I met Alexia, Blake was in a lockdown treatment facility in Utah for an attachment disorder, and it cost nearly $10,000 a month to keep him there.

In 1999, Reed was struck by an eighteen-wheel truck while repairing a flat tire on the road. Days after Reed's death, while Alexia was still in the depths of her grief, she was going through a stack of mail and came across his corporate American Express bill. She opened it and soon discovered that Reed had spent a weekend with his secretary not long before he died. His paramour had even signed for several charges, including lingerie.

Soon enough, Alexia discovered more and more evidence that Reed, the love of her life, had been cheating on her regularly for nearly two years. She had never once suspected it. Within a month of Reed's death, Alexia received a huge insurance settlement: $2.6 million.

The night after Reed's memorial service, she had a date with his old college roommate. Within a week, she went dancing with a lawyer friend who had been flirtatious with her for years. Within a few brief months, they became lovers. After that, there were several others—six in all—over the course of fewer than two years.

I believe that's why Alexia essentially asked me to marry her on our second date. As a child of missionaries and raised with a firm moral foundation, I believe that she was tired of the self-loathing that came from promiscuous living. She had also been frivolously spending her settlement money, and she needed to stop her financial hemorrhaging. Because of my neediness, which had never healed, I entertained her marriage idea rather than dismissing it as foolishness—like any sane person would.

By the time I met her, two years after Reed's death, half of her funds had been squandered. Her job as a lobbyist paid her very little, so Alexia was terrified of being broke. Both of her children were huge expenses—each having an attitude of entitlement, which Alexia simply wasn't strong enough to hold in check. It was too much for her. Blake's professional care to correct his behavior cost Alexia more than $250,000, but there was no change whatsoever. Tiffany was living just as extravagantly. Alexia needed help—big time, and I was the guy she needed to help her, which was fine with me.

Chapter 49

We'll Have Fireworks

Alexia knew she was taking a gamble by marrying me because of my numerous marriages, which does sound a little risky, doesn't it? My kids were upset when they found out, saying, "No, Dad, not again!" Others warned me that Alexia was still so fragile, and that it was too impulsive of me to get married so quickly. I didn't listen to any of it. Like always, *I was sure this time.*

We went forward with our plans. At first we planned to go down to City Hall and have a civil ceremony—just the two of us—with Jade and Sterling as our witnesses. Many in my family said that they wanted to come, and we began to grow excited. Soon, a judge and courtroom service didn't seem sufficient, so we opted for a more extravagant wedding ceremony, which included fireworks at Alexia's request. Everything was set for a beautiful wedding in May 2002.

A week before the wedding, one of my daughters called, who has asked to be unnamed regarding this topic. When she called, I thought she was going to congratulate me, but she had a far different agenda.

She said, "I have something I need to talk to you about."

"Sure. What is it?" I asked.

"I don't know how to say this," she continued, hesitatingly but determined. "I have a memory of you sexually molesting me when I was very young."

"What!" I exploded—unable to believe what I had just heard. "You can't be serious."

"It's in my memory, Dad," she said without a trace of anger or bitterness.

"That's nonsense," I thundered in disbelief. "I would never do that—

never!" I added, bewildered, horrified, and deeply wounded. When the conversation ended, I remained in shock. She couldn't believe that—she just couldn't.

Within ten minutes, I called Mona, thinking that even if she hated me—which she did—she wouldn't stoop low enough to support this. She knew it wasn't true. Because she could tell her that there was no possibility this was true, I appealed to her for help. While we talked, Mona was very supportive and said she knew these "memories" were inaccurate.

After my initial shock and embarrassment, I thought about it a little more. I knew there was no validity to the accusation, which meant it was either a false memory or someone else had molested her.

At the same time, I felt like a scarlet letter had been emblazoned across my chest, announcing to the world that I was a pervert. It was crushing, especially since protecting my kids was always so important to me. Feeling as low as I had felt for several years, I called Dick and told him about it while, at the same time, swearing him to secrecy.

Several days later, when Victoria called about some Watts & Associates business, I told her about my conversation. Having slept on it for several nights hadn't helped. If anything, I was more upset as each day passed. As I was relating the story, Victoria cut me off midsentence and said, "Dad, I was also molested."

I stopped instantly. "What?" I said incredulously.

"When you were telling me what happened," she said, "I had the flash of a memory. But it wasn't you. It was somebody tall with blond hair."

"Are you sure?"

"Yes," she said with conviction. "I just remembered it. The memory just flashed in front of me."

As our conversation concluded, I realized that something had happened decades earlier, and I was unaware of it. All I had ever wanted to do was to protect my family members, and I had failed. My sister, Jean, had been molested, then Jordan by Papaw, and now this. The pain was excruciating. I was about to get married, which was exciting, but I was deeply troubled as well.

Chapter 50

"Leave Me Alone, Pervert"

I pulled myself together for the wedding, which went off perfectly, and we liked to say it ended with a bang—because of the fireworks, of course.

Before we married, Alexia insisted on a prenuptial agreement, which didn't bother me at all. Because of this, I was reluctant to give her advice concerning her financial affairs. When she asked, however, I had plenty to say. One day, within two weeks of the wedding, she did ask for help, which I gave gladly. She was relieved to have me there to take the decision-making burden off her hands.

We initiated several major changes, which made more sense, helping her financial situation significantly. By putting Blake in affordable care, selling her house, and having Tiffany transfer from a California school, which she hated, to Ole Miss, which she loved, we ended up cutting our combined expenses by nearly $20,000 a month. The financial part of her life stabilized immediately.

My brother Danny, now living in Hawaii, had been teaching as an adjunct professor at various colleges and penal institutions for years. We corresponded occasionally by phone or e-mail. Evidently one or more of my anecdotal messages—perhaps my assertion that he had cheated Mom out of $26,500 with the Vermont home—offended him because he sent an e-mail that said,

> I hate you—bastard. Why don't you diddle" girls from our family. "Leave me alone, pervert, I know what you did. Dicky told me.you molester! Leave me alone. I will delete your message like i've deleted you, perv.

I was stunned when I received it. I couldn't believe how vicious it was. To begin with, I was irritated with Dick for breaking his promise, but that actually had a purpose, too—although I didn't realize it at the time. What I couldn't understand, however, was Danny's assumption that I had done such a thing. Even if he did think it was true, what would make him so accusatorial? It seemed very bizarre. Furthermore, upon looking at his fractured, disjointed, and poorly punctuated reply, I noticed something far more interesting. He wrote about it as plural and not singular. Nobody else had made a public accusation—just the one. Then why would Danny make reference to more than one? He had no idea about Victoria's memory. He couldn't have. I hadn't even told Dick at the time. This was very perplexing—and disturbing.

Danny's stinging accusations hurt, especially since there was no truth to them. For decades he had been my hero, despite his repeated ugliness toward others. He was my brother and I had continually forgiven him. Even when I mentioned the money he had stolen from our mother, I had done so in a lighthearted tone to try to show him that I loved him in spite of his selfish actions. So I couldn't figure out where all of his malice toward me originated.

———————

In mid-fall 2002, Sterling and Jade were married in her home with just a few close friends in attendance. When the wedding was over, I helped clean up in the kitchen. Because I bent over the sink and washed dishes for hours, I wasn't surprised when my right shoulder hurt the following morning. I thought the pain would subside as the day wore on, but it didn't—it intensified. Within three days, it was nearly unbearable. To deal with the pain, Alexia made an appointment for me to see a chiropractor. Since she worked as a lobbyist for chiropractors, she was adamantly opposed to seeking a medical opinion. I just wanted relief.

I went to see the chiropractor several times. He thought my pain originated from a sports injury because of all of the basketball I played. So he pushed on my shoulder to put everything in alignment, but the pain became worse—much worse. A rash appeared as well. He dismissed the rash and continued pushing, telling me it would be better by the end of the weekend.

By Sunday afternoon, however, I was in excruciating pain and told Alexia I was going to see a medical doctor. When I walked into the examination room and showed the doctor my shoulder and rash, it took him less than ten seconds to say, "You've got shingles."

"Are you sure?" I asked.

"As sure as the other two thousand times I've diagnosed it," he responded confidently.

Obviously he knew what he was talking about, while the chiropractor didn't have a clue. The physician gave me a prescription but told me that since the shingles had not been treated promptly, I was going to have significant pain for a long time. I just shook my head.

What made this significant was that Alexia's job—and her passion—was to lobby for chiropractors to become primary health care professionals in Georgia. After my terrible experience with the chiropractor—my only experience with one—I distrusted them and expressed that to Alexia. Perhaps I shouldn't have categorically dismissed the entire field because of my painful experience, but I did. And perhaps I shouldn't have told Alexia my feelings, especially considering how passionate she was about the subject, but I did. If I hadn't been in so much discomfort from the shingles, I probably would have been a little kinder, but I wasn't. From that one incident, however, part of the foundation of our marriage was shaken.

————

During the early months of Alexia's and my marriage, I had two meetings with the daughter of mine who had accused me of molesting her, but nothing was ever resolved. I felt so wounded, hurt, and embarrassed that it's hard to imagine. We had dinner both times. I tried to tell her that I loved her and would never do anything to harm her. My reassurance seemed to sink in at the time, but it didn't last. I really didn't know what to do; it was such a helpless feeling.

Otherwise, life was progressing very well. Alexia's parents came often and always stayed with us for several nights, which made my wife very happy. Tiffany joined a sorority at Ole Miss, where she thrived.

Jordan was doing well in high school. She was secretary of the National Honor Society, captained the volleyball team, became homecoming queen at Norcross High, and spent substantial time with me, which made me very happy. Finally, things were working out. We also started participating in a small group Bible study as a part of the church's ministry program; we actually studied the Bible. I loved it—as did Alexia.

One Sunday, while all of this was going on, Dick called. He was very upset about a conversation he had just had with Danny, who was now back in Boston, teaching classes at various institutions—classes no one else wanted to teach. Dick said, "Jack, do you have a couple of minutes? I need to talk to you." He told me that while he and Nancy were having lunch with Danny in Boston the previous day, Danny had been particularly vitriolic, saying horrible things about me, Murph, and, of course, our father. But that wasn't the worst of it. Dick's voice was utterly distressed when he reported that Danny had told him a particularly hurtful story.

"What story?"

Dick took a deep breath. "Danny said that Ellen got drunk one time when I wasn't at home, and she asked him—*no, begged him*—to screw her," Dick, close to tears, told me in a quivering voice. Pausing to calm himself, Dick added, "Danny said he refused because he wouldn't do something like that to me."

This was low. And particularly low because Ellen, Dick's second wife, had been deceased for many years and was deeply loved by Dick.

"Do you think that really happened, Jacky?" Dick asked, again in a trembling voice.

"No," I said adamantly. There was no way. Ellen loved Dick, and Danny's spite and cruelty wouldn't work on me any longer.

"Ellen hated Danny," Dick reasoned. "She couldn't stand him."

"I know, Dick. This is just like Danny—being as cruel as he can. Think about it: Have you ever known him to pass up sex—regardless of the consequences—with anybody, ever?"

"No," he said as the truth started to dawn on him. "I haven't."

"Have you ever known him to restrain himself because it might hurt another person?" I asked.

"No."

"Neither have I," I continued. "Something happened, but it's much more likely that he made a pass at her and she said, 'No.'"

"Do you really think so?" he asked, seeking as much reassurance as possible.

"I'm certain of it."

After we ended the call, I thought about what had been said. I was convinced that Danny was the one who initiated the incident with Ellen. When he told Dick he "wouldn't do something like that," I knew that wasn't true.

But I was deeply troubled by my brother's truly sinister behavior. I knew he was a cunning, explosive man, but this was a new low—even for him.

Chapter 51

I Didn't Have a Clue

The following spring, Dick's two sons got married, and each wedding was a lavish affair. David, the elder, married first, and the Watts family from Georgia was well represented. At some point during the wedding, Jean and Victoria came together to chat privately, and Victoria told me later that the conversation turned to the molestation controversy in our family.

Victoria had asked if she thought I was capable of doing such a thing to my daughter, and Jean immediately answered that she knew it wasn't me. Hearing this later, I was not surprised by the response, but I was grateful for her affirmation.

Looking keenly at Jean as she filled her glass with red wine, Victoria then asked, "Who do you think it was, then, Aunt Jean?"

Jean's response was to just shrug her shoulders, so Victoria added in a small voice, "I think it was Uncle Danny."

"Danny?"

"Yes," Victoria said. Continuing, she asked, "What do you think, Jean? Do you think Danny is capable of molesting us?"

After a moment, Jean said, "I remember more than forty years ago when Danny slapped and shook his nine-month-old son, while in the crib, because he wouldn't stop crying. A man who would do that could do anything." She added, "Yes, I'm sorry to say it, but I think he's capable of molesting you—absolutely."

Victoria looked at Jean and simply nodded her head as aunt and niece deepened their bond. Neither spoke for a few minutes as both sipped their Merlot, contemplating what had just transpired.

When I left to return to Georgia after the wedding—as yet unaware of this conversation—Victoria and her family remained to visit Jean and her family. While at Jean's house, the molestation issue became a major topic of conversation. Victoria confided in Jean, telling her about a tall, blond man coming into the bedroom, when she was a child, and molesting her. Jean, of course, was keenly interested and wanted to explore what Victoria remembered. They talked at length about what had happened. Victoria was candid with Jean, who quickly became a supportive listener and trusted confidante.

Several weeks after returning to Atlanta, Victoria called Jean, distraught about what she remembered and upset about what she still couldn't remember completely. Jean's repeated efforts to calm Victoria had a hypnotic effect on Victoria as additional memories of what had happened in I.V. flooded Victoria's mind. As these memories surfaced, Victoria once again was overcome with distressing feelings. Understandably, her emotional state was quite fragile.

Jean finally said, "Victoria, calm down. Take deep breaths." After helping Victoria regain her composure, Jean added, "You need help, and I mean today. Victoria, let's get you some professional help, someone who can help you remember what happened and how to deal with it."

Victoria agreed and went to a therapist named Deborah to sort it all out. For a while, Victoria went to therapy several times a week—then less often. She had to; what she remembered troubled her that much.

When she was able, we had several lengthy, detailed conversations about what she remembered. In the first conversation, she said, "Dad, I know who the tall, blond man was who molested me."

"Who?"

"It was Uncle Danny."

"What?" I didn't believe it at first.

"It was Uncle Danny. I'm sure of it."

"When did he have the opportunity?"

"When you were gone on business trips in California," she said. "Do you remember him coming when you weren't home?"

"Yes," I said. Then a thought hit me. "But Danny isn't tall. He's shorter than I am. And his hair isn't really blond."

"It's blond in the front, Dad." Continuing, she said, "And he was tall to me. Remember, I was five."

"Right, that makes sense," I said. I knew Victoria wouldn't lie, but this was something I had never considered. No matter how malicious my brother had been, I would have never imagined that he was capable of molesting my children. But from that moment forward, I couldn't stop thinking about it.

Danny did make several surprise visits to California in 1974—in addition to two planned trips. He came all the way from Boston to see us, something he had never done before. But this still seemed so bizarre and difficult to swallow. And what about Mona? Where was she when all this happened?

I woke up in the middle of the night with complete clarity. Suddenly, everything clicked into place, and I was certain I knew what had happened.

Chapter 52

In Love with Being in Love

In subsequent conversations, Victoria slowly revealed some of the specifics about what happened to her when she was so young. I knew I needed to hear it all from her, but she was reluctant to discuss her experiences openly and freely. This forced me to be patient because each attempt by me to push her proved to be counterproductive. She had to reveal the specifics at her own pace, which I learned to accept. This is often the way it is with kids who have been molested. Some of her memories were graphic and detailed. When Victoria explained them, I was deeply disturbed; I still am.

———

As all of this was unfolding, I developed some large red bumps on my legs that spread to my arms, back, and chest. They were sore and depleted me of nearly all my energy. All I could do was sit in front of the TV; I was exhausted all the time. Alexia was very concerned about my overall health and had been during our entire marriage. She purchased numerous supplements from a health-food store for me to take—six times a day. It seemed like all I did was swallow pills. Nevertheless, my condition continued to deteriorate. I finally said I was going to a doctor, knowing it would cause trouble with my wife.

After my initial examination, the internist was so alarmed that she sent me to a dermatologist for an immediate biopsy of the red bumps. Several days later, I was called into the dermatologist's office to discuss the results. He informed me the bumps were from an acute allergic reaction to something in my system. With Alexia standing beside me, the doctor inquired, "Are you taking any over-the-counter health-food supplements?"

"Yes, lots of them," I said.

"That can't be what it is. They're all good for him," Alexia challenged.

"That's not necessarily true, Mrs. Watts," the doctor explained calmly. "In fact, an allergic reaction to supplements is something we see every day." He then asked me what I was taking. When I told him Alexia was giving me colostrums harvested from New Zealand sheep, he gave me an open-mouthed gasp.

That was all Alexia needed. She pitched a small fit right there in the office. As the doctor and Alexia were going at it, his physician's assistant touched my arm lightly to get my attention. With obvious concern in her voice, she said, "Jack, it's unwise to take colostrums from a DNA group that's not your own. Stop taking those supplements, and the welts will go away."

I never took the supplements again. Within a few days, the bumps started to subside, and they were gone within a couple of weeks. My strength, which had been significantly diminished, returned to me, and I felt wonderful.

There was a price to pay with Alexia, however, because the subject of my lack of support for alternative medicine returned. At this point she asked for a divorce, which she announced as "God's will" to the members of our small group Bible study—much to their shock and horror.

In her mind, I had broken a wedding vow. That's how important her commitment to alternative health care was. At the same time, I had returned to complete health by simply discontinuing all the supplements she had given me, but this didn't seem to matter to Alexia.

I didn't want another divorce, but I couldn't remain unhealthy just to please her either. Still, things settled down for nearly a year, because we really were very compatible and genuinely fond of each other.

If I had been as committed to the marriage as I should have been, however, I would have been more vigorous in my efforts to ensure its survival, but my dedication was lukewarm at best. So was hers. For me, being married—versus being single—was important because it seemed normal, while being single didn't. If you're single, people ask questions about your past, which I wanted to avoid at all costs. It was just too embarrassing and I didn't want to be forthcoming. If you're married, that's all that counts. It makes you impervious to the legalistic scrutiny of self-righteous Christians, which I needed personally and professionally, especially being employed by so many ministries. Obviously this was flawed thinking, but that's exactly how I felt.

Truthfully, I was in love with the idea of being in love with a beautiful Christian woman—someone who would be a real helpmate and partner in life—but I was not in love with Alexia, not really. And I couldn't support her passion for alternative health care. To me, it was a little wacky, and whenever she talked about it, she was more than a little wacky. Consequently I passively allowed events to take their course, rather than provide the stabilizing leadership I promised in our wedding vows. Because my enthusiasm and passion for her evaporated, she must have felt emotionally abandoned, which she was.

Alexia finally decided to leave. I had planned to go on a business trip to Michigan on a Monday morning right before Halloween when I discovered late Sunday night that Alexia had movers coming in the morning—just hours after I left for the airport. I thought, *Here we go again.*

Chapter 53

Exactly the Opposite

The following morning in the fall of 2005, I got up, showered, dressed, packed for a business trip, kissed Alexia good-bye, and left for Michigan—as planned—for three days of meetings. While I was away, my wife of four years, with the help of her daughter and her sisters, packed up her belongings—plus a little more—and left. Everybody knew she was leaving, except for my family and me. I felt like Billy Crystal in *When Harry Met Sally*. The movers knew before I did. It was painful, sad, and tragic, but most of all, it was surprising. I didn't think it would happen; I really didn't, but I should have. Nobody wants to be married to a man who has become apathetic about the relationship, which was exactly how I felt.

Alexia wanted me to be gung ho for alternative medicine and I wasn't, but I simply couldn't imagine she would divorce me over it. As the events unfolded, for a long time, I wouldn't acknowledge my role in the failure of the marriage. Instead, I chose to blame her, self-righteously taking the high ground, which I really didn't deserve.

When I returned from the trip, my house was a mess, having been completely dismantled, and she was gone. Her abrupt departure hurt everyone—especially Jordan, who opened her heart completely to Alexia. I think Jordan was hurt more than anybody.

Alexia left at Halloween, and I was served divorce papers the Sunday evening before Thanksgiving at 10:00 P.M. Once again, a policeman was standing at my front door. It was a devastating blow, bringing a sense of finality to our relationship. It was over, and I felt the pain acutely. I also was embarrassed. I didn't want anybody to know I was going through another divorce. I couldn't believe it was happening—*not again*!

But it was. She wanted the divorce immediately, so she didn't contest a thing. What was mine was mine; what was hers was hers—period. We didn't even retain lawyers.

———————

Once again, I went into "soul-searching" mode, but this time it was different. I knew what had happened and why. Now sober for more than a decade, wisdom had begun to enter my heart, providing much-needed clarity, maturity, and acceptance.

Finally, I was thinking and acting like an adult. I was lonely for quite a while, but I got over it. My life became peaceful, even pleasant, and I was able to enjoy the simplicity of my solitude. It was a relief to realize that I no longer required a woman to validate me or make me feel whole. I knew I would be fine by myself, and I was. I could function much better than I ever had before. Although I would have preferred to have a relationship, being alone felt normal—at least most of the time.

My biggest problem was dealing with my embarrassment. I was absolutely mortified. Being divorced so many times is difficult to deal with and nearly impossible to explain. It made me appear so unstable and flaky, and although I could understand the perception, I genuinely believed I was exactly the opposite.

Chapter 54

Stand Up for the Truth

Over time, Victoria had been slowly telling me small details about Danny's molestation—each detail more revealing than the last. I knew that eventually I would need to confront Danny, which I decided to do in February 2007.

With my goal established, I called Dick, saying, "I'm coming to Boston to confront Danny." Waiting a moment for him to take in what I said, I added, "And I want your help."

After a short pause, Dick answered, "Are you sure you want to do that?"

"I'm sure."

After thinking about it for a minute, he said, "Okay, let's do it."

As soon as I announced my plan, numerous people—especially Victoria and Jordan—tried to counsel me to abandon my decision, saying it would be fruitless and possibly even dangerous. I understood their rationale, and from their perspective, I also realized why they thought my plan would be unsuccessful. Each told me they thought my chances of obtaining a confession from Danny were slim to none.

I also doubted I would get an admission of guilt from Danny. He was far too enmeshed in his depravity and narcissism to admit guilt about anything. Additionally, because his behavior was so volatile and unpredictable, numerous family members, including Jordan, also were concerned for my safety.

But I knew that confronting Danny was my duty and my responsibility, regardless of the fact that more than three decades had passed since his offenses against my family and me. I had to stand up for the truth and for my daughters. I would be unable to live with myself if I shirked this responsibility.

———

Now that I had decided to confront Danny, I hoped Victoria would finish putting the pieces of the story together for me. I asked her if we could have a joint session with her therapist, Deborah. Before dealing with Danny, I wanted to be crystal clear I had my facts straight. Because verbalizing her memories was so difficult, Victoria was hesitant but finally consented, and we had the session. It lasted nearly three hours.

After some initial small talk, Victoria looked at Deborah, took a deep breath, turned to me, and began. She said, "Dad, when I was five, Uncle Danny came to visit us when you were away on a business trip. I didn't know he was coming, and Connie and Brenn didn't know either. He just showed up at the front door and slept on the couch in the living room. He did this more than once. Do you remember that?"

"Yes, I do."

I could tell Victoria was having difficulty discussing this with me, her father, but her therapist, who was very supportive, gave her a reassuring nod to continue.

Victoria proceeded, "One time, when he was there, I woke up and heard Mom and Uncle Danny talking in the living room with someone who came to the front door."

Victoria continued, "That night, as Mom was introducing Uncle Danny to the people who came in, the noise from their conversation startled me. For some reason, I felt uncomfortable, so I got up and went into your bedroom. I got into bed on your side and fell asleep. Mom came to bed a little while later and let me sleep beside her."

I nodded as she spoke, remembering that it wasn't unusual for the girls to sleep in our bed, especially when I was out of town.

Continuing, Victoria said, "After Mom was in bed, Uncle Danny came in and gave her something to drink. He said something like, 'Here, Mona, drink this. It'll stop your headache.' She drank it and went to sleep. Some time after that, he came back into the room and got on top of Mom, and they moaned for a little while as the bed rocked back and forth. They thought I was asleep, but I wasn't. As little as I was, I didn't have any idea what was going on, but I didn't like it. It made me feel very uncomfortable, but I didn't say anything. After a while, Uncle Danny got off of Mom and left."

When she said this, I was sickened. I assumed that Mona and Danny had had sex—that part of the story had become clear to me—but I had no idea Victoria was in the bed when it happened. Neither had I suspected Danny of drugging Mona, which undoubtedly impaired her memory of the incident.

Victoria went on, "A little while later, Uncle Danny came back into the bedroom and lifted the covers. I can still remember the cold on my back— as the cool night air hit me and made me shiver.

"He stopped, looked directly at Mom, and said, 'You pathetic snatch. Did you think you could satisfy me?' Those were his exact words. I can remember it like it was yesterday."

With moistening eyes and trembling hands, I asked, "Did your mother say anything to Danny when he said that?"

"No," Victoria said.

"Do you think she heard him?"

"I don't know, Dad, but I know he said it." Looking at me, she added, "I didn't know what it meant. That's what made me remember it so vividly."

Apparently Mona just stayed in bed during the entire episode, either too scared or too sedated to move—probably the latter. At this point Victoria paused, and I became overwhelmed with sorrow. I started to cry, and I couldn't stop. As I wept, the therapist and Victoria sat silently, allowing me nearly five minutes to regain my composure.

What she told me didn't make me angry. It wasn't like that at all. Instead I felt an overwhelming sense of loss—a loss that could never be restored, not for any of us. I also wondered if Danny could really be *that* evil. It was difficult for me to comprehend such depravity.

As I wiped my eyes and blew my nose, with trembling hands, I nodded for Victoria to continue.

She said, "Dad, looking back at this as an adult, I believe Mom gave herself to Uncle Danny to protect us, but it didn't work."

"Do you really think so?"

She nodded. "I've come to believe that Mom was probably molested herself when she was a girl, which explains why she responded to the entire incident like a little girl and not like a mother. That's why I think she wouldn't tell you about it and has remained silent all these years. She doesn't have the emotional tools to cope with her complicity to what Uncle Danny did."

Later, after I thought about it, I remembered Mona telling me about a time when she was a little girl at the movies—perhaps seven or even a little younger. While sitting there, a man asked her if she wanted some popcorn. When she reached into the bag, it wasn't popcorn she found. The man told her he "would get her" if she ever told her parents, which she never did.

Victoria continued, "Dad, it's been more than thirty-five years since Uncle Danny molested me, and Mom still can't admit what happened. She's never told any of us the truth about her part in covering up Uncle Danny's behavior either. Because she has kept quiet for so long, she thinks she has no choice but to maintain her silence."

"Maybe," I said. I realized how difficult Mona's position was. At the same time, I thought about how harmful her silence has been over the years; but I chose not to bring that into the conversation. I wanted to hear everything. This was not the time to scrutinize Mona's behavior, so I nodded for Victoria to continue.

She said, "None of us told you about it. How could we? We were little girls and didn't know what was happening—let alone how to describe it. Mom certainly didn't tell you either."

After looking out the window and thinking for a moment, Victoria said, "One time, I do remember asking you what a snatch was. Do you remember that?"

"No," I said.

"You never connected my question with Uncle Danny's visits. I didn't go into detail. That's the closest I ever came to telling you. After that, I eventually forgot or suppressed the whole incident.

"When all of this happened, we didn't really know what Uncle Danny was doing to us. Before he came, we had no sexual awareness, so everything he did was confusing. We had no reference point. We were so little—but we didn't like it. Connie protested, Dad. When she resisted him, Uncle Danny hit her with a closed fist and knocked her out."

"What!" I said, as my muscles tensed and I became angry. I wanted to get up and pace, but I couldn't. I needed to calm myself and pay attention to what Victoria was saying. This was the information I had sought for so long—presented clearly and cohesively, so I had to sit there and remain focused. I took a deep breath and forced myself to keep my emotions under control.

"Uncle Danny came more than once to molest us, Dad," Victoria continued. "On another occasion, Uncle Danny put a pillow over Connie's face and held it there until she passed out and finally complied with his desires. As a little girl, none of this made any sense to me.

"After all of this happened the first time, Mom called us into the bedroom. It was just before you came home. I remember sitting on the comforter in your bedroom. It always made me feel warm and safe, and I liked to rub it between my thumb and forefinger. As we sat on the bed, Mom said, 'Your daddy will be home in a few minutes. You can tell Daddy about running through the sprinkler, doing gymnastics on the lawn, staying with Uncle Danny while Mommy got her hair done, going to the park to swing, and having lots of fun. But you can't tell him anything else.'"

Again, I was finding it hard to sit still, but I knew I had to.

Victoria continued, "After Mom said this, we all nodded our heads and promised not to tell you anything. Mom explained to us carefully and slowly, 'You can't tell Daddy anything else because Daddy might get mad and leave us. If that happened, *we would never see him again.*'"

At this, I groaned audibly—exasperated by Mona's betrayal.

"When you came home a few minutes after our conversation with Mom, you were really glad to see all of us, and you were happy to see Uncle Danny, too. Do you remember that?"

"Yes, I remember that vividly," I said.

"When you came in, you picked me up, and I remember asking you, 'Are you going to leave, Daddy?'

"You just looked at me and laughed. Then you said, 'No, Pooh. I just got home.'" I smiled because I frequently called Victoria "Pooh." Winnie the Pooh was her favorite childhood character. She loved being called Pooh, she still does.

Reflecting for a moment, Victoria added, "I can't remember if it was on that same visit or an earlier one—probably earlier, but Mom came into our bedroom to make the beds. When she bent down, she noticed some stains on the sheets. She put her nose right next to the stains and smelled them. Then she took the sheets off the bed and held them up to the window to examine the stains more closely."

Continuing, Victoria added, "Mom put them down and left. A few minutes later, the lady from across the courtyard came into the bedroom with Mom, and they looked at the stains as Mom held them up to the light from the window again. The lady was alarmed and said, 'Could Jack have done this?'

"Mom said, 'No, he's been away all week at a business meeting in Los Angeles.'

"I remember the woman was very concerned about the stains and so was Mom. I think Uncle Danny had gone back to Boston by then, but I'm not sure. That same day, Mom took us to see the doctor. It wasn't our regular pediatrician. I knew that because the office was on the side of a mountain with a view of the ocean. I remember how nice it looked. The doctor gave me a vaginal examination."

After pausing for a long moment, she continued, "As I was seated in the waiting room, the doctor talked to Mom on the other side of the room. I remember how distressed Mom was about what he said. When he was finished, she shouted, 'No!' At that point, Mom became extremely upset, and the doctor had to give her some pills and a glass of water to calm her down."

I wanted to ask Victoria a million questions but didn't. I just let her continue—fearful that any interruption might prevent her from completing her story.

"I also remember the nurse saying, 'The best you can hope for is to forget everything and have no memory of this.' Nothing happened after that—except I remember the lady from across the courtyard telling me to never drink anything Uncle Danny gave us—never, under any circumstances.

"Another time, when Uncle Danny came for an unannounced visit, we weren't home at the time. When Mom saw his rental car in the driveway, she backed out and drove off real fast. We didn't go home until you came back from your business trip. We kept asking Mom when we were going home, but she wouldn't take us as long as you were out of town. It seemed to me we were away quite awhile. All of us kept asking Mom to take us home, but she wouldn't budge—not as long as you were gone."

"Thank God for that," I said. "I didn't have a clue, Victoria." Looking at her, I said, "When your mom went into that two-year-long depression shortly after Danny left, I never connected the dots. I should have, but it never occurred to me."

"I know, Dad," Victoria said as she straightened her shoulders a bit. "There's something else. Years later, I remember when you were at the foot of the stairs in our house in North Atlanta and we were all standing at the top when Connie told you that if anyone had to leave, we wanted it to be you and not Mom. You remember that, right?"

"Of course, I have never forgotten it," I said.

"Dad, you had no way of knowing what happened shortly before Connie's announcement. Mom called my sisters and me into the bedroom and said, 'I can leave for good in just a few minutes if you want me to.'"

Collecting herself, Victoria continued, "We told her we didn't want her to leave. That was a terrifying thought for us. We were teenagers and didn't want our mom to move out. So Mom manipulated Connie into saying what she did. When you walked into the house, Mom said very softly, 'Connie, isn't there something you want to say to your father?' With that, Connie stepped forward and spoke. That announcement changed all of our lives, but Connie was manipulated into it, Dad. It wasn't her idea."

I shook my head, appalled by this unexpected revelation.

"There's one more thing, Dad."

"Oh, boy." I sighed.

"During a conversation with Mom a few years ago, I asked her if she keyed your Cadillac at the gymnastics meet when I was in high school. When I asked her, she squirmed in her seat for a few seconds, but she finally said, 'Yes, I did it.'"

Victoria continued, "I asked her, 'Why would you do something like that, Mom?'"

"'I don't know,' Mom said. 'It seemed like a good idea at the time,'" Victoria said, giving me a small smile as she did. "But all I cared about at the time was that nobody was there to see me stick my routine on the beam! My performance won the meet for Alpharetta High, and neither of you were there to see it."

When she said this, I began to laugh, and Victoria and the therapist started laughing, too. In the midst of all of the unfolding tragedy, this provided much-needed comic relief.

After the meeting concluded, I found it difficult to drive home and nearly impossible to sleep. I was unnerved and deeply disturbed by the enormity of what had been revealed. Even though I had heard bits and pieces before, it was upsetting to have it spelled out so thoroughly.

The meeting ended on a Wednesday evening at 6:00 P.M. The following morning, I left bright and early to fly to Boston at 8:30 A.M.—armed with the truth and prepared for whatever was to come with my impending confrontation with my brother Danny.

Chapter 55

"Secret Friend"

As I flew to Boston, my thoughts were focused on the conversation with Victoria. I thought about Connie, who had been especially subjected to Danny's violent brutality. Perhaps her uncle's assault was why she became a bully toward her sisters Victoria and Brenn—just like Danny had been a bully to Dick and me. Even Connie's stealing from me was no different than Danny's stealing from Mom. Each felt entitled to do so, never acknowledging their actions for what they were: theft.

I began to feel far more compassionate toward Connie than I had in the past. Although she was ultimately responsible for her actions, her betrayal became easier to comprehend. I finally understood what was behind it—a horrific childhood trauma.

When I arrived at Logan International Airport, it was a cold winter day in late February. I rented a car, drove to the suburbs, and met Dick for lunch. We visited for a short time and discussed our plan. Danny had done a masterful job of disappearing. He had made it clear that he never wanted to see any of his siblings again, so none of us had a clue about how to contact him. We had only one lead.

As we played a game of amateur sleuth, it reminded me of the make-believe adventures Dick and I had had when we were little boys. In spite of the seriousness of the situation, or maybe to cope with it, we had a lot of fun as we searched for Danny. We knew where his good friend lived, and we also knew he lived with him periodically. Perhaps he would even be at his house and our job would be easy.

Driving to the guy's residence, we walked up to the front door and knocked. Nobody was home, and there were no signs that Danny might live there either. With no other leads, we went back to his house at least four more times that afternoon and early evening. Finally we decided to simply leave a note and ask him to call. After that, we went to Dick's house, nearly forty minutes away. A return call from him was our best chance to find Danny.

He didn't return the call that evening, and it snowed several inches in the middle of the night. When I drove back to his house the next morning, I could see there was a place in the driveway where there was no snow, so I knew that a car had been parked there overnight. The note also had been taken from the mailbox, so I knew we had made contact. Both of these signs were encouraging.

After Dick finished work, he met me at a coffee shop, and we talked about what to do next. While we discussed options, Dick's cell phone rang. It was Danny's friend. Dick told him I was in town, and we set up a time to have lunch the following day. Dick said that Danny's buddy sounded glad that we had called.

We met at a local restaurant the following afternoon and had a lunch that ended up being pleasant. We learned that the guy had recently returned from his second, month-long stay at a rehabilitation facility for alcohol abuse. Tragically, he had already started drinking again, in spite of having been diagnosed with hepatitis C, which requires complete abstinence. Clearly his alcoholism was out of control, and my heart went out to him. Without dramatic change, which was unlikely, his future would be grim and short.

After a lengthy visit, he gave us a number where we could reach Danny. We had him! Using the reverse white pages, we quickly obtained an address for him in a small town on the North Shore. The next morning, Dick went to work, and I set out to find Danny. With the windchill near zero, I was reminded of why I didn't miss living in New England.

When I arrived at Danny's home, I stopped and reflected at what I saw. He didn't live in a nice house—far from it. He lived in government-subsidized housing. It was small, dirty, dismal, and depressing—far from the pomp and splendor he always thought should be his station in life. I learned later that he was living on welfare and food stamps. Without family or friends, Danny had relegated himself to a dingy state of subsistence—a prisoner of his own devices.

I knocked on his door, holding my nose to ward off the foul odors, which seemed to ooze out of every crack and corner of the building. He

wasn't at home, which didn't surprise me. From there, I went to six different gyms looking for him before I discovered where he worked out. But he
wasn't there either. I searched the entire day without spotting him.

The next day I went to Dick's house, where Sunday dinner had been
planned with Jean and her family. Three siblings were together—with
Danny being conspicuously absent. As I reflected on this, it dawned on me
that he had spent his life being unwanted: resented when he came into the
world, alienated throughout most of his adult life, and unwelcome with his
family in his senior years.

We sat at the table for three hours, allowing ourselves to relax a bit,
laughing and joking and reminiscing. Embracing everybody warmly as I
left in the early evening, I drove to the North Shore one final time to try
to find Danny. Dick and I told Danny's friend I would be leaving Sunday
morning instead of Monday. If he had warned him I was looking for him,
Danny would have felt safe by Sunday evening. This was my chance.

As I drove up to his housing project, I could see that our minor deception had paid off. I was a little disappointed that Danny's friend had given
away our scheme, but it didn't matter. A light was shining in his apartment,
and his TV was on. He was there! I knocked but he did not answer. He must
have seen me approaching. I knocked repeatedly for several minutes—like I
had years earlier when I confronted Mona at Milton's apartment. Finally, I
called him on the phone. He answered—probably because he didn't realize
I had his number.

"Hello," he said.

"Danny, this is Jack."

"What do you want?" he challenged.

"I want to talk to you for a few minutes." I added, "Would you be willing to open the door and talk to me?"

"No. I don't want to talk to you ever again. You're nothing to me," he
hissed. "I've cut you out of my life."

"I've come a long way to talk with you, Danny," I responded. "Please, let
me in."

"No, I don't care what you've done," he said with a snarl. "Don't ever call
me again, fat boy." With that, he hung up.

I redialed, but he didn't answer. As I stood there just a few feet from
him in the bitter cold, I realized I had accomplished part of my goal: I
had confronted him. From his perspective, I had invaded his world. I had
rattled him. It was a start.

In that moment, I realized that he knew I knew the truth. He was afraid of being confronted. Ultimately I know that he is as confined and chained by his behavior as if he were in prison.

Realizing the bondage he was in, I walked to my car and drove away, just as I had years earlier when I left Mona to spend her days in ignominy with Milton Bingham.

As I drove away, I felt at peace. I had done my best. The rest was up to God.

I thought about the choices Danny had made in life—as well as their consequences. Because of his egregious behavior, he is alone, completely alienated from those who should be close to him. He is bitter, angry, unfulfilled, and friendless. Nobody cares whether he lives or dies—not really. Truly, the consequences of his actions have produced a living death.

While driving back, I called Dick and told him what had happened. After I finished my narrative, Dick said, "Danny is a decrepit old man who is financially, morally, and spiritually bankrupt. He doesn't want to face you because he doesn't want to remember."

"Yeah, that's what I think, too," I said.

About thirty minutes later, Jean called—after having spoken to Dick. When I answered, she said, "Hello, fat boy." With that, we both broke into fits of laughter at the ludicrous insult Danny had launched at me.

The next morning, I left for Georgia amid another snowstorm. While flying home, I had an idea. I had Danny's phone number, and I devised a plan for another confrontation. There was one more thing I had to communicate to Danny.

Waiting several weeks before contacting him again, I called early one evening. He picked up the phone on the second ring.

"Hello," he said.

Without hesitation, I spoke, "Danny, I know what you did—exactly what you did."

"What?" he said sheepishly, consumed with apprehension. I could hear in his voice that he had finally been made vulnerable. He sounded scared.

"I know what you did in 1974, Danny, and *I forgive you.*"

He didn't respond for at least five seconds. Finally he said, "I'm a professor, and you're nothing. You're not at my intellectual level. You're a moron, and I want nothing to do with you. Never call me again." With that, he hung up the phone. At least he didn't call me "fat boy" again.

I tried to call the next day but he had changed his cell number.

Shortly after I hung up with Danny, Jordan called me. I told her about the entire conversation with her uncle Danny. Jordan said, "That five seconds of silence tells you everything you want to know, Daddy. He's as guilty as sin."

"I know" was all I said in response.

As Victoria, Jordan, and I discussed my encounter with Danny, each pressed me for every detail I could remember, asking me hundreds of questions—most of which never occurred to me. I've always thought how amazing it is that women can do this. They think of things men never do. Nevertheless, I was glad I had forgiven him. It freed me from the past, which still enslaves him.

———

Several weeks after my phone conversation with Danny, he left Dick a voice message, that said:

> *Dick, this is Danny Watts. Jack called . . . raving about something—he was going to forgive me. . . . I have no idea. I haven't seen Mona since I was maybe twenty-eight. He's really sick. I'm very happy to be away from all of you. You won't know when I die because none of you will be alerted—not that you care, but that's fine, too. . . . I don't want anything to do with you people. Please, please . . . stay out of my life.*

After listening to Danny's message, which said he hadn't seen Mona since he was twenty-eight, I looked at my photo album and found a picture of Danny sunbathing in my backyard in I.V. He was sitting on a lawn chair with a pillow in his lap, and the girls were playing in the background. The date on the photo was April 1974, when Danny was thirty-nine—not twenty-eight.

I scanned the image and e-mailed it to everybody in the family. When Victoria saw the photo, it triggered additional memories for her. Being as forthright as I had ever seen her, Victoria responded to the photo by e-mailing her mother and copying the rest of us. In the e-mail, which made me overflow with pride at her maturity and grace, Victoria wrote,

> *Dad kindly thinks he's protecting us by using the word molested, but the correct word is rape. Danny used that same pillow to hide his "secret*

friend, who did a magic trick." He used the same pillow to suffocate us to the point of passing out; then he raped us. . . .

Enough time has passed. Enough lies and manipulations have been told to cover these events. Let's spend this next decade in forgiveness and healing.

I know everything that happened and am willing to help you all. I have dredged through excruciating and painful memories, even some at the point of hypnosis, but only feel stronger after facing my fear and shame. . . .

Mom, it's time to tell the truth. There is no need to hide anymore. Your family will still love you. You were more heroic than you realize.

She concluded by saying that everyone will know the truth about "our family's past."

—————

As I thought about my older brother, who had been my hero when I was a little boy, I wondered how he could have fallen so far. I wondered what was behind such pathology. What caused it? His behavior seemed so bizarre that I wondered what grievance could create such aberrant behavior.

Could it be that Danny grew resentful toward me all those years ago when I confronted him while he was assaulting his wife, Erica, and kept him from nearly killing her? Could it be that he always resented the fact that my father had welcomed my birth and not his? Probably. Those factors—plus, I'm sure, several that I don't even know about—combined to make a person so hardened and dark that he seemed almost beyond the point of redemption.

I had my theories, but soon enough, I discovered more concrete answers to my questions, which came from a source I never would have imagined: my ninety-two-year-old paternal aunt, Sweetie Pie.

Chapter 56

"Get an Abortion"

In 2008, I decided to drive to Louisville to visit Sweetie Pie, my dad's younger sister. Although I hadn't seen her since his death in 1976, she knew that I was trying to discover the truth about the origins of our family dysfunction, particularly regarding Danny. Having been recently widowed, Sweetie Pie was now living with her daughter in a suburb of Louisville, not that far from Atlanta.

When I arrived, I was surprised by how spry and lucid she was. An accomplished artist, in some ways, she hadn't lost a beat. After a few minutes to get reacquainted, she surprised me by saying, "Jack, I admire you for your commitment to pursue the truth. Because I know how important this is to you, I'm going to tell you a story I've never shared with anyone—a story I was certain I would take to my grave."

She had my undivided attention. "What story?"

"The truth about how your mother and father got married," she said.

"Oh," I said, a little disappointed. "I already know about that."

"No, you don't," she insisted.

Surprised, I motioned with a simple nod for her to proceed.

Sitting straight in her chair, Sweetie Pie said, "When your father was a young man, he played in a band and loved the wild side of life. He played the trombone. He was very handsome, and the girls fell for him easily. He had any girl he wanted, and he had a string of them."

Smiling, she continued, "He got involved with one girl and got her pregnant."

"I know, Sweetie Pie; it was my mom."

"No, it was another girl," she corrected me.

"What?"

Sweetie Pie nodded. "Her name was Maxine, and when she turned up pregnant, she assumed your dad would marry her. But he didn't want to get married. He said to Maxine that he didn't want to marry her, and he wasn't going to raise her 'little bastard' either. Maxine loved your dad and was crushed when he said this, but he wouldn't budge. He was so cruel to that poor girl."

"What happened?" I asked.

"Your dad told her to get an abortion, which was rare in those days—and dangerous. It also was expensive, and your dad didn't have any money. He begged our mother to give him some money, but this was during the worst part of the Great Depression. She didn't have two nickels to rub together. She told him, 'You should have thought about the consequences before you had sex with her,' which infuriated your father. He backed her against the wall—his own mother—and hit the wall. He knocked a hole right through it. I started to cry because I thought he was going to hit Mother, too. He didn't hit her but she was afraid he would, so she gave him the money. The following weekend, Mother and I took Maxine across the river to East St. Louis, where there was a nurse who performed the procedure. I was only twelve, but I remember the ride home like it was yesterday. Maxine sat in the backseat with a blank stare that still sends chills up my spine. That poor woman! Your dad never even bothered to ask about Maxine. He didn't care two hoots about her after she got pregnant."

"What a story," I said, thanking her, but she cut me off before I could say another word.

"There's more," Sweetie Pie said. "Less than a year later, Bill got another girl pregnant—not your mother."

"Are you serious?"

She nodded that she was. "I can't even remember the girl's name; it's been so long, but it was the same story. Your dad refused to marry her and told her to get an abortion. This time, however, Mother wouldn't give him a dime—even though he begged her. She said, 'Are you going to knock another hole in the wall, son, or are you going to knock a hole in me?'"

"Did he hit her?" I asked.

"No, but that poor girl, who thought she was going to be a wife and mother, had to pay for her own abortion. Your dad didn't help her at all."

"I can't believe this," I said, shaking my head in dismay.

"It's true," Sweetie Pie said. "And when your father got your mother

pregnant a year later, he said the same thing to her. He refused to marry
her and said he wanted nothing to do with the little bastard she was carrying. But your mom was different than the other girls. She said, 'We'll see
about that!' She was Catholic and refused to even consider the possibility
of having an abortion. She insisted that he marry her, but he absolutely
refused. Then she informed her four older brothers about her situation,
telling them what your father's intentions were. The next night, they found
your father and beat him within an inch of his life."

"They literally beat him up?"

"Yes, they did."

"Good for them," I said. I was proud of my uncles for standing up for
Mom. It reminded me of when I had stood up for my sister when Timmy
Brinson molested her. I knew exactly how Murph's brothers felt. My dad
was always a bully, but like all bullies, he was a coward at heart.

Sweetie Pie reached over and held my hand. After a short pause, she
continued, "From then on, your dad was scared to death of Mary's brothers. When one of them came around—especially your uncle Jack—your dad
would always find some reason to leave. And after they knocked some sense
into him, your father agreed to marry your mother, but he never wanted
the child—your older brother, Danny. Your dad always considered Danny
to be in the way—an undesired nuisance. He blamed Danny for ruining his
life."

I knew that Danny wasn't a wanted child, but I didn't realize the depths
of my father's resentment. "Danny used to say he was unwanted all the
time," I responded. "I didn't realize how right he was."

"It was so sad, Jack," she said. "When I would babysit for Danny, your
dad was so cruel to him—even when he was a toddler."

I just shook my head. Because I hadn't yet been born, I never witnessed
my father's cruelty toward Danny when he was a young child, only when
he was older. It seems my father's resentment toward Danny never relented.
Surely this must have been when Danny's personality became twisted—as
a toddler.

Changing direction, Sweetie Pie added, "Having to get married like
that affected your mother as well. I really think it's the reason she started
drinking so heavily. In her heart, she knew your dad didn't love her and
didn't want to marry her."

I was heartsick, but the story connected all the missing dots for me.

Looking at my aunt with tears streaming down my face, I said, "Thank you for telling me the truth, Sweetie Pie. It explains so much."

"You're welcome, Jack."

As I drove back to Atlanta after lunch, I realized I had been given a gift. I had clarity about everything. My father's hostility toward Danny is where it all began. Danny was nothing but a bastard to my dad—never loved, never nurtured, and never a son. My father's heartlessness was much more cruel than I had ever realized. I also understood why my aunt had kept the story a secret for more than three-quarters of a century.

Chapter 57

Squirmed in Her Seat

After talking with Sweetie Pie, I decided that I also needed to confront Mona. Besides the fact that I desperately wanted to clear the air with her, I also needed her help. There were still several people in the family who believed that it was I who was the molester. I knew that if Mona would admit it was Danny, the doubt in the rest of the family's eyes would subside. To my pleasant surprise, after I contacted Mona, she agreed to meet with me.

We met at a coffee shop in Vinings, which was near my house. It was a beautiful spring day, and we sat outside. After some initial small talk, I said, "Mona, I've been to Boston to see Danny; and I want you to know that I have learned the details of what happened in I.V. when he came to visit in 1974. I want to talk with you about it because I need your help."

When she heard this, I had her undivided attention.

Gently I said, "I know you had sex with Danny. After Danny had intercourse with you, I also know he molested Victoria. I know he did it."

"What?" she said with obvious surprise. This meeting, incidentally, was before Victoria sent out that revealing e-mail, which explained Danny's behavior. "I never had sex with your brother," Mona said. She seemed genuine.

I was confused, but just listened as she continued.

"Back then, I wouldn't have done that. Later on, I did a lot of stuff, but back then, I didn't."

From the way she said it, I could tell she was being as forthright as she knew how to be. Victoria was right—Danny must had drugged her and she seemed to have no memory of the event. At the same time, I also remembered how often—and with what sincerity—Mona has lied to me for years about practically everything. Plus, hadn't she told the girls not to relay to me what had happened back then? She told them that they could tell me about the fun times they'd had with Danny but never the darker times—or I would leave and they would never see me again.

So what didn't she know, and what did she? I realized that although she was quick to defend herself about having sex with Danny, she didn't say anything about his molestation—a glaring omission.

Pressing her, I stated, "Mona, it was Danny who molested the girls, not me. And I believe *you know that*," I said with emphasis.

Mona just squirmed in her seat, fidgeted with her clothes, and avoided eye contact. What I said distressed her, clearly, but she didn't respond. She didn't say a word; she just sat there quietly, allowing the tension to mount. After a few minutes, she changed the subject and acted as if I hadn't addressed it in the first place.

Not wishing her unnecessary anguish, I relented. A few minutes later, however, I redirected the conversation back to my purpose of the meeting. "Mona, we have to discuss this. It was Danny, and not me. You know it wasn't me, and I need you to tell the girls the truth about what really happened. Will you help me?"

Again, she just sat silently, adjusting her posture and smoothing her clothes. The whole conversation was disconnected and very uncomfortable for me. I can't imagine how difficult it must have been for her. Finally she changed the subject again.

Within a few moments, I brought it up another time with the same result: dead silence. This happened four separate times in the course of our conversation, and Mona never said one word about my repeated allegation that Danny was the perpetrator, and I needed her help to set the record straight. With nothing left to discuss and no progress made, we said good-bye and left.

As I was driving home, I thought about our conversation. Although I hadn't obtained an admission, which disappointed me, I knew it was all I could do. Once again, I left the outcome in the hands of God.

But I did wonder about Mona's reaction or, more accurately, her lack of a reaction. When I told her I knew it was Danny, she never asked me a thing about it—not one question. She didn't ask, *How do you know? What makes you think it was Danny? Did he confess to it? What do we need to do—as parents—to help our daughters understand the truth? How can I help you resolve this? What proof do you have? Does Danny want to make amends for what he has done?*

Surely she would have asked these questions and dozens more if she was genuinely surprised by the assertion. Of course she knew the truth, but she just sat there, stoically maintaining her silence, which she has maintained since the Watergate era. Her fear of exposure, I knew, was too great for her to come to the light. It was obvious to me that I would never get a straight answer from her. I had to accept that.

Obviously I had hoped for a *Perry Mason* moment—with both Danny and Mona—but real life is not that simple. Both Danny and Mona are far too steeped in their emotional prisons to simply come forth with the truth. Each, for their own reasons, has a vested interest in perpetuating the darkness by covering up their behavior. But cover-ups don't work; darkness is always revealed by the light.

For Danny, not only will the time come when he has to stand before God to give an account, but he also has to live his fractured life in a corner, avoiding the truth and the light. He has no abundance or joy—just fear, bitterness, and alienation. The chains he has to carry make Marley's manacles of greed seem light by comparison. Covering up his crimes against innocent children has been his only option. But it hasn't worked.

Being forthright is what works, and I am humbled that God allowed me to see clearly the destruction that came from all this. That's why I've chosen a different course: complete authenticity. In AA we say, "You are only as sick as your secrets." That's why I have told my story. I refuse to nurture secrets or to live a secret life. By making myself vulnerable, I've invited criticism, but I've also freed myself to walk into the future unencumbered by the chains of the past. I'm free, and it feels great. Because I believe that the Lord restores the years eaten by the locust, I look forward to the rest of my life, knowing that He has good things in store for me and not bad.

Conclusion

My Goal Is Fulfillment

I began telling my story the day I went to AA to pick up a white chip. That's when I acknowledged publicly that I was powerless over alcohol. But joining AA involved more than admitting I was an alcoholic. In many ways, that was easy. The other part—realizing that *I thought like an alcoholic*—was really difficult.

It wasn't simply giving up my addictive behavior that was required. I needed to change the way I thought about life, which has been more challenging. Drinking caused me problems—no doubt about it—but it was thinking like an alcoholic that made my life a wasteland. It produced chaos, dysfunction, and insanity, each requiring years of sobriety to transform. At the time, I had no idea what would be necessary to make me whole; I just knew I needed help and lots of it.

My surrender also was an admission that I needed God to heal me and restore me to sanity. Every successful AA story is a God story. Even though I had been a Christian for years, it wasn't enough. I couldn't solve my problem with alcohol on my own, most people can't. I needed recovery, not abstinence.

As I end my story, perhaps the best place to do so is where it all began—at an AA meeting.

A year after my meeting with Mona, I went to a 5:45 P.M. meeting at Triangle, where I have been a regular for years. I brought Jordan with me. She had just graduated from the University of Georgia with a degree in psychology. She was getting a graduate degree so she could counsel children who have been sexually abused. Obviously I'm very proud of her and the choice she has made.

As the AA meeting ended and the chips were being given, Jordan stepped up and said, "Hi, my name is Jordan."

"Hi, Jordan," several hundred people responded in unison.

She continued, "I'm not an alcoholic, but my dad is. This is his fifteenth anniversary of sobriety, which is a special milestone for him. That's why I want to give him his chip." Turning her eyes to me, she said, "I'm very proud of you, Daddy." With that, she gave me a blue chip as tears started to fill her eyes.

Accepting the chip with misty eyes, I looked at the crowd and said, "Hi, my name is Jack."

"Hi, Jack," came the familiar response.

"I'm an alcoholic, and it's been fifteen years since my last drink."

The audience, which was filled with familiar faces, all clapped, smiled, and hooted their approbation. It was a wonderful moment.

As the applause subsided, I said, "I remember the day I picked up my white chip like it was yesterday. I was determined to stop drinking, but I had no idea how to do it. It took about a year for me to come to the point where I no longer craved alcohol. I thought that was all I needed."

When I said this, most people laughed. Like me, they knew my journey to sobriety had just begun.

Continuing, I said, "By the time I picked up my five-year chip, I no longer thought like an alcoholic. It took that long for me to become sober—completely sober."

Several newcomers groaned when I said this, recognizing the daunting task that lay before them.

"When I picked up my ten-year chip," I said, "I had finally learned how to incorporate my recovery tools into other areas of my life. And from then until now—my fifteenth anniversary—I've learned how to live day by day in recovery, especially the value of transparency."

Looking at Jordan, who was beaming, I smiled. "Most people don't learn to live until they are told they are dying," I said. "I want more for my life than that. From this point forward, my goal is fulfillment, which is achievable, as long as I remain sober in body and spirit—one day at a time. Thanks for being there for me when few others were. It means the world to me."

As I sat down, I realized I was no longer a prisoner of my past. My chains have been broken, and I'm free to go forward, embracing the truth and the light. I'm free to finish strong.

As the meeting ended, Jordan and I drove off in my Volvo convertible. The weather was lovely, and everything felt in sync.

With the top down and the wind gently blowing, Jordan turned to me and asked, "Dad, do you think you'll ever get married again?"

It was a great question. After so many failed attempts, sobriety and counseling had taught me that I was okay the way I was and didn't require a woman to feel good about myself. Perhaps Humpty Dumpty would have to remain broken forever.

At the same time, I knew I didn't want to spend the rest of my life alone; so I answered, "I'm not sure whether or not there will be a caboose to this train, Jordan." Smiling, I added, "I'll keep you posted."

Knowing me as well as she does, Jordan just grinned mischievously; so did I. I guess we both knew the answer.

LOOK FOR *RECOVERING FROM RELIGIOUS ABUSE,* ANOTHER GREAT BOOK BY JACK WATTS

RECOVERING FROM
RELIGIOUS
ABUSE

11 STEPS TO SPIRITUAL FREEDOM

JACK WATTS
Foreword by ROBERT S. McGEE

HOWARD BOOKS®
A Division of Simon & Schuster
A CBS COMPANY